'66 FRAMES

'66

FRAMES

introduction by
Jonas Mekas

GORDON BALL

coffee house press
minneapolis

AUTHOR NOTE

'66 Frames is a memoir, centered in perceptions, memories, and reflections of one individual. It is therefore subjective. Aware of possible sensitivity of persons depicted, its author has sometimes altered identities.

Coffee House Press is supported in part by a grant provided by the Minnesota State Arts Board, through an appropriation by the Minnesota State Legislature, and in part by a grant from the National Endowment for the Arts. Significant support has also been provided by The McKnight Foundation; Lannan Foundation; the Lila Wallace Reader's Digest Fund; Target Stores, Dayton's, and Mervyn's by the Dayton Hudson Foundation; General Mills Foundation; St. Paul Companies; Butler Family Foundation; Honeywell Foundation; Star Tribune Foundation; James R. Thorpe Foundation; Dain Bosworth Foundation; Pentair, Inc.; the Helen L. Kuehn Fund of The Minneapolis Foundation; the law firm of Schwegman, Lundberg, Woessner & Kluth, P.A.; and many individual donors. To you and our many readers across the country, we send our thanks for your continuing support.

Coffee House Press books are available to the trade through our primary distributor, Consortium Book Sales & Distribution, 1045 Westgate Drive, Saint Paul, MN 55114. For personal orders, catalogs, or other information, write to: Coffee House Press, 27 North Fourth Street, Suite 400, Minneapolis, MN 55401. Good books are brewing at www.coffeehousepress.org.

LIBRARY OF CONGRESS CIP INFORMATION
Ball, Gordon.
    '66 Frames : a memoir / by Gordon Ball.
      p.   cm.
    ISBN 1-56889-082-9 (pbk.)
      1. Ball, Gordon. 2. Motion picture producers and directors—United States
Biography—. 3. Mekas, Jonas, 1922 − . I. Title. II. Title: Sixty-six frames.
PN1998.3.B315A3   1998
791-43'0233'092—dc21
  [B]   98-56279
                                                             CIP

10 9 8 7 6 5 4 3 2 1
printed in Canada

3   DEPARTURE

acknowledgements

The names of those who've assisted the author in the preparation of this book over the last six years are legion: they easily match the number of its characters. The paragraphs below, extensive as they may be, recognize those whose contributions were the greatest.

Several people gave extremely lengthy and detailed attention to the manuscript. They are my wife Kathleen and my friends Bill Morgan, John Leland, Nancy Peters, and Michael Schumacher. For the generosity of their considerable labors, insights, and frank criticisms, I feel a profound affection, and am indebted more than I can ever say. Whenever asked, Allen Ginsberg answered question after question pertaining to events or persons in my story, and helped as a researcher himself. He and my daughter Daisy photographed the author in front of old haunts; back home, daughter remained patient with father as he continued work in his study.

Alan Baragona not only loaned me his Toshiba laptop, on which the great part of the manuscript was typed, and without which it might not have been completed; he devoted uncountable hours to every computer problem that arose. Jonas Mekas answered my every question, from long distance telephone to his Anthology Film Archives office, to Mars, the bar across Second Avenue and down a block, to his home. Townsend Ludington carried and read the six-pound manuscript in Germany and on the flight home, and phoned me his comments.

My friend Eddie Rivers also reviewed manuscript portions, took great pains to retrieve and share valuable visual artifacts, and constantly encouraged, going far out of his way to try to help me find additional time in which to complete my work. Friend and former employer Leslie Trumbull survived stroke and heart attack, and cheerfully summoned up information and history whenever asked. My friend Jane Hunnicutt was always helpful with valuable reminiscences.

Bob Rosenthal and Peter Hale in Allen Ginsberg's office were generous with assistance—as ever. My department head at VMI, Emily Miller, encouraged and supported this work at every opportunity, as did friend and colleague Rob McDonald, who seemed to come up with helpful ideas almost daily. The Research Committee funded summer research in New York. The entire staff at VMI's Preston Library and Washington and Lee's Leyburn Library were consistently of aid.

I also wish to thank other friends for help: especially Bill Trotter, Ken Siman, Bill Wiseman, P. Adams Sitney, Preston M. Faggart, Jr., Toby Mussman, Yves Le Pellec, Tom Chomont, M.M. Serra, Tom Whiteside, David Carter, Oscar Janiger, Jeff Rosen, Ken Jacobs, Fred Kirsch, and Martee Johnson. For their vital contributions at Coffee House Press I'm indebted to editor Allan Kornblum (who believed in this from first look) and his skillful colleagues Kelly Kofron, Jim Cihlar, Jana Robbins, Christopher Fischbach, and Zeth Lietzau. Ann Charters, Marjorie Perloff, Bill Ferris, Eddie Rivers, and Allen Ginsberg wrote recommendations for the still-elusive Guggenheim Fellowship.

To Jonas Mekas
And the Memory of Allen Ginsberg

ABOUT THIS BOOK WHICH IS A SLICE OF LIFE

This book is a peek into a time period. I say a peek, because Gordon Ball is telling things that I myself, being a shy person of relatively strict upbringing, would never tell. There is almost an aspect of the peeping Tom for the reader, peeping into the personal and not so personal life of a young man trying to grow up in New York in the sixties, surrounded by drugs, sex, music, and underground movies.

When Gordon first asked me to write an introduction to his memoir of the sixties, I enthusiastically said yes. Not because of the sixties but because of Gordon, who is a good friend. I could not have written this book, because I am not a child of the sixties. I am a child of one of the most horrible periods of this century: WWII. I grew up in a rural, farming village in Lithuania; after the war I spent time in a series of Displaced Persons camps; and I came to New York in 1949. My experiences of New York and the cultural movements of the day were colored by this generational difference. But now, reading Gordon's recollections, I recognize all my friends of that period, because they were, or became, friends of Gordon. They all liked him—this twenty-year-old, All-American boy from North Carolina. I was forty-four, with my own different experiences and background. While Gordon was immediately caught in the very middle of the sixties scene, I was both outside of it and in the middle of it at the same time.

Because I was also twenty, in the sixties. . . . You see, a strange thing happened, when the Russians marched into Lithuania, and later the Nazis, and then the forced labor camps. At the moment that history took over, I and my brother Adolfas froze in an interrupted explosion or expectation, and we remained frozen there until the end of the war. Then we woke up, and we discovered there were things in the world like the writing of Rimbaud and Cocteau and all the rest. We had lost one decade from our lives. Instead of aging, though, it was as if we woke up ten years younger.

As you'll find out while reading this book, I played a big part in Gordon's sixties life. But lives have this interesting way of branching out. Thus, while I was familiar with some of Gordon's life branches, including his work in film, I was totally ignorant of some of the others, which I found out about while reading his memoirs. One of those branches, unknown to me, was his involvement in the drugs and free love of the New York of the sixties.

I have to admit, I am still naive even today about some of the social and cultural phenomena Gordon comments on in this narrative. Andy Warhol used to ask me, "Jonas, tell me what drugs are you on, what are you taking to keep yourself going like you are going?" To tell you the truth, the biggest mental and psychic experimentation that I have ever gone through was at Wiesbaden and Kassel, in the Displaced Person camps, with my brother Adolfas. After the long, horrible war and the deprivation that followed, we discovered Rimbaud and Valéry and Rilke and Trakl and Baudelaire and Artaud. We were so intoxicated with these new discoveries that our brains boiled over. No drug was a match for that.

In 1965 I visited Timothy Leary, and one morning he took me for a walk, and we walked and talked. Then we stopped on a little bridge and he said he was amazed that here I was, in Millbrook, and there were all those great gurus and LSD and Baba Ram Dass, and all, but the only thing I did was shoot film or read. (Actually, I was reading an amazing book I had found about Meher Baba and his work with the mentally disturbed.) Tim was wondering why I didn't take LSD. (I did once, though, for Barbara Rubin—because I loved her.) I said, "But I have already my Rimbaud and my Baudelaire and my Rilke and my Trakl—and my body cells are still reverberating with their words, their rhythms, and their incredible spaces." Tim stood silent, then we walked back to the mansion silently.

Andy Warhol used to ask me, on observing my close friendship with P. Adams Sitney, "When are you two going to come out of the closet?" But we were completely someplace else. When I first came to New York, I did not even know there were gays and lesbians. Of course, it did not take long for me to get to know many people who are gay or lesbian, many of whom are artists, and to respect and admire them. I'd go so far as to say there virtually would not be an avant-garde cinema in America without such sensibilities.

When a journalist asked filmmaker Ken Jacobs what it was like to live in that turbulent time, he answered, "I didn't know then that I was living in The Sixties." That's how the legend goes. Yes, each of us had our own sixties. This book is about the sixties—Gordon Ball's sixties. I was thrown into the sixties, and I became a part of it. And I recognize it all in Gordon's memoir. This book is a slice of sixties life.

—Jonas Mekas

1966 FROM 1999: A PROLOGUE

One evening a few years ago, after decades of travel, jungle, foreign jail, farm, study, romance, books, movies, photography, marriage, father-hood, professorships, house moves, and a child grown into teenage, I found myself—now teaching at a military school—settled with my small family into a new home. Alone in the torn overstuffed chair of my log cabin study late at night, I recalled my brief moments with Robert Du Peintre and many others I first encountered at twenty-one: all the hope, imagination, fantasy we shared (even my own early youthful fancies, confusions and failings feeding into it), all the reality and marvel of rec-ollection—fragments, really—of a life, a generation gone. Like bright receding voices the recollections came to me, stuttering, echoing, vanish-ing. Lest I write them down, they live only in memory, fading as sunlight swallows shadow.

1 FOREPLAY

ROBERT AND OTHER EARLY PHENOMENA

①

The image of a moment, late September 1966—a gathering at an artist's loft—plays in my mind: I was in the midst of one of my first DMT highs. Feeling I was in heaven, I turned and saw a short, slender fellow with wavy black hair, wearing a white sheet over street clothes—and thought him an angel.

②

The name of the young man in white at mixed media artist Richard Aldcroft's—where I'd originally gone to interview Aldcroft for *Film Culture* magazine—was Robert Du Peintre. I—an extremely young twenty-one —ran into Robert several times soon thereafter, but it was one encounter a few weeks later, at the First Avenue apartment of his friends Art and Richie, that was extraordinary.

Let me explain. By early October, I'd taken LSD (lysergic acid diethylamide) five times since arriving in New York around the tenth of September. I remember thinking how—unlike others whose psychedelic experiences I'd read of—I hadn't really seen God at all. It had been a miracle-level phenomenon, yet with none of the supernatural or divine.

Such was my line of thought, at any rate, one quiet Sunday evening as I set out, lackadaisical, ruminating and observing—not quite sure why I was invited—for Art and Richie's. On foot, I'd left other friends I'd been visiting in the lower end of the West Village, and skirted an almost sleeping Little Italy. I cut through Washington Square, where one night three years earlier, after my freshman year at a white men's college down South, I got my first marijuana through a black friend, a dollar a joint; where I, who'd once slept nightly in a bed made daily by maids, stretched out all of one warm evening on a park bench, and spent another nearby at the bums' Hotel Greenwich, listening to the all-night ricochet of old men's coughs, old men's creaks.

At some distance I passed a policeman, his shiny night stick reflecting, like memory, an arc of mercury vapor from the streetlight overhead. I crossed Astor Place and Third Avenue, came upon Richard Aldcroft's at 12 St. Mark's. Had there been sufficient illumination, I could've seen the large beige block lettering—DEUTSCHE-AMERIKANISCHE SCHUTZEN GESELL-SCHAFT—that projected (and projects still) from the lintel between second and third stories. Three generations earlier, this Greek revival townhouse had been erected for socially and legally sanctioned activities—beer drinking included—of the German American Shooting Society. Across the street at 23 St. Mark's sat the now quiet Dom, where upstairs at the Balloon Farm, Andy Warhol's Exploding Plastic Inevitable with the Velvet Underground and Nico appeared Friday and Saturday nights. Down St. Mark's a few shadowed young people milled about in denim, paisleys, and old coats. The window display in the closed East Side Book Store was still visible under street lamp and full moon. There, among many other items, was a multi-media group's mandala, a large silk screened Buddha head on bright poster paper; the Beatles' new LP, *Revolver;* R.E.L. Masters and Jean Houston's *The Varieties of Psychedelic Experience; Psychedelic Prayers* by Timothy Leary; and *Allen Ginsberg Reads "Kaddish"* on Atlantic Records.

At the corner, Gem Spa's eerie electric luminescence fell upon its snared bundles of *Times, Village Voice, East Village Other,* and its egg creams alike. I was just two blocks from Art and Richie's. As the light changed from unspeaking red to unspeaking green, I headed north then east, thinking that LSD was phenomenal, extraordinary, good play, unbelievable sex, energy, sound and color, but not God. Or certainly no anthropomorphic God.

Art and Richie were brothers. I never knew their last names, and I never asked. Behind a door thick with red paint, they lived in a second floor walk-up on First Avenue between St. Mark's and Ninth. When I'd run into Robert after Aldcroft's, he'd say he wanted to trip with me (perhaps at Art and Richie's), and I'd respond very casually each time. I was, in fact, somewhat puzzled. What was so important about tripping, about doing it together? About planning to do it together, as he seemed to want? It was just a form, if an absolutely, amazingly, utterly extraordinary one, of recreation, discovery, and play, wasn't it? We'd do it if and when it happened.

Now it happened. Art was short, brown-haired, freckled, bearded; Richie, tall, slender, longhaired and blond, good-looking, sexy. In the course of the evening Art would open the frost-lined freezer door of their fridge to tumbling icy smoke and point deep inside to fifty tiny white tabs wrapped in transparent plastic: they were dealing.

And now the four of us were tripping. Through his vibrating voice and hands—and his commanding presence—Robert made himself the center of our attention. As at Aldcroft's, he wore a white sheet; only this time he also held in his hand a sort of dime-store, bejeweled Aladdin's lamp or censer—a psychedelic toy which (through eyes dilated by LSD) sparkled like many glowing diamonds and rubies. Early on, as we watched, he wept: Art or Richie or both of them had let him down, or not appreciated him, in some way he—and possibly they—knew but I did not. He wept almost as if he were a sort of suffering savior, struggling with the burden of all the energy in the room, all the burdens of unredeemed humanity, crying at not getting through to anyone. Then his tears subsided.

Soon I realized he could—as I called it at the time—"polarize" consciousness: make our several consciousnesses one. The move of his extended, darting hand left a trace of bright silvered energy hanging visible in the air an instant, like a child's sparkler at night. The nonverbal deep-throated trills flying fugue-like from his lips in rapid chant or incantation startled all the space around us, as if rearranging its molecular formation. All of our consciousness rushed toward Robert and his censer.

Then we played, timelessly, good-heartedly, and in utter amazement, with the shimmering, multicolored, myriad energy of sight and sound, of vibration and wave, of which we were all a part. We saw the toy-like resplendence, the sacred marvel of common everyday items—not only of the dime-store censer but of glass ashtrays, a hookah, a child's kaleidoscope. We too darted our limbs and cavorted as sea waves of energy rushed through us. We were jugglers of the universe, delighting in its infinite constituent particles. Robert made jokes about our molecular systems and levels of consciousness, and we lost much of our everyday sense of separate being. Any lines of demarcation one from the other were as arbitrary, tenuous, and quickly vanished as breath.

Then gradually we became more diffuse as a group, each began going his separate way in the small two-bedroom apartment. I went into Art's or Richie's room, took off my clothes except for my underwear, and sat on the white-sheeted bed, my head on a pillow. I stared at the opposite wall. Once or twice on earlier trips I'd gazed at white-plastered pale Lower East Side apartment walls and seen seventeenth-century Chinese merchants, locked in discussion of trade as they sat at dark lacquered tables in long silk coats, long generous sleeves drooping to delicate wrists. They projected slightly from the relief of the cracked, repainted plaster and its swirled spatula tracks, as if in mute three-dimensional Answer and Solution to unasked Question and unknown Mystery from my childhood in the Far East. Now I stared at the upper part of the wall's whiteness and saw deep ruby red diamonds, in neat squares and rectangles, patterned, growing, glowing, breathing from the whiteness. I realized this trip was taking me deeper, and farther, than I'd ever gone.

Robert entered the room, his sheet gone. In just his dark shirt and brown corduroy pants, he came over to me, and sat on the edge of the bed. I sat straight up, and saw that his eyes were directed at something below mine; I looked down. Very slowly, my right hand was rising in the direction of his, which was extended, palm down like mine, pointing toward mine, his fingers contiguous. Small electric-like bands of energy—arcing lines with rainbow hues—bridged the gap between our opposing fingertips. There seemed to be a slight high-pitched whirring sound, and a coolness emanated from the lines or bands. I looked at him and he looked back at me, bright-eyed and knowing, with a quiet smile. Gazing upon our hands once more, I began to weep just a little. This was it, that for which I'd always yearned: the union of mortal souls beyond physical convention, the chance to know one another beyond limitation of word or practice, in a psychic realm that bridged the gaps of material reality . . . even to know, perhaps, people in all times, all places: to play with the building blocks of the universe! Travel in time and space, even that might be possible! Exultant, anticipant, I found myself in the midst of the wondrous.

"You didn't know?" he asked, his dark eyes reflecting the light overhead as they fixed on mine. A proud knowing grin took over his face.

"No, not at all." I looked back at him for an extended moment. Time was passing, and I could sense the acid beginning to weaken just slightly.

"Want to lie down?" he asked.

"Okay, it's time for sleep."

We went into a much smaller room with a single bed. He brought himself close to me, his face only inches from mine.

"Listen, I'm sorry, but your breath smells bad," I told him quietly with blunt truthfulness. "And . . . and," I stuttered, "I . . . I don't want you sexually, Robert."

His lips rumpled, he cast his eyes to the floor as he turned off the light. We lay down on the narrow bed and shared it for the rest of the night, but it was a frustrating one for him, as it would turn out to be when he was with me thereafter. "Gordon's half a loaf," he'd sometimes tell friends in my presence, loud and laughing. When he got really worked up, his words tumbled forth in riotous cackle.

(3)

It was around this time, at the Filmmakers' Cinematheque (I was working for filmmaker Jonas Mekas), that I first saw Candy O'Brien—her pleasing face, her eager smile, her vividness, her vibrancy. In profile: her large brushed mass of auburn hair splayed from her head and down her back, her large breasts pressed firmly against a white sweater struggling to enclose them above tight brown bell-bottoms. She was looking for someone else; neither of us spoke to the other. Then I saw her again at another gathering at Richard Aldcroft's, gazed into her bright dark eyes, listened to her warm sexual and vaguely whiskey-like voice, felt her eager, galvanic energy. "I'm Candy," she began, wrist bracelets jangling, Camel Filter between index and middle finger, "Who're you?"

She was originally from Maryland, had traveled some, and now lived below Houston Street. She was sixteen months older than I, and seemed to meet the world head-on with self-confidence. She was generous, talky, brassy, and bright. And some months earlier, she confided, she'd separated from her husband.

She'd noticed me at the Cinematheque. And now it seemed she liked me. She smiled eagerly, brushing my hands with her fingertips as we spoke of our lives. Under a blanket we lay side by side on the straw mats at one end of Aldcroft's loft, his New World Church Meditation Center, and watched the large projection of his Infinity Machine on the white wall opposite: roiling, superimposing, geometric forms shifting and interchanging in wondrous fluidity, their colors common as vibrant primaries, rare as exotic magentas, chartreuses. Then we left for her place.

'66 Frames

I stayed. Robert visited, dominated, and nearly stayed himself. To my initial surprise, he and Candy seemed to get along—almost enthusiastically—and for several weeks on and off he became part of our casual group lovemaking on the six sheeted mattresses that made up the floor of our "living room." He had a slender pale face with large shiny dark eyes, a long nose, large white teeth. At times on LSD he'd look like a goat-faced shaman. He was as slight as Candy was large. He kept his black hair relatively short and neatly combed, almost like a courtier, with flounce and wave. He was always "Robert," never Bob or Rob, or perish even the thought, Robby or Bobby. A few years older than I (I never learned how many), he had a bearing that was utterly aristocratic, with a jutting lower lip and eyelids that nearly kissed each other in simmering hauteur when he was offended or angered. But he was at the same time disarmingly down-to-earth. Along with his psychedelic skills, he could be immensely funny, and Candy seemed nearly as drawn to him as I. He had narrow shoulders and a flat chest beneath his large long head, and—as I saw when he screwed Candy—a big dong.

Once, as he rode her with power and ease, his pale upper body upright, he laughed, with a delighted cackle, about being a "fag." Another time, clothed and standing upright, he ridiculed me for thinking I'd never get crabs when he and Candy and others had them. With a great tilting back and opening gesture of the raised palm of his hand as he teetered on his feet, he told me I thought I was "too white" to ever get such things. And he was right.

Despite my hesitations and rejections, and despite my obvious affection for Candy, Robert wasn't giving up on having me as a lover. That, presumably, was his ultimate reason for hanging around. Late one evening in our 57 Thompson Street living room, after much smoking, talking, laughing, as Mick Jagger and the Rolling Stones pleaded to "Lady Jane," as Miss Lyn, Candy's part Russian Blue cat, lounged and rolled among us, we turned off nearly all the light, and Robert—he was one of our two visitors that night—asked me to join him. Our other guest, who like him had been sitting up against the wall, was my closest friend from college, Billy Trotter. Billy, who had moved to the city from North Carolina a month before I'd shown up, was short, broad-shouldered, good-looking, and intense. Literarily gifted and in some ways tradition-minded, he was passionately loyal, and on occasion—in New York 1966—could be stodgy. Or worse.

Now he was morally offended by Robert's invitation, for suddenly we heard him challenge, "You try that shit and you're gonna have me to reckon with!"

"What?! You're threatening violence?" The even shorter Robert, vivid, reddened, and outraged, raised up and clattered out his great cackle.

I looked for Billy's brooding face in the darkness but could sense nothing. Then I heard him say "You heard—!" and Candy shout "Billy! C'mon now!" from the center of a warm, disbelieving laugh. I realized that hard as it was, much as I dreaded it, I had to speak. Yet since I didn't like Robert erotically there was no real problem—except in Billy's mind.

"Yeah, c'mon, Billy," I managed, my heart in my throat as I turned to my older, emotional friend. "There's nothing for you to worry about."

Though I felt sure that from his perspective his intentions were good, I didn't like his moralistic presumption. I could join Robert if I chose. On the other hand, I didn't want to join Robert—not in the manner he most ardently hoped for. As I thought to say more, I saw the shade of Miss Lyn jump onto Billy's lap. Perhaps the surprise of it tripped some final switch within him, for, distracted, he relaxed, and the Rolling Stones and their Lady came to the forefront once more. I moved slightly closer to Robert, although given the confined space on the mattresses, I had moved closer to everyone else, too.

The tension was eased nonviolently, but it bespoke, loud and clear, my own ambivalence. Robert was extremely intriguing, and I appreciated his regard for me; yet I always hesitated to respond in kind.

I never hesitated responding sexually with Candy. She was luscious and voluptuous and we made love to each other almost daily, in as many different ways as we wanted. She generally accepted my sex with other women as I hers with other men: her sexual curiosity and sense of adventure matched mine. Our living room of sheets on mattresses constituted invitation and blessing for all that took place, like some sort of white, unscathed, sanctified land. She read books, she worked nine-to-five, she was immensely sociable, she did most of the looking-after of our tiny household, and she seemed to love me.

Robert claimed, almost proudly, to have never learned to read, and even seemed to disapprove of such activities. Once, when I memorized a phone number, he chastised, "It'll rearrange all the other data in your

'66 Frames

consciousness!" He didn't have a job, and how he managed to always bear his share of expenses I never knew.

Nor did I ever learn anything about his past, except that he'd once lived in Philadelphia. One weekend when Candy went to her sister's in Connecticut, we visited a queer friend of Robert's in his Rittenhouse Square loft. We arrived very late on a Friday.

As I looked around the next morning, I noticed the loft's broad floor of highly varnished hardwood was scarcely interrupted by furniture; through huge high windows generous to light, its whole long street side looked out upon cobbled alleys, bare trees, charmingly aged red brick buildings. We'd just risen, and were in the underclothes in which we'd slept. Robert made a kind of presentation of me, or rather, I might say, shy as I was, I made one of myself. "This is Gordon," Robert said to our host, an attractive enough young fellow in his mid- or late twenties, with medium length blond hair. His right sleeve, partially pushed up, revealed a small tattoo—unusual for those days—of a small globe in indigo over a fine chevron of joined lightning bolts.

Suddenly, on a whim, I was disrobing, twirling, pointing one foot in front of another, raising one leg high, pirouetting—making up all steps on the spot, having had no dance study at all—displaying myself eagerly, freely, pleasurably, before two admiring male companions. I danced, voluntarily, spontaneously, naked, for some short moments, in front of both men. And that was all. Once, as a virgin sophomore in college three years earlier, I'd fantasized becoming a catamite. But I hadn't reconciled that momentary intention with the fact that I basically didn't like men sexually. Now, here in Philadelphia, I was gliding across brilliant dark hardwood that glowed a rich deep orange in the early winter light, inspired by the admiration.

(4)

As time passed and weeks began to turn to months, I became much closer to Candy than Robert, even though he'd continued to visit our tiny apartment where socializing was intimate, psychedelics familiar. And Candy and I saw more of her friends, and of the new ones we were making together. Yet she seemed to remain favorably disposed toward Robert, and once argued, to Billy Trotter's disgust, "He may become another Buddhist leader." Certainly Robert was smart, intriguing, and delightful. But he'd continue, time and again, to seek my favor as more than a friend. I can remember an extended moment one mild November afternoon on Thompson Street in front of our apartment, just opposite the bodega next door. I was sitting with him in my large green Chevy, and had just turned off the engine. He'd kept pressing me, "Well, do you like me as a friend or companion, or do you think you could love me?" And every time I'd begin to try, feebly, to articulate how I felt, he'd take the dialogue further, fleshing out my thoughts as he imagined them. I couldn't keep up with him. Mentally, I turned and twisted like blown linen on a line.

I wasn't as bright as he, or at least not nearly as articulate. I wasn't accustomed to speaking about how I felt, and growing up had known few people who did so. For me the gap between word and feeling was often far beyond reach. But late that afternoon, parked on Thompson Street thirty years ago, I couldn't have begun to explain such things.

Nevertheless, even though our relationship had perhaps reached its maximum intensity that moment in the car, one or two additional extra-ordinary events—like lightning striking snow—were to occur before Robert and I eventually fell out. Once on acid as we stood together in a lumbering subway car, shiny gray plastic grips clasped in our hands, Robert claimed he could slow time. For the next couple of minutes he did; the seconds expanded as we stared at each other. Seated passengers read books and papers, eyed ads overhead for Preparation H and marriage counseling and Kool cigarettes, squinted up at the recessed fluorescent tubes, yawned, or grabbed their child as the train shook its way through darkness to the next stop, doors spreading themselves to the metallic blast of ozone. We looked at each other; our sense of time seemed to melt, to become like dry rain.

That same month we went, at Robert's instigation, to a midtown Chinese movie theater to see a film without English subtitles or dubbing. The movie dramatized warring Chinese monks from hundreds of years ago, whose psychic feats—telekinesis, teleportation—were their exclusive weaponry.

Within the theater, no signs were in English or any other non-Chinese language—except "EXIT." Everyone else appeared to be Chinese —except one couple. As we began making our way farther inside, the somewhat darkened lobby was filling with palefaced, dark-topped Asians leaving the earlier showing. But ten or twelve feet in front of us, within the crowd yet apart from everyone else—Robert pointed them out—came an older, high-cheekboned European gentleman with cane and black cape and a long thin silken moustache ending in a pointed tip that protruded inches from each cheek. At his side walked a light-haired woman in an overcoat. It was Salvador Dalí and his wife Gala, and we were approaching each other. "Hello, Mr Dalí," Robert volunteered, stepping toward them, hand extended. "Enchanté," Dalí shook both our hands as Gala, remaining one step to the side and one behind, smiled.

Then one day late in the winter—months after losing touch with Robert's friends Art and Richie—I happened to pick up the New York Daily News. Its big black block front-page letters, in all their upright, righteous, square citizen stolid massiveness, proclaimed a drug bust. The person busted, I saw upon reading within (the immense capitals ate the front page whole), was Art. I remembered reading an earlier article about another bust back in September. A young public schoolteacher and his wife had been arrested for making grass and LSD inexpensively available. The Daily News had been horrified that a schoolteacher could be involved in such wickedness! I had wondered why a man was being punished for (allegedly) making available an agent of discovery, a means by which we can learn more about ourselves, the universe to which we are electro-magnetically and biologically connected as one, and all our silly hopes for this poor pitiful race of roiling humans and their doomed and spinning planet. That he was a schoolteacher and was, according to the article, seemingly quite an "upstanding" fellow, to me invited once more a different conclusion: perhaps we don't understand this subject well. Perhaps our laws—and the new ones being passed—are wrong.

But now the person busted was someone I knew. I had to find out what was going on. Immediately I phoned Robert (who'd recently moved into an apartment with friends across the street from Candy and me). Art, out on bail of four figures, was unreachable. The bust had been made by an undercover agent posing as a buyer.

"What did Richie say the narc looked like?" I asked Robert.

"Like a storm trooper."

⑤

This event made me extremely paranoid. Who could I trust? Was my judgment any better than Art's? I bought something only once—an ounce of grass for a cute girl I met in a laundromat on the hill in Syracuse the preceding summer. Often grass and acid alike were free; sometimes Candy, whose nine-to-five clerical work gave her an income several times mine, would buy. We used grass and acid and other substances such as DMT frequently, even though just possessing them was illegal. And some of our generous friends who visited us dealt.

Directly or indirectly, Robert continued to press me to be his special companion. Though the pressure had nothing to do with the sale of drugs, I now became only more uncomfortable with him. Certainly we'd shared extraordinary experiences. Yet his pressuring, at its worst, could be suffocating, like a lead mask on one's face. We'd given him a key to our apartment so he could come over whenever he liked, and now that too worried me. There he was, unemployed and living across the street. What might he fall prey to, under the power of a State which lavished rewards on those who extended its power, trammeling any human relationships that might lie in its way? I knew it was possible that I was being totally paranoid, but Art's bust left me profoundly cautious. I spoke with Candy, then approached Robert.

"Robert . . ." I began one day as we stood together in the tiny kitchen at 57 Thompson, just inside the door.

"Yes . . ." He was curious; he could sense something was up.

"You know, we're going to need our key back . . ."

"Oh, okay," he eyed me. "Why?" He continued staring, mouth partly open.

"We just feel it would be better . . . we . . . we may have other people coming over, and . . . you know, we have to be careful, and . . ."

He was already sticking his hand into the front pocket of his dark corduroy pants. He fished the key out and over to me, eyeing me an instant as his lips rumpled. He turned and raised the long, creaking police bar that stretched from door to kitchen floor. And let himself out.

I seldom saw him again.

⑥

By this time Candy and I were quite established as a couple, her friends had become ours, and our circle was growing. But for me to enjoy such a (relatively) settled yet expanding social scene, only a few months after coming to the city, invites questions. To the extent that I'd done so, how had I made—or bumped—my way, with no real plans or resources and very few contacts? Of course I was young and—I've been told—outwardly quite attractive (inner character was another matter). Some who knew me then have recalled alabaster skin, deep-set large liquid brown eyes, sensual lips, longish hair with a little wave, and other features both men and women found appealing. ("You looked like a Greek god," a poet confided to me years later.) Yet I was socially inept, shy, acutely self-conscious, and, on many occasions, almost mute—an alien to much of car-crazy, war-crazy, money-crazy America.

The question is answered only in part by telling of encounters with Robert Du Peintre, Candy O'Brien, and many others. Some of it had to do with Louise Matthewson.

LOUISE

On one of my very first days in New York, September 1966, before there was ever a Robert Du Peintre or a Candy O'Brien in my life, I was introduced to a pretty, small, blonde woman with short straight hair and blue eyes who resembled movie actress Jean Seberg. Louise Matthewson, five or six years my senior, had just received some LSD, and she offered me one of her two doses. That first night together was my first trip. She'd taken acid several times previously.

I'd enjoyed very much the erotic effects of marijuana my final year in North Carolina, and most recently on the streets of New York near Tompkins Square Park when I walked with a young woman I'd met at the apartment of a Hungarian countess on a spring break visit a few months earlier. But half an hour after Louise and I took acid, as we walked at evening across cobbled Sheridan Square, orgasms suddenly exploded in my thighs. I'd never felt anything so sexual. As we passed people on the thronged street they looked deliciously funny; life was a vibrating bounce of laughter and amusement for our sake. We were witnessing a part of a great pageant and it was extremely vivid and very, very funny. All the faces coming toward us were outlined in rich reds and blues and greens, as if I were seeing far more variety and depth of form, shape, color, and space—and yet more clarity—than I ever had.

When we got to Louise's apartment, several of her friends were there, and the sounds of their voices took on added resonance. New sounds, sounds I'd never heard, cataracts and baroque bendings and hieroglyphs of hearing that I could almost touch. This too seemed very, very funny and had aural resonances that went on infinitely. And the people themselves— all I saw, in fact—looked vividly different, with bright vibrating bands of primary colors; when we came into the kitchen and suddenly switched on the light, even cockroaches shimmered with dark brilliance as they scuttled away. The round, amber-colored wooden dining table of this West Village apartment was now rich with a breathing ocean of desert flowers. All was alive, and "Reality" was liquid. There was, ultimately, no demarcating one phenomenal entity—myself, a cactus, a table—from another.

Though we scarcely knew each other at all, Louise and I could feel ourselves coming closer and closer together. We descended some stairs into a cluttered, low-ceilinged basement and sat inches apart on a mattress, looking into each other's eyes, yearning. Our faces pressed together, our tongues reached sweet secret recesses of our mouths. It would be my first time with an older woman—did I dare? She was resplendent with unbounded mystery. . . . Why not?

Unconcerned that anyone else might start down the stairs (telling myself they knew what we were up to anyway), I unbuttoned her white blouse and reached around her back, felt for the hook to her bra. . . . Then spreading her loose blouse open at either side like curtains upon a window of flesh, I buried my face in her warm skin and sucked and kissed and drove my tongue up and down her utter bareness nipple to navel. I took her dark skirt as she my jeans, and then we were fucking. We were the universe and we were fucking, we were the universe fucking, an organism endlessly expanding, contracting, rippling in rhythm of sweat and cock and heat and vulva, breaths and heartbeats one in universal resonance.

At 7:00 in the morning—we'd had no sleep, felt not the least need—we went upstairs and across the hall to greet her young slender Puerto Rican neighbor, just returned from his night's work. Raul let us in, gave us each a beer, complained about higher tax rates for singles, and played the Beatles' new album, *Revolver,* which I hadn't yet heard in its entirety. He handed us the slipcase, with its black-and-white Klaus Voorman sketch on the cover: tightly framed close-ups of the four Beatles, at askew angles. Though the overall representation was flat, the strands of their hair were depicted with almost vermicelli-like thickness and depth. On the cover's upper half, a potpourri of smaller Beatle images cascaded over and down between their heads, mixing with their hair; at bottom, the album's title— no mention of its artists—proclaimed itself in modified black blocks.

We heard the first cut, which was, ironically, "Taxman." Second, "Eleanor Rigby," which I'd enjoyed already several times on the air waves. Then, backed by East Indian drums, came the sound of a driving sitar (I didn't even know, then, of such an instrument, though one was on the the Stones' "Paint It Black," which I'd listened to again and again in May and June). The sitar would eventually represent, for me, the sound of Time, of Infinity uncoiling itself.

After "Yellow Submarine," McCartney's shouted exuberance, "Good Day Sunshine." Then I listened, puzzled, to the sitar-like moans at the beginning of the very last cut, "Tomorrow Never Knows," feeling uncertain all the way through to the end. It was almost as if I were in the midst of the LSD—though I knew I was not. We'd peaked a number of hours earlier, and now everything had assumed its ordinary cast. Yet Lennon's filtered voice urged ego surrender, and the tape loops and electronic strangeness abided throughout the cut, as weird bird cries faded in and out, blending with electric guitar warps, bringing us back to the LSD experience.

Only many years later would I learn the words were adapted from *The Psychedelic Experience: A Manual Based on the Tibetan Book of the Dead*, by Timothy Leary, Ralph Metzner, and Richard Alpert. Overall, as I heard *Revolver* then and again many times that autumn, I was struck by its playfulness and invention, its crispness and condensation: something as simple as "She Said She Said," or the syntactical inversion and surprise of "I love her and she loving me." I didn't then know, let alone use, such words to speak about music and its lyrics (even in college, poetry had been something we found flat on the pages of school books, and approached largely by scanning and deliberating, not joyfully declaiming or even singing). But I knew that here was strangeness, mystery, oddness, unpredictability, invitation.

And as I heard, puzzled, the electronic playfulness on the "Tomorrow Never Knows" of *Revolver,* I was aware of the beer as a small enclosed can of beer and the city as a city, framed within the wooden-silled window through which I looked out onto gray rooftops and old dark red brick and knew that everything was the same, and different, from here on.

MYSELF: TOKYO TO NORTH CAROLINA

As 1966 approached its end, I planned to head briefly to my family in
North Carolina at Christmas. My parents had recently retired to
Winston-Salem—near my brother and sister—after forty years of bank-
ing in China and Japan. I wasn't eager to return—that much is clear from
a paragraph in a letter I wrote my mother and father:

> Was sorry not to be with you for Thanksgiving. I may have the same
> difficulty in getting down there for Christmas, too. I am hesitant to
> drive over a holiday season, and since going by bus would mean a
> much longer trip, I'm not sure if I'll be able to. My work is such that
> it keeps me busy 6 – 7 days a week and I don't yet know if Christmas-
> time will offer a lull in things that need to be done.

Perhaps an offer of a ticket persuaded me. For four years ending in
June 1966, I'd been supported generously at Davidson, a somewhat upper
crust college. My educational expenses were covered, and, until I ran into
financial difficulty at Harvard summer school between junior and senior
years, I enjoyed a monthly allowance that went as high as $120. This
Christmas visit would be my first one home following those four years of
my life, those four years of my parents' investment.

My A.B. degree in English, from a college that was regarded within the
South as "distinguished," had purchased little on the job market. Much
of that summer after graduation, I languished with a girl in Syracuse,
where I worked the docks in a candle factory. By late August, I'd resolved
to go to New York and look up avant-garde film pioneer Jonas Mekas,
whom I'd brought to Davidson the previous spring. Determined that my
life be meaningful, that my work have something to do with something
inside me waiting to grow, I'd offer to work for him.

Having connected with Jonas in September, I wrote my father in
October asking him to send winter clothing, especially my "heavy green
hooded coat." I explained that my work paid little (it was $25 a week).
Several hours a day I was seated in front of Jonas's old upright Smith-
Corona typewriter—old even then—and his Wollensak reel-to-reel
tape recorder. I often did work-related tasks afternoons and evenings.
I thought I could manage $100 a month car payments, I explained, by

renting my Chevrolet to Jonas's brother Adolfas on weekends. I was doing what I wanted to, I reassured him, and in fact the night before had helped Andy Warhol with a film. Though I hadn't asked for anything, in response to the bare-bones conditions I described, my father had sent $10 with the winter clothing.

Just before Christmas, Candy left for several days with her family in Somerville, New Jersey. Taking LSD on Christmas Eve, Robert and I searched for a Christmas tree, a challenging mission so extraordinarily late in the season, let alone at the pocket-change prices we sought. We rushed through the cold dark streets serried with myriads of other hurrying bundled figures, their palpable breaths preceding them. Suddenly in a magical instant they and we and all that was around us were blessed by descending whiteness. Finding a tree at last, we fairly charged with it back to 57 Thompson, apartment B. Pausing at the door to brush the snow from its tender green, we squeezed it inside, set it on a stand in a corner, and dressed it in bright green, red, blue, and yellow lights that flared amidst dark boughs, shimmering colored balls, and vibrating tinsel. The whole tiny apartment seemed to grow, in complex webs of brightness, hue, energy. We were pleased, we were exhausted, and it was already late at night, nearly Christmas Day. We lay down next to each other on sheeted mattresses and slept.

At 6:30 Christmas morning the alarm clock rang, I spooned some cereal into a bowl, and dropped a Black Beauty—a strong, speedy diet pill with amphetamine—into my mouth. I left the apartment, took the subway to Grand Central, the bus to the Eastern terminal, and flew to the Winston-Salem-Greensboro-High Point airport.

And I was accepted into what I saw as the sober, awkward pleasantness of "home." At the Christmas afternoon dinner table were our hostess and host, my sister Maylee (Marilyn—Chinese amas "renamed" her) and her husband Harold; my brother Edgar and his wife Paula, and my mother and father, Daisy Belle and Gordon. My three young nephews were also there.

Over the years, I'd enjoyed with Maylee—ten years my senior—a relationship almost as close and passionate as those of platonic soulmates in Dostoevsky, starting with the early days when she bounced me on her knees as we sang "Hello my baby, / Hello my honey, / Hello my ragtime gal"; with the night when she swooped me in her arms and eased my tears after my father spanked me for throwing my shoe through the frosted glass bathroom door. And though I'd come to think of her as anchored in what seemed our traditional family Republicanism and authority, I knew there was more there, too: she once confided to me years later that in 1960 she'd voted for John Kennedy, not Richard Nixon. Our affections had diminished some with her marriage and childrearing and my growth and fallings in love and profound disillusionments. But I always felt the base was there.

Edgar, who like my sister had adopted North Carolina as home, was eight years older than I. He was extremely quiet, shy; my sister once told me that when grown-ups saw the two toddlers together and asked Edgar how he was, "Ask Maywin" (Ask Marilyn) was his reply. However, for me, he was bigger and stronger, an object of esteem. But since he and Maylee were shipped to prep school in the u.s. when I was seven and a half, that esteem came to be held at some distance. And as in time physical difference narrowed and he began making educational and professional comitt-ments, a psychological and social distance widened: in later adolescence I'd wonder if he were not only bookish but smug.

At the same time, he too had suffered the disruptions of family life: while our parents and I remained in Tokyo, he was at Hebron Academy, Maine, a freshman, then in the mountains of North Carolina at Asheville School for Boys, a sophomore. His very modest allowance and lack of social contacts may well have made him feel all the more abandoned. Staying with our sister and her family as he finished high school, he met a schoolmate who virtually saved him. Paula, as straight and bright as he but more outgoing, was the daughter of a supermarket meat manager and a housewife; she lived with them and her three brothers and sisters in a white frame house in a solid middle-class area of Winston-Salem. In spite of the many constraints on the higher education of females, she too, like he, aspired to a Ph.D.

Edgar, a year older than Paula, was driven to the large University of North Carolina at Chapel Hill for his freshman year by his one-handed Uncle William McKinley Ball. "Kin" had lost a hand when he stuck it in a corn grinder at age ten, then made his own way in life and expected everyone else to do the same. "Here it is," he said, pausing at the low Franklin Street wall at the edge of the main university quadrangle. Edgar hauled all his bags and belongings out onto the sidewalk, and Uncle Kin drove off. But Edgar managed to make his own way extremely well there beginning with his first year, and before his second Paula joined him as fellow student—and wife.

Through their smarts, commitment (my brother worked his way to a B.S. in Business Administration in three years), and thrifty manner of living, they both won Ph.D.s. And though to my eyes they might appear thick-skinned and preceptorial, on occasion they transcended the text-bookly stiffness and disapproval I sensed, and revealed themselves as "good eggs." Certainly, they both welcomed me when I returned to the U.S. for college.

In the summer of 1962 they hosted me for a week, and Edgar arranged for an alumnus friend to take us on a day visit to Davidson. At the time I was in a quasi-mystical state, trying to perpetuate a love relationship (that existed almost exclusively in my own head and heart) with a young woman who'd left Tokyo a few months before I. Almost daily I'd sing the words to *West Side Story*'s "Somewhere," full of promise that there was a place and occasion for true love; I'd identify Evelyn and myself with the doomed modern Romeo and Juliet of Russ Tamblyn and Natalie Wood. "Somewhere," my brother would mock, with the clarity of everyday responsibilities.

Certainly my sense of reality was as incomplete as my sexuality. Doubtless through Edgar and Paula's eyes I was unmotivated, dreamy, and spoiled. Soon I'd make college grades as poor as theirs were good (they were both Phi Beta Kappa). "You don't have any initiative," one once offered gratuitously; "When will you start supporting yourself?" the other returned when I asked to bum a cigarette. I was proud of a long, earnest autobiographical short story, "The Boy Who Couldn't Understand," which I'd written on that failed love relationship (a year later, novelist Reynolds Price would give it Davidson's prize), but Edgar and Paula were reproving. "Why write just about the beautiful things of life? Why not the ugly, like Dostoevsky?"

I was born at the end of 1944, a year after my father returned to the U.S. as an exchange prisoner of war on the Gripsholm, following one year of house arrest in Shanghai and seven months in a Japanese concentration camp (Daisy Belle, Maylee, and Edgar had been sent home just before the Japanese came.). My father had worked from 1926 for National City Bank of New York (what is now Citicorp) in the foreign concessions of Shanghai, Peking, and Canton; my sister and brother were born in China. After the war, Gordon Senior ("an expatriate at heart," my sister declared decades later, although I never knew his heart) resisted Daisy Belle's urgings to stay in Parkersburg, West Virginia and take one of several available banking positions. National City sent him back to China, from which he later got one of the last two planes out before Mao secured Shanghai in 1949. He remained in Japan for his last decade and a half of service with the bank. My mother, sister, brother, grandfather, and I joined him in Occupied Tokyo in 1950, when I was five and a half.

I recall—before Toyko—an idyllic American red-brick home life and neighborhood in Parkersburg, West Virginia. My "girlfriend" *was* the one next door. With awkward affection, Mary Nelson and I garlanded each other's hair with clover in our back yard where my grandfather had tomato plants every summer and baby chicks at Easter. In our family household, with my father abroad, my mother's father, then in his seventies, was my best friend. "Bopsie," I called him, snuggling up to him in bed at night.

I remember evenings at home, mother and sister at our piano, brother and chums singing: bright faces, voices harmonized and askew in music and laughter, red-and-black checked lumberjack shirts. Unlike in Tokyo, with my father and a chauffeur doing the driving (and maids cooking and housekeeping so she could concentrate on hostessing and attending ladies' teas and receptions), my mother drove a car: "Mother's going forty," Maylee or Edgar once sang as Mother picked up speed crossing the broad Ohio to Marietta.

Arriving in Yokohama July 1950, I was excited as our big s.s. President Wilson dropped anchor and the first of many fathers in khaki uniform, with shoulders of silver or gold and chests full of rainbows, began entering the children's playroom. Their little boys and girls—with whom I'd been in close contact half a month on the Pacific—rushed them in utter joy, arms raised and spread. But when my father finally appeared it was not in khaki, silver, gold, or rainbow, only a dark, faintly striped double-breasted business suit—I burst into tears.

Scarcely two years later my brother and sister were back in the States, and a declining "Bopsie" would before long pass away. No more did Sunday drives in our snout-nosed 1949 Studebaker take us to distant hairpin peaks and isolated villages and resorts; the larger texture of family life was thinning. We three would come to seem increasingly separate individuals.

Doubtless my own growth had something to do with it. But my father favored remoteness, even when we shared the same house, when bank and foreign community business did *not* require his being away. Once, I used his Vitalis hair oil and left the top off; when he discovered it a few days later, half the contents had evaporated. Getting such commodities in Occupied Japan was difficult; the bottle had likely come through the black market or a friend in the military whom he felt he couldn't ask again. He didn't spank me with his hard, open, stinging palm as he sometimes did. Instead, he sat on the tiled verandah that extended outdoors from my grandfather's soon-to-be-vacant room on the first floor, and silently held his bowed head in his hands. I stood in the yard and looked up toward him, almost in disbelief. It hurt much more than a spanking.

When I was eleven, visiting the u.s. on furlough, I asked my sister, then the mother of a baby boy, where babies come from. Two people love each other very much, she said; their love starts a seed, from the seed grows a baby. On return to Japan I heard a sort of rough-and-ready classmate, himself recently returned from a year at a boys' school in a western state, say the word "fuck." Later the same day I asked my mother what it meant. "That's not a nice word," she answered. When I asked her where babies came from she gave me a general idea, saying "You should talk to your father." That evening my father, seated at the far end of our carpeted silent living room, addressed me. "Your mother tells me you want to hear about the birds and the bees."

After his brief exposition I remained confused. What if the male "wanted to do it" (it hadn't quite been connected in my mind with having an erection) while he and his wife were at a party? I thought of the many receptions my mother and father went to, with other business and diplomatic people . . . sometimes, even, members of the Imperial Family were there! I also labored for months with the impression that the male stuck his cock into the female's bottom. I kept observing the size of women's bottoms, wondering if some were simply too large. Finally I asked my mother, "What if her bottom's too big?"

———

By the age of ten, I'd become a great lover of film. In Tokyo there were at least half a dozen first-run American movie houses and more theaters for older releases. Many a Saturday morning while my father worked at the bank, I'd see a movie with my mother: technicolor epics celebrating Vikings; good-spirited Danny Kaye films; *Knights of the Round Table.* From my velveteen seat—close as my mother could tolerate—I'd eagerly consume the large-screen action. Occasionally, I'd try to figure whether the momentary fading in of one image on another was really happening on-screen or in my mind. Through transparent rimmed glasses, my mother, seated next to me, remained quietly studious of the flickering dance of light and darkness.

Though as time passed we did less as a family, weekend evenings sometimes found the three of us at the movies. In those we saw, like all films from abroad, a transcribed soundtrack, sometimes embellished with commentary, ran down the right side of the screen in bright, crisp silver kanji. Whenever we took in a Hollywood film having to do with the Pacific conflict between Japan and the United States—a popular subject those days in Tokyo theaters—we'd hear the almost entirely Japanese audience clap and cheer uproariously as their Zeros scored a hit against American aircraft carriers: no side titles were needed.

And we'd see many other sorts of new releases, as well: *The Brothers Karamazov,* with its orgiastic scene of the father tickling a young woman's foot; *The Caine Mutiny; The High and the Mighty.* (During this time, Kurosawa Akira, Ozu Yasujiro, and others were making internationally acclaimed monuments of cinema; yet we saw none of them.) I kept going to movies from the States at every opportunity; I saw so many, in fact, that the editor of *Far East Film News,* a dinner guest in our home one evening, proposed an illustrated front-page feature on my love of cinema in an upcoming issue.

One movie stood out immeasurably from the others. I first learned of it through a glass-cased preview display outside the theater, as my mother and father and I returned one night to the rainy sidewalk from the warmth within. On exhibit were small black and white stills of American men in Western outfits, facing off, fistfighting, drawing guns. Beneath each was a caption in calligraphy; the whole display was centered by a bilingual *Shane.*

Gordon Ball

As much as anything, it was the strangeness of the name which struck me. Two weeks later, when I saw the movie itself, I was affected by much more. Though I couldn't have put it into such words, it was the sense of a perfect grown-up male role model that came through: understated, handsome, strong, with ringing words of instruction and inspiration for the young boy who loved him and who would be with him. I contemplated writing Alan Ladd a letter, inviting him to stay at our house if he came to Tokyo. I imagined him appearing suddenly some rainy spring evening, hatless, wet-haired, blue-eyed, in a light cloth raincoat, at our door, a little like his entrance in one scene in the movie.

I even liked Jack Wilson, the wicked gunslinger hired by the ranchers, played by Jack Palance. I couldn't reconcile Wilson's wanton, brutal slaying of a homesteader with my own sense of right and wrong, nor with my own love of the American South (Wilson used his opponent's southernness to taunt him into drawing first on the single muddy street of Jackson Hole), but that didn't stop me from loving the film.

One morning in Shinjuku I bought a thick bilingual paperback, *Sweet Jazz,* its cover a shot of Danny Kaye and a blonde actress in Santa suits, smiling heartily into the camera as theatrical snowflakes descended. Inside were lyrics and music for dozens of popular songs from American movies of the day. I memorized and sang the theme of *Shane,* "The Call of the Faraway Hills," over and over, at home, at school, and as I rode across Tokyo, in the back of our 1952 Plymouth, down clogged streets, past great canals. Amidst graceful bicycles, spokes flickering into bright light when caught by sun, past huffing three-wheelers and exhausting trucks, the words always came:

> Shadows fall on the prairie.
> Day is done and the sun
> Is slowly fading out of sight—
> I can hear—oh so clear,
> A call that echoes in the night.
> Yes I hear sweet and clear,
> The call of the faraway hills . . .

I began signing my name *Shane* on my papers, and my fourth grade teacher Mrs McClure seemed dutifully to understand. For Christmas I was given an imitation buckskin fringed jacket like Alan Ladd had worn. I even hoped to someday search for the historical Shane in the American West. And though I was let down by its more "grown-up" perspective, I read Jack Schaeffer's novel *Shane.* By age ten, I'd seen *Shane* four times, from the large commodious first-run theater to an extremely small, packed, steamy one on a rainy night where admission was forty yen (ten cents).

My father had been one of eleven children raised on a large, somewhat impoverished West Virginia farm near the banks of the Ohio. His father had made the mistake of accepting books as payments for rent at the small riverside hotel he'd once owned, only to then find them worthless. As a result, my grandfather and father (supported by my grandmother) argued about the value of learning and education. When Gordon left the farm for West Virginia University, he stoked boilers at night, made good grades, and got a job with the bank—which eventually sent him to Shanghai.

He'd first met my mother—barely fifteen, blue-eyed, shy, and endearingly attractive—when, as Ravenswood High School year book editor, he visited her father's portrait photography studio in Parkersburg to inquire about senior class pictures. Returning from China in 1931 from his first stint in Shanghai, he proposed to her. She was willing, but her parents—white southern middle-class, reserved—wouldn't let Daisy Belle go halfway around the world from them. Two days later, on a scheduled stop in Iowa in his model A as he began his way back to the Far East, he was greeted by a telegram from her best friend:

DAISY BELLE CAN'T LIVE WITHOUT YOU

He returned to West Virginia, they married, and after the reception my father was so excited he inadvertently lost the road and ended up driving on the railroad track. My mother's favorite uncle, Buddy Charles, who'd had the impish good sense to follow them in the April dusk, found their car on the tracks, all four new tires split into shreds, and took them back to Parkersburg for the night.

In China my parents, like most white foreigners who weren't missionaries, lived as aristocrats, in elegant quarters, with servants to maintain them. My father wore tweed suits with knickers and took a walking cane with him on his walking tours of Shanghai and the countryside. He had a folding seat to take to the races where he could use United States

Navy binoculars, bought cheaply on Chiang Kai-shek's black market, to see the horses up close. He had a still and a movie camera. Many years later I saw a black-and-white film of him walking in a Shanghai park where a sign was posted in Chinese and English: "No Chinese or Dogs Allowed."

Unfortunately, my father's words to me about China and especially his concentration camp experience were as brief as those about sex. He did once allow that he'd studied Yoga because he knew the Japanese were coming. He thought that if he were arrested, it would prepare him for confinement in close quarters. He'd stopped, he confided, "When they tried to tell me that I didn't exist."

I did learn that he was "Assistant Sanitary Engineer" (latrine orderly) in the concentration camp, spending several hours a day digging ditches. As he later reported confidentially to the bank, it was work he appreciated, for it was "good, hard, physical labor which kept me out in the open and was completely tiring so that I had no trouble sleeping at night." And he did tell me that the prisoners played the guards in baseball a few times. But we exchanged no more than two dozen words apiece on this or any subject, as he devoted himself to bank and foreign community affairs, school board (he was chairman four years), and church.

My relationship with my mother had been much closer, perhaps almost too much so. In any case, I loved her greatly, even as I was starting to grow apart from her. On first Saturday mornings in Tokyo when we lived far on the outskirts, I'd lie in bed with her while my father was at work. Later there was our morning moviegoing; often on afternoons she'd ride with the chauffeur to pick me up after school. "Eek a freak!" I once greeted her as in the company of a fourth-grade classmate I descended the stairs at the very moment she was starting up. Returning to school in a walking cast after having broken my leg, I was accompanied by my mother, who helped me between classes (a big galoot from the high school basketball team, on seeing me alone one day, sneered, "Where's your mother?").

She often helped me with homework by quizzing me on assigned reading, and once or twice I confided in her, however haltingly, dread secrets I'd never tell my father. But as time passed, I found communicating with

'66 Frames

both parents more and more difficult, especially when I began to wonder out loud about the unconventional, the socially inappropriate. One day at age fifteen a classmate—the son of an emissary from the Atomic Energy Commission, sent to Tokyo just over a dozen years after Hiroshima and Nagasaki to persuade the Japanese to consider nuclear power—told me of a group of people on the coast of California who spent their days painting and reading and writing poetry. They were called "Beatniks." I came home from school that afternoon and told my mother what Steve had said. "After all," I added, "what else is there to do?"

For an instant she looked me in the eye. Then she was saying, bitterly, "If you don't know"—tears started down her face—"I won't tell you," as she turned and left the room.

I'd just turned twelve when my leg was broken in six places in "Japanese Bulldog," a football-like outdoors game at a Boy Scouts gathering. As I lay in bed at home two months in a crusty cast from hip to toe, I put on weight. When I returned to normal activities, all the fat disappeared, except a very small pocket behind each nipple. It made me suddenly shy of my daily mile of summer swimming at the American Club, a social organization for the foreign business community, located just behind the Embassy of the Union of Soviet Socialist Republics.

When I was thirteen, I had my first girlfriend. Some schoolmates whose parents were in the American military had a party, and I lay on the floor all evening—on top of twelve-year-old Alice Reznik. In the same room, other couples sat together on furniture, the lights very dim. As Elvis Presley's "Wear My Ring Around Your Neck," the Dell Vikings' "Come Go With Me," and Johnny Mathis and other slow songs made their way mutely from a distant hi-fi, I kissed and kissed Alice, on her lips and cheeks and forehead and neck and ears, and lay with her in excitement and wonder. . . .

But when June came I avoided my familiar pool, afraid that Alice would see me—and discover I was a girl. While my mother was offering, "I hope that little Reznik girl wouldn't let you kiss her on the cheek," our relationship crumbled.

———

As I lived with my parents in a rapidly modernizing Tokyo, we sometimes had dinners for visiting VIPs associated with the bank, including Saki, an actor in the film adaptation of *Teahouse of the August Moon*, and John Paul Getty, Jr. More often, my parents attended evening receptions or dinners. After I returned from my American international school, maids would serve me dinner alone at 4:30. I'd read the *Asahi Evening News* and the *Stars and Stripes* as I ate; then until (and even sometimes after) dark, I might play imaginary American major league baseball games by bouncing a ball off an outside wall.

When we'd return to the U.S. every few years on furloughs, adult Americans would often say what an extraordinary experience it must be growing up in Japan. In the early fifties, when it was still occupied, I'd see bombed-out buildings; open sewage gutters lined some streets. I was forbidden to eat in Japanese places. "Honey" buckets were still used as vegetable fertilizer ("Owai! Owai!" came the collector's call). And even in the later fifties and early sixties, as Japan careened through a political and economic "miracle" of which I was almost oblivious, I'd still sometimes be chauffeured through the thronged, dynamic streets in our large black Plymouth. In my last years, thousands of anti-U.S. Zengakuren students, their foreheads embraced by white cloth vivid with red or black kanji, snakedanced their way down narrow alleys and broad boulevards just minutes from the walls of our housing compound. For me, "growing up in Japan" was an experience so protected it was almost denied.

In college my friend Eddie Rivers would tell me, "You seem still a child, Gordon." In Tokyo I grew older with an extraordinary lack of self-reliance, yet feeling I had to be president of the student council (which I did become my senior year), thinking the ideal world was the real world, not knowing the language spoken all around me. When a junior in high school I wrote a note to myself—in block lettering on white 8½ by 11— revealing that what I wanted most in life was a woman. I didn't know how to say it to anyone, let alone how to act on it. And I continued to assume that the United States was the world's vital center, an assumption that showed not only in my relations with Japanese in general but in the haughty manner in which I'd sometimes relate to the Japanese closest me.

'66 Frames

For years I'd been in the habit of baiting, ridiculing our maids, often for their ignorance of an American culture from which I too was distant. "Who's this?!" I once challenged as I held before our younger maid, in all the innocence of her baretted hair and starched white uniform, a close-up photograph of Louis Armstrong from the *Asahi Evening News*. Then some months later, at fifteen, I sat under a green gingko on a golden afternoon at a Shinto shrine and had what I took to be a religious experience. I resolved to mistreat Noriko and Chieko no more—and told no one of the experience.

Two years later I prepared to leave for the States and college. A photograph—I don't know who took it—from a mid-July evening in 1962 records a last, posed moment with my parents before I boarded a large Pan American jet. A "special" arm band allowed Mother and Daddy to accompany me to the foot of the very stairs rising metallically into my plane. Mother, in patterned summer dress, string of pearls, small hat and white gloves, is making a smile as she clutches a white sweater—perhaps there's a cool breeze out on the tarmac at Haneda Airport. At her right, heavyset husband and slender son remain tight-lipped. In a dark two-buttoned suit, dark necktie pinned to white shirt, Daddy looks fatigued, eager to exit the frame. I'm grim-jawed in suit and tie similar to his, my left hand displaying the glass imitation ruby ring I once bought Alice Reznik. Angry, eager to depart, I hold my bag at my knees with both hands, as if to ward off both presences.

Four years later, my retired father and mother had settled into a modest new stateside home, just two miles from my sister's in Winston-Salem. Though few signs of it were recognized at this time, within two years my mother would be diagnosed for what was being called Alzheimer's Syndrome.

During that four-year interval, my assimilation into American culture had bumped along: late, slow, and problematical. Before college I hadn't a crack at certain things which many young Americans in their midteens took for granted. I quit my first job of any sort—part-time busboy in the cafeteria at Davidson—early in my freshman year, after failing my first test in psychology, a subject I'd considered majoring in. I didn't learn how to drive a car till spring break of that year, when I took a week's course with a professional driving school. Two days after getting my license, just after buying a seven-year-old Chevy far on the other side of Winston-Salem, I made a discovery in unfamiliar, slow-moving bumper-to-bumper five o'clock traffic. Catching sight of an appealing young woman on the opposite corner, I found that the basic makeup of cars was cellophane as I jammed the rear of the Buick in front of me.

So after four years back in the United States, I'd held no "real" job, and was in fact indisputably irresponsible. I'd gone over $400 into debt at Harvard in the summer of 1965 when I had my first charge card (with the Harvard Coop); made a number of long distance calls to my girlfriend Anna Marie in Charlotte; and, after loaning her my Chevy (now nine years old and ailing) for the summer, I covered repairs when she drove up to see me. Even after cutting expenditures considerably my senior year, I'd received notice before the end of second semester that my checking account was being closed "to protect the community." I'm sure I often seemed—and was—outlandish, prodigal, inarticulate; the evidence was certainly there for siblings to think of me as wastrel, ne'er-do-well. Likely my parents had a similar impression, though my mother held hope. "Have you thought of becoming a minister?" she once tried in a letter from Tokyo, early in my undergraduate career. Undoubtedly she and my father had been profoundly shocked when in September of my freshman year they received a telegram expressing my desire to renounce citizenship, and quit compulsory ROTC.

So there I was on the afternoon of December 25, 1966, sitting in a high-backed, peaked bishop's chair for Christmas dinner. In front of us, a large turkey roasted crisp and juicy by my sister, accompanied by canned peas, sweet potatoes, and cranberry sauce in rose medallion dishes. Most of us were in fairly formal wear: my father in one of his dark sober suits, my mother in silk blouse and blue wool suit. I wore a green velour shirt, broad leather belt, tight bell-bottoms, and a pair of leather boots, a gift from Candy. The lulled sounds of polite intermittent conversation, silver sliding over rose medallion, weight-shifting creaks in the high stiff bishop's chairs, the tiny silver butter knife clinking in collapse upon its glass dish, all took hold. My slender, lean-faced brother-in-law's Blue Ridge drawl as he addressed my parents; my brother's quietness (Was it glumness? Judgment?

'66 Frames

Suffering? I never knew.); the wincing pleasantness emanating from my
mother's compacted, birdlike frame; my father's abstractedness; my sister's
diluted emotion, passion; the stiff, practical, polite assertion of my sister-in-
law as she addressed my mother and father . . .

I tried once or twice to offer up a playful or even mischievous remark,
but no one indulged. Later in my brief visit, several of us went over to that
rather modest red brick home into which my parents had moved in early
1966, nine thousand miles from Tokyo, eleven thousand from Shanghai.
Not far from my sister's Meadowbrook Drive, it was what you'd expect for
a relatively comfortable family of four, its new foundation rising humbly
from its bed of red clay. But inside the living room were several of the arti-
facts from four Eastern decades: Indonesian teakwood figurines (a pair,
one male, one female) sitting erect on a Chinese ebony sideboard; a nest-
ing set of elaborately carved cherry wood Chinese tables; an ebony, ivory,
and jade Chinese screen of infinite Vairocana Buddhas.

From a closet my father lifted out a small, somewhat jittery 16 mil-
limeter Kodak projector he'd bought in Shanghai and shipped home with
my mother, brother, and sister. I then gave my family one of the first
screenings of *Georgia,* a silent, plotless, multi-imaged, four-minute color
film I'd recently completed—my first! I held my breath as the only 16 MM
print I had began to make its way off the revolving reel, squeeze under the
first sprocket wheel, loop and then plunge straight down through the
ancient gate and eventually rise again to curl round the takeup reel.

Without tear or mutilation, my film made its way through the worn,
clattery, gray machine. Perhaps equally a matter of good fortune and cir-
cumstance was the making of the movie itself half a year earlier. When in
late April 1966 Jonas Mekas had stepped off the train in the Charlotte sta-
tion, he'd presented me with a small, strong and heavy regular 8 mil-
limeter Revere movie camera. In just a few minutes he'd explained all I
needed to know to use it—including how to superimpose, to place one
layer of imagery atop another. I took it with me riding north eight weeks
later with my friend Jon Mullis, and I had it in hand when we stopped in
Richmond to see Jon's ex-wife, Margaret. Within minutes upon meeting
her as twilight began to fall on a warm, expanding Saturday night in early
summer, I began shooting a movie.

Margaret—"Georgia"—was petite; her high cheekbones and large
deeply set green eyes pleaded intelligence, sensuality. As dusk gathered

the three of us began driving down Richmond's august Monument Avenue, where enormous statues every few blocks celebrated in bronze and stone the heroes—J.E.B. Stuart, Stonewall Jackson, Robert E. Lee— of the white southern cause. As night fell we stopped at a large traffic circle fountain, where I was immediately spellbound: lights and fountain and mist and the beauty of Georgia's face became one.

On the spot, in the course of two hours, I shot a single magazine of regular 8 MM Kodachrome. Camera in hand, barefoot in my chinos, I stepped about within the calf-high waters of the pool and the enveloping mist of the fountain, holding Georgia's green scarf over my lens, diffracting light into explosive gossamer brilliance far beyond the power of the moist air, shooting her from one angle, then another, shooting the lights of the fountain, of the traffic beyond. Then, right at the heart of our evening, the police drove up.

"What are y'all doin'?"

"We're making a movie."

Politely they drove away, baffled but unremonstrating. As I shot I reinserted the single magazine over and over so there were up to four levels of imagery at once, superimposed: a "tone poem," a "film portrait" others called it on seeing the rhythmic, rhapsodic, baroque variations of Margaret's face appear and disappear in gossamer mist, impressionist light, velvet darkness. When he first saw it at an open house at the Cinematheque four months later, Jonas Mekas hurried out of the auditorium immediately afterward, asking, exclaiming, "Was that yours? That's a very good film, a very good film."

Following the family living room projection at Christmas 1966, I snapped on the light and glanced toward the wrinkled, ruddy, pleasantly somnolent face of my father, beheld the puzzlement on my mother's brow. The light overhead reflected off my brother's glasses, shielding what lay within his brown eyes. The moments ticked, or seemed about to, when suddenly I heard Paula, a clinical psychologist who was characteristically a little more given to speech than our reticent family, offer, "You really have a kind of molecular feeling for your subject."

"Molecular," for me, was a code word: Timothy Leary had spoken of LSD opening up "cellular" consciousnesses, and Robert Du Peintre spoke of our "molecular systems." My eyes suddenly brightened. "Yes, right into the old molecular system!" I affirmed to my well-intended sister-in-law. Did she know my particular connotation? What did the word really mean for her? Fearing to find out, catching a glint of what seemed Phi Beta gold from the corner of my eye, I left the subject at that: perhaps being understood was riskier than not. In her modified dark blue empire dress, front tips and heels of her low black pumps vanishing into the soft light gray wall-to-wall carpet, she smiled back pleasantly. My parents and others sat quietly: but they had sat there, and watched my film. Still I remained struck by the enormous sense of difference I felt, and I didn't know how to close the gap.

Such, outside of playing with my nephews and a few quiet moments alone with my sister, was essentially my day-and-a-half or two-day Christmas visit. Another plane ride and I was back in New York. On December 30 I turned 22, as self-absorbed as ever; though I may've been superficial in some ways, I was seeking to penetrate the depths of Absolute Reality. I was now the same age as Jonas Mekas when, twenty-two years earlier, he and his brother Adolfas were captured by the Nazis and placed in a work camp outside Hamburg. Twenty-three years earlier, my father had marked his last days in the "Chapei Civil Assembly Center," the concentration camp across from Soochow Creek, on the outskirts of Shanghai.

NEW YEAR'S EVE

Candy was back from Christmas in Somerville, revived and even talkier than usual after several days with her large Catholic family. Minutes after I'd gotten in I heard her key in the lock for the long police bar, turned to see her rush from the cold, beaming, lips glowing with fresh gloss, cheeks far redder than the reddest of her auburn hair. "Oh, Baby!" she shouted, we embraced. Then we stepped out across the hall a moment, to the neighbor who'd asked to keep Miss Lyn, Candy's cat with satiny silver tipped gray hair and white paws. Then back in apartment B, we hit the mattresses to catch up.

On December 31st, Candy and I took acid. Hours later, en route to the Cinematheque for its last program of the year and a party afterward at filmmaker Shirley Clarke's Chelsea Hotel penthouse, we pushed exuberantly up the steps of the Times Square subway. In visible white traces, Candy's breath tumbled upward as she exulted, "It's like we're a whole new race!"

We'd been chattering about the entire subterranean youth culture of which we felt a part, loosely connected in ethos, in the hermetic or gnostic values we cherished, with thousands of others of the same age. We were horrified by many of the values of dominant, mainstream "overground" culture that was leading our American War (there were at that time 385,000 lethally armed Americans in the Republic of Vietnam), sending fellow human beings to death in the electric chair, disenfranchising blacks, and imprisoning many of our peers for following curiosity by ingesting beneficent herbs and profoundly valuable chemicals. It abused language for commercial and political gain; it substituted meretricious competition for profit in place of cooperation, imagination, spirituality, aesthetics.

The Cinematheque program, "The Last Open House of 1966," featured a number of unscheduled films and presentations. At its center Ronna Page, a young actress friend, spoke breathily from the stage before showing her own film, *Himalaya West: Children of the Lower East Side.* Celebrating "a silver-haired pop artist," her words seemed to suggest that with the New Year, Andy Warhol would bring a New World.

After the program's end, Candy and I mingled in the rather small, spartan lobby of the subterranean Cinematheque, talking, laughing. Still under some effects of the LSD, we found ourselves alone at one moment. Without deliberation I extended my hand so as to begin to raise Candy's—without touching it. I looked down and could see the same bands of energy I'd last seen with Robert now connecting us—fine thin graphite-like arcing lines with rainbow emanations. And as with Robert, I could hear a slight sound from within those few inches of extraordinary activity. A few dozen other people, many somewhat older, many with heavy coats and warm hats, milled about in twos and threes and larger groups, talking of Artaud, of war, of Bob Dylan, of city zoning and fire regulations—and perhaps even LSD. Candy and I looked at each other, delighted, and exclaimed, "We can do it too!"

Shortly we were to leave midtown basement for Chelsea penthouse. As it happened, we were driven there along with several others, from 125 West Forty-First Street near Times Square to West Twenty-Third between Seventh and Eighth, by Allen Ginsberg's companion Peter Orlovsky. Wearing a Tam O'Shanter, he called out to Allen in his gruff lilting voice—"Huh, hoh, Allen!—This way?"—from his driver's seat at the front of an off-white Volkswagen bus (even though Allen too was right there in the front). Boney-faced and extremely animated, with black horn-rimmed glasses, Peter had long straight thick blondish-brown hair hanging so far down it seemed to have a life of its own, responding to the movements of his O'Shantered head like a tail on a tadpole. Once he emerged from the car, his ass and elbows (the former taut, with scarcely more fat than the latter) likewise seemed to express a life of their own, as he strutted and "Harrumphed" up the pavement, toward the electric-lit pointillist paintings of the Chelsea lobby.

Up in the rooftop home of filmmaker Shirley Clarke (who'd made *The Connection* and *The Cool World*) we could see more clearly some of our fellow passengers. Allen and Peter were on either side of a young Puerto Rican to whom Allen offered a joint. The boy—age sixteen?—seemed shy, hesitant; Allen encouraged him. Also in their company in some sense was a silent, sullen fellow with something of a scowl on his face, just slightly short, lips glued together in a downward slant. Socially, he seemed to absorb—or reflect—nothing. He simply stood there in his crewcut: a white T-shirt stretched its bottom half over a pot belly. Was he retarded? A juvenile delinquent? I realized afterward—or someone said—that he was Julius Orlovsky, released in 1964 from twelve years in an asylum.

Gordon Ball

Things settled down after midnight. Shirley, a slender demonstrative woman with short dark hair, was joined by her black companion Carl Lee, who'd played Cowboy in *The Connection*. Candy and I met her flamboyant black drink-mixer Jason, a self-proclaimed hustler who loved telling stories, giggling, eyeing you brightly from behind large black horn-rimmed lenses. He rolled joints with panache, capping them with a quick lick, a suggestive head-on thrust inside his mouth. He was so vivid of manner and speech, so given to performance, and so complex a personality, that Shirley would soon shoot a feature-length film of him.

There were maybe a dozen guests. Allen became engaged with a small group seated around a sort of bed or couch that was flush with one wall, covered with Indian paisley cotton. He sat upright against the white plaster; resting next to him was filmmaker Jack Smith. As they continued talking with several others who sat on the other end of the bed, Allen put his arm around Jack's shoulder, tenderly, companionably, close. How much I admired the statement of freedom and comradeship and togetherness and brotherliness and affection it made! How outré, unacceptable, and downright forbidden it seemed in America, 1966!

The conversation (was it about the continuing problem of censorship of literature and film in America?) among their group of five or six was subdued, serious, quiet. Long after Candy and I had settled into each other in a nearby corner, talking and playing languidly, their intimate all-night voices continued.

When one or two hours later we all rose to go, Allen came over and planted a kiss on Candy's forehead. Minutes later, in the hush-tired dark of a 3:00 A.M. taxi heading back to 57 Thompson Street, a few distant straggling revelers visible on the cold side of our warm windows, she exclaimed from our quiet back seat, "Allen Ginsberg is a saint."

EARLY ALLEN

I didn't talk with Allen that night, though I'd chanced to meet him briefly, earlier in the spring before my move to the city. Visiting New York a week in the company of a friend, I stayed with Panna Grady, Hungarian countess and arts patron; she threw two big parties in her extremely large Dakota apartment. To one of them, Allen came. I'd seen him early in the evening as I passed by: he was standing up against the white wall, in black beard and black cape, seeming to expound to a huddle of more than half a dozen other guests in tight semicircle. Aw, I told myself, what's he got to say more valuable than I?

Enjoying mixed drinks in unusual quantity (usually, I took none), I circulated among the other guests. To José Garcia Villa's request, moments after we met, that we spend the evening together, I responded insensitively, "There are lots of other interesting guests here and I'd like to meet some of them, too." One of the first to arrive had been Norman Mailer. The black-uniformed maid had greeted him, "Good evening, Mr Mailer," as she freed his coat from his dark suit. His mass of gray-and-black hair curled almost uniformly above ears poking up and out; with broad smile and bright little blue eyes, he looked resplendent, all set for a charmed evening. But later on, when I was speaking with Andy Warhol, he came in between us and greeted Andy by exclaiming, like a loud carnival barker with entrepreneurial Brooklynese flourish, "Oh, Andy, it's guh-rate to meet a real movie directah!" (Andy's response was a blank-faced "Oh.")

A few exchanges later I turned to my left, to Andy's right, and there was Allen, facing me. He extended his hand, "I'm Allen," his look so soulful we continued one more instant, as if seeing deeply into each other, while my hand took his: "I'm Gordon." Then, with drunkenness approaching sickness, I turned and left, went to my room, lay down.

Five months later, I looked up his address soon after coming to New York in the fall—his number, 777-6786, along with his 408 East Tenth Street address, was listed in those days. I even walked, once or twice, on East Tenth among the heavily Puerto Rican alphabet avenues hoping to run into him. Then on a warm night in early autumn I saw him around East Sixth or East Seventh between First and Second walking with a friend, absorbed in conversation, wearing a white cotton suit of the sort I imagined he'd brought from India—loose-fitting homespun khaddar cloth like Mahatma Gandhi wove and spun, challenging the English manufacture of Indian cottons.

My first visual image of him had come several years earlier, soon after my first year at Davidson College, when—with total determination—I made my first trip to New York. I left the company of my mother, who'd arrived a few days earlier from Tokyo for a family visit. Feelings hurt, she said I shouldn't go. But I'd won a small amount of prize money for my fiction, and longed for New York—on my own.

Browsing at a newsstand one New York morning, I picked up the mid-summer issue of a major periodical. Inside was a large glossy color photo of Ginsberg, a hearty, robust, ecstatic expression on his face, dripping head to toe with water from the Ganges. There in the holy ancient river he stood, nearly naked except for the thin white muslin that clung wetly to his torso. The photograph impressed and intrigued me with its sense of something primally, atavistically vibrant, ecstatic, and sacred—something absent from sober, Presbyterian Davidson College, from life as I was finding it.

Two years later in Charlotte, North Carolina, pinned above Billy Trotter's work desk, I saw the news photo of Allen Ginsberg walking through falling snow in front of a Manhattan courthouse, carrying a placard, "Pot is a Reality Kick." A year after that, summer 1966, on the university hill in Syracuse, New York, I bought the small black-and-white City Lights Pocket Poets series number four, *Howl and Other Poems,* for seventy-five cents. I read some of the title poem and wasn't sure I understood it. But I kept it.

DAVIDSON, *FLAMING CREATURES*, AND JONAS

(1)

Five years before *Howl,* LSD, *Revolver,* and life in New York City—five years before touching a movie camera—I was a senior at the American School in Japan, applying to colleges in the United States. Davidson, set in a small, tree-lined North Carolina town, had come highly recommended by sister and brother. Among National Merit Scholars, even Rhodes Scholars, it was well-represented. And, though 9,000 miles from "home," if I were at Davidson, brother and sister would be nearby.

I was rejected at Harvard and Swarthmore and applied late to Duke, where I was put on a waiting list. I chose Davidson, which like Harvard then was all-male but without a Radcliffe next door, or a Cambridge, or a Boston. It was a much different place from today: strongly Presbyterian, with mandatory vespers (Sunday evening worship services) and tri-weekly midmorning compulsory assemblies that were for the most part secular, but were required nonetheless. I told myself that the lack of women wouldn't matter—I was going to study.

A land grant college founded by Scot-Irish Presbyterians in 1837 in southwestern North Carolina, Davidson lay twenty miles north of Charlotte. I can still see the catalog that traveled nine thousand miles to our home in Tokyo, its brown cover emblazoned in magnified federalist script, "Sir, Having a young man of genius . . ." My mother wept in joy upon learning of my acceptance, embracing me.

Davidson seemed ever to champion itself—even a Main Street marker celebrated it—as the alma mater of Woodrow Wilson, in spite of the fact that, having found Davidson "rough" (one had to start one's own fires in winter) he transferred after a year and a half to Princeton. William Styron (class of 1946) also attended, transferring to Duke because of the heavy dose of Old Testament fundamentalism he encountered. Davidson's most celebrated contemporary graduate was Secretary of State Dean Rusk, one of the prose-cutors and defenders of America's Vietnam War. Rusk admirably demon-strated the Davidson ideal of soft-spoken loyalty to the power at the helm.

Once I came to the Davidson of the the early 1960s, I found much of the faculty provincial, with one of its icon-like members valued supremely—by students!—not for any ideas or enthusiasms of his own, but for his having had a high grade point average in his own career there four decades earlier. Indeed, within its faculty and administration, the alma mater was more than generously represented—eleven of the fifteen major administrators, from the president down, were alumni. Ideas, except for those approved as safe by long-established traditions, were not in the habit of being discussed. "Homosexuality, Mr Rivers," the venerated, spectacled, white-mustached philosophy professor slowly and pontifically addressed a question from my friend, "is a subject for the clinic, not the classroom."

There were of course other reasons for my disaffection, including my own extreme youthfulness and personal shortcomings, as well as the thicket of long-developing problems with my mother and father in Tokyo. And there was the whole enormous cultural shift from a cosmopolitan environment in the largest city on earth to a small, isolated, religion-based college of sons of the white upper class from the southern states.

Alienated, I fell early on through a series of social and academic disasters: being blackballed by a fraternity after I reported, as my "Big Brother" had requested, that I'd been hazed; failing one semester of freshman math twice; being identified by the dean, in a letter to my parents, as one of a few dozen "underachievers." Part of my problem perhaps also lay in feeling, as I often did in those days, that—much as I thought I wanted to live my own life (whatever that might mean) and much as I already lived, to some degree, in a sort of fantasy realm—the larger world of "reality" and social norm ultimately had to be yielded to. I hadn't sought fraternity life, but chose it—the dominant mode then at Davidson—on family recommendation. When asked to "defend the Constitution of the United States against all its enemies, so help me God," I tried to resist compulsory ROTC, then gave in to peer pressure.

By and by, I came to make my separate peace by chairing the Student Union Film Committee my last two and a half years there. This was work I'd live and die for, and its by-product was an ad hoc education, even if limited and haphazard, in American and European narrative film, which made up for the lack of movie courses of any kind at the school. In front of my large magic-markered poster extolling "The Film Scene at Davidson," I excitedly greeted entering freshmen at orientation, urging the interested to join. Capitalizing on some of the many great recent works of international cinema, I developed "Film Friends," a special semesterly series of movies to be shown at the new Fine Arts Center across campus from the Union. Rentals of these "finer" films—from Eisenstein and Murnau through Mizoguchi and Agnes Varda—would be supported by the full-house receipts we'd get from showing the commercial films—the first James Bond, *Cool Hand Luke,* and the like—that we screened regularly at the Union.

Viewer response was never stronger than on an evening behind pneumatically closed, rubber-bordered doors in the Morrison Room of the David Ovens College Union. Then and there, perhaps two hundred young, close-cropped, fresh-cheeked sons of ministers, bank managers, accountants, physicians, missionaries, and lawyers sat elbow-to-elbow on skeletal metal folding chairs in a darkness violated only by a streaming, splaying light that emanated far above and behind them, growing vortically as it passed overhead and in front of them until it smashed against a flat silver-stippled screen at which they all stared. At flickering configurations suggestive of sexual arousal, they would all shout en masse, "Take it off!" and "Do it!" and—when subsequently disappointed—"AAAWW, SHIIT!!!"

Such was the dominant aesthetic. Meantime I worked in our small office area at the Union, holding meetings, talking rates and dates with distributors like Brandon Films, Cinema 16, New Yorker, and Janus. In solitude, I looked up reviews of coming films for my own information and for potentially useful promotion copy. I loved all of those activities, as well as using the microfilm readers in the library to read *New York Times* reviews: I loved that illuminated dark cave-like work.

Often, since films generally came in three or four days early, I had an opportunity to project some of them, for myself and/or an occasional friend or committee member, ahead of time. When I saw Andrzej Wajda's *Ashes and Diamonds,* I was completely taken visually, dramatically, with the ghostly Polonaise near its end, with the death of the bleeding young Zbigniew Cybulski, clutching white linen in a desolate field of hanging white sheets. Immediately I reached for magic markers and large white posterboard and made a new entry for our Union lobby display, proclaiming *Ashes and Diamonds* the greatest film ever made.

Just a little later that fall—it was my senior year—a classmate lumbered through the green plastered second-floor corridor of Duke Dormitory one evening. I looked up and saw a small round head on a long frame in my open door. "You ought to invite Jonas Mekas down," George Williams told me almost matter of factly.

"Who's that?" I asked. When I read *The New York Times* Sunday magazine article George handed me—"Voice of the 'Underground Cinema'" by Alan Levy—I knew he was right. Levy described a man of great singleness of vision and devotion to the aesthetics of cinema and the social and cultural revolution it could bring. Organizer of and fund-raiser for independent and avant-garde cinema from production through showcasing, a filmmaker himself, and the author of a controversial weekly film column in the *Village Voice* where readers had characterized him as "going mad," "a catalyst," and "a firebrand," Jonas Mekas in the eyes of Levy was ". . . a gaunt thin-lipped bachelor with the face of a Slavic martyr . . . 'I am a poet,' [Jonas] explained softly, 'whose involvement comes from inner need, whose language is film, and to whom going to jail is not just a human experience, but a moral obligation. I *see* more than others.' "

And he seemed a man of some wisdom: " 'Children and wise men never argue about movies,' he says. 'Everything is clear to them. Only we—those in between—are all shook up, confused, lost in the pastures of art.' "

Simone de Beauvoir and Jean-Paul Sartre were admirers of Mekas's most recent feature-length work, *The Brig*, a documentary so unconventional that after it won First Prize at the 1964 Venice Film Festival, Mekas informed jurors that in reality it was not a documentary but a filmed performance of a play. His view of the potential of cinema was limitless: "Salvador Dalí is working on contact lenses which will throw color images on our retina while we sleep. It is from here just one step to the absolute cinema—Cinema of Our Mind. For what is cinema really if not images, dreams and visions? We take one more step, and we give up all movies and we become movies. . . ."

And here was a call from somewhere other than the gross material world. Levy reported that not only did Mekas receive no salary from his writing and administration, but that his estimated total personal income for the preceding five years was $2,000. "Films," the filmmaker-poet concluded, are made with " 'belief, passion, enthusiasm, persistence—anything but money.' "

Mekas's jail experience related, in a way, to some of my own recent involvement with movies. Twice within the last year or so he'd been arrested for showing two films declared obscene by the police—Jack Smith's *Flaming Creatures,* and, soon thereafter, Jean Genet's *Un Chant d'Amour.* In the first instance, Jonas was alerted by phone that film and equipment were being seized—and that manager and cashier (Ken Jacobs and his wife-to-be, Flo), as well as ticket taker, were being arrested. Jonas hurried to the theater and demanded that he too be arrested. In the second, he went to jail with a copy of William Blake's *Poetical Works* in his coat pocket; it was later forced from his hands with the explanation that it was a potential weapon.

I'd first heard of *Flaming Creatures* from another student at a college Union convention the previous spring. While the bus taking us to afternoon events shifted into second past the rolling green hills, million-dollar horses, and fresh white fences of Lexington, Kentucky, we spoke of intimate depictions of sexuality in cinema. My seatmate confided about *Creatures,* "It has everything!" Though I also, perhaps foolishly, sought, yearned for aesthetic, transcendent dimensions in film, I was every bit—perhaps even more than they—as interested in sex on screen and off as schoolmates who shouted "Take it off!" Back at Davidson I managed to find a little writing—not much—on this particular movie, including Susan Sontag's five-page essay that would appear over a decade later in *Against Interpretation.* What my friends and I took to be the film's unrestricted sex—with some dimension of art—was of course at the heart of our interest. And, I felt determinedly, sex could, after all, be art. But what Sontag's several references to *Creatures*'s homosexuality as well as heterosexuality would actually mean when full-blown and moving on a vacant screen, none of us could say.

Creatures was distributed from New York by Filmmakers' Cooperative, whom I'd reached on the phone. The Cooperative was one of the several small organizations involved in showcasing or distributing the "New American Cinema"—independent, experimental, noncommercial, personal, avant-garde works—which Mekas had pioneered. He'd done so out of his belief that movies need not be the product of thousands to make money, but that they could be as personal, as individual, as inspired, as poetry or any other art.

His commitment to the art of film was long—and rock-solid. After more than half a decade of flight, internment, and relocation from refugee camp to refugee camp in west central Europe, enduring hardships that were often extreme, Mekas with his younger brother Adolfas, had entered the U.S. in 1949, a Displaced Person. Their first two years were spent loading trucks, washing dishes, and assisting plumbers. Then they bought a 16 MM Bolex and documented the Williamsburg section of Brooklyn in which they lived. And always, always, they went to the cinema. Moving to the Lower East Side in 1953, Jonas began a series of avant-garde and other kinds of films; two years later he began editing a new journal devoted to foreign, narrative, and experimental work: *Film Culture.* In 1958, he began weekly columns in the *Voice,* and shot his first feature-length film, *Guns of the Trees.* Soon, he was founding the New American Cinema Group to look out for the interests of noncommercial creative films; taking a program of American independent films to Europe; setting up the nonprofit Filmmakers' Cooperative, which rented movies to colleges, museums, film societies, individuals; shooting *The Brig;* and creating the Filmmakers' Cinematheque, a small showcase for independent film. As the audience for independent, avant-garde films continued to grow, the spring of 1966 found him and several colleagues founding a Filmmakers' Distribution Center to release experimental works to large commercial first-run theaters.

The movies which Jonas championed, supported, and defended in action as well as written and spoken word, represented a great variety of genres, from diary and autobiography to narrative to film portrait to animation. Each was part of filmmaking traditions going back through Maya Deren, Luis Buñuel, Sergei Eisenstein, and Man Ray to Méliès and the Lumières at the turn of the century. Through Jonas, such traditions were connected to the narrative experiments of contemporaries like John Cassavetes and Robert Frank.

Of course, some—not many—of the films Jonas stood for dealt directly with sex. His efforts to show them sometimes got him in trouble, as in his U.S. arrests, and in an earlier contretemps at the Third International Experimental Film Festival at Knokke-Le Zoute, Belgium, 1963. After showing works by the great American filmmaker Stan Brakhage and others, Jonas was denied his showing of *Flaming Creatures* by the Belgian Minister of Culture, who in full authority stood before him in front of a packed auditorium. Mekas responded by projecting the film on the minister's face and well-dressed body—until the electricity was cut.

My own efforts to show the Smith film were as star-crossed—but I lacked Jonas's wily magic. As word grew of our hopes to book it, contro-

`44`

versy flared within the student body. Handwritten and typed statements and even posters were tacked onto the Union's large "Wailing Wall" bulletin board. "But what about decency?" one short-haired earnest young schoolmate asked heatedly, as we argued face-to-face one afternoon in front of the colorful board. Shocked by the narrowness I sensed, I didn't think till later of responding, "What *about* decency? What about art!"

Other schoolmates—having heard that homosexuals appeared in the film—attacked *my* sexuality. In the eyes of many, grounds to do so were already ample, since for a male to have long hair as I did, mid-South fall 1965, went far beyond the pale. My friend Billy Trotter posted a defense, citing the "handful" of young women he knew I was then sleeping with in Charlotte—they might indeed have something to say about my masculinity! In large blue magic-markered block letters, one righteously offended student identified me as "the Mario Savio of Davidson"—and I appreciated the undeserved, unintended compliment.

My friend Eddie Rivers displayed a 2 by 3-foot poster speaking out for "pansexuality" in the face of two millennia of Christian repression. I was afraid for smart, bespectacled Eddie—and admired, almost loved him for it:

> A Counterblast Against "Preversion"
> I am shocked & outraged that the Union would entertain for a moment the idea of an open showing of a film as potentially harmful as *Flaming Creatures*. We must NEVER allow our boys to suspect that there are other kinds of sex than the heterosexual, genitally-organized kind. What would become of the Great Institution of the Family, on which our Nation, under God, was founded, if we should be assaulted with, and forced to give serious consideration to, the idea that sexual love among members of the same sex is not only possible, and does occur, but that it can be downright Enjoyable? Or that there are ways to get Kicks with a girl, or with three or four or five at the same time, without anybody's ever actually getting screwed so she can get kid & continue the race?? (I'd tell you how, but I don't want to make you any sicker.)—Let's not kid ourselves; aesthetic detachment is practically impossible when sex is the subject being treated, and nobody is going to see a film about blow jobs without getting SEXED OFF!!! Which is criminal—CRIMINAL! I hate the thought that I might see something on the screen

Gordon Ball

that could stir long dead urges in my psyche and whisper to me something about myself, about the race, that I'd rather not know. We all know that what's important in sex is the big boobs in *Playboy*—and Nothing Else! (big boobs means she'd make a nice mother means she's like our mother means she wants to be our mother means a happy medium between sex and security so I can go out & make $1,000,000 and not worry about being castrated). It's taken me 2,000 years to get my Dionysian and pan-erotic proclivities under lock & key in my subconscious, and By God, YOU'RE NOT GOING TO STIR THEM UP NOW BY MAKING ME WATCH TRASH LIKE *FLAMING CREATURES*.

Eventually we realized, of course—as Union Director C. Shaw Smith, more than two decades our senior, "helped" us see—that we couldn't show *Flaming Creatures* at the Davidson College Union. Many students (and likely, parents and alumni) would be outraged, and we—and he—would be called to task for it. Finally, if that weren't persuasive enough, he'd say "No" anyway. So we asked two friends in Charlotte if we could use their house.

Helen Mullis—Jon's second wife—was pretty and perhaps thirty; Jon was good-looking, five years younger. Bohemian and generous, they managed somehow to survive in middle-class, or lower-middle-class, white Charlotte, and several times had hosted Billy and me and our young women companions in their large frame house. Now again, for *Flaming Creatures,* they were agreeable.

Since the Mullises lived deep within the city, we drew a map for all who paid their $2.00. Billy added an injunction on the map in block letters: "DON'T LEAVE THIS LYING AROUND," which I saw and erased immediately, fearing further difficulties from anyone who, interest piqued, might decide to crash the affair, or pass the map on to the police. It might not have been legal for them to bust a showing in a private home, but the Charlotte gendarme who thrust his face and flashlight into the back seat of a car one night during my freshman year seemed to have no qualms about following his whim. "If you're gonna sit in the car," he spat down at my lady friend and myself in the depths of the seat, "sit up!"

That fall a bespectacled, bearded, learned new philosophy professor, Neville Douglas, had come to Davidson; my friend Rick Jensen had exclaimed about both his mind and his nine-foot long living room bookshelf. In discussions of film—*Creatures* in particular—he and a few other instructors had seemed supportive. But I found myself saying, awkwardly, "You don't know what you're missing," when Douglas, responding to my call to his home two days before the showing, told me he wouldn't attend. I'd wanted to convey something of my disappointment, but still leave a door open—and almost immediately regretted my words. Philosopher Douglas was of course interested in aesthetics, and had seemed a "bona fide" intellectual, in contrast to our perception of the many provincials, "fossils" and "prunes" long resident within the Davidson faculty. Now, faced with putting down $2.00, taking the risk of being seen by students and, possibly, strangers, he and several like him backed off. We were left with Billy and myself and our small gang of friends, and perhaps a dozen jocks hungry for flesh—and generous Jon and Helen.

"Thank you for coming," was all I said to the much larger, broad-shouldered, short-haired, big-biceped and unsmiling young men who in dormitories, locker rooms, and frat houses were the wellsprings of ebullience. At the end of the hour-long *Creatures,* they quietly trickled out. In spite of what I'd been told in the spring, the film—which all of us, myself included, had just seen for the first time—did not contain "everything;" it was a merry, campy transvestite romp, with a mock gang bang, a jiggled limp penis, and an unaffectionately jiggled female breast, but little actual sex. The mood of the piece, with its ancient victrola music (1930s crooners and rhumbas) and costumes (women and men in lipstick, second-hand store lace, silk, hats, scarves) was of some interest to me. But it was all from a world beyond Davidson College, where wise men directed discussions of the varieties of sexual experience to the clinic. I sympathized with the football players who paid and drove at least an hour—perhaps getting lost on the way!—to see something that might certainly have satisfied them for strangeness but surely, sorely disappointed, outraged, and confused them for sex. At the same time, I remained drawn to the mystery. What kind of films were being made in New York? Who were these people? What were they really like? What were their other movies like? What was going on in New York?

Gordon Ball

②

I connected with Jonas Mekas on the phone, and we talked of the possi-
bility of his visiting and showing films in the spring. But C. Shaw Smith
—portly, jocose, a magician on the side—acted apprehensive. "Is he a
communist?" he asked. It was one of a series of questions displaying
the fear that Jonas might politically, culturally, sexually, or religiously
threaten community values.

Strengthened by the Sunday *Times* article and an occasional *Village
Voice,* I put aside the offense I took at such questions, and tried reassur-
ance: Jonas had fought the Nazis with his own underground paper during
World War II, and his independence of mind had steered him away from
most political groups.

In a sense, Smith was a "chummy" adversary. Brutally, we—our
"gang"—enshrined him and several other administrators and faculty
in the myth-making cartoons, skits, and routines we'd improvise daily.
Luckily, we kept our parodies to ourselves: I was able to relieve C. Shaw
of his apprehensions, and, promising not to show Kenneth Anger's *Scorpio
Rising,* win permission to invite Mekas.

But funding would be limited: I had to look beyond our college Union
film committee budget alone. For consideration by the larger college-
wide Fine Arts Committee, which brought to campus once or twice a year
such performers as Odetta, Hal Holbrook ("Mark Twain"), and the honky
tonk pianist Max Morath, I prepared a special manila folder portfolio. It
contained my own 200-word exhortation for funding assistance (". . . we
would like to ask for help in bringing to campus a man who we believe
is one of the most exciting, enthusiastic, and voluble individuals in film
today . . ."); two sample issues of *Film Culture,* and the Sunday magazine
piece from the *Times*; as well as British, French, and Italian reviews of
The Brig. I capped it all with a special label for the front: THE CASE FOR JONAS
MEKAS.

I affixed it to the cover in earnest schoolboy fashion using one of those
special labelers of the day which you held in your hand and squeezed hard
and tight to make it slowly crunch out embossed individual letters one-
by-one, in permanent-seeming "official" white plastic against a flat back-
ground of blue adhesive tape bordered in burnished gold.

Still, I didn't know this Jonas Mekas, and I wondered what he was really like. The Sunday *Times* contained but a single photographic glimpse of his physical likeness. I imagined a relatively old sort of man, with a fedora in a heavy wool overcoat, braving the cold of New York like some kind of wintry Chicago, with temporary respites of hot soup or coffee clutched by cold ruddy hands in public cafeterias.

Spring Break came three weeks before his visit, and at the start of our temporary liberation from Davidson, Billy Trotter and I joined poet Carolyn Kizer in Washington. Kizer had founded the literary journal *Poetry Northwest,* befriended Mark Tobey and other painters and poets in the Seattle area, where she had been married to Stimson Bullitt, a prominent attorney. A year before coming to Davidson, she taught in Pakistan as a U.S. State Department Specialist—but she left early, she would later say, because of the United States' war in Vietnam.

Once she was back in the U.S., about to become director of literary programs for the National Endowment for the Arts, a poetry reading circuit announced her forthcoming arrival at Davidson. Gazing upon two slim books (*The Ungrateful Garden* and *Knock Upon Silence*) and a full-length photograph of her in a long silk gown, Billy and other friends and I stood before the glassed-in college Union display case like children peering into a forbidden candy store. None of us had "had" an older woman (two or three, perhaps, hadn't "had" any woman at all, not to mention knowing one as an actual friend). What was she like? We were eager to see.

Some twenty or twenty-five students, five or six of them from our "gang," attended her reading in a small room upstairs in the Union. A large and vivid woman, she read poems of love, of gardening, of baseball, of—of—but my mind wandered! (as it often did, and still does, at many readings). Later I mentioned such wanderings to Billy. "My mind was between her legs," he answered.

Reading over, she went beer-drinking with us "up the road" (alcohol was forbidden on campus), and the next evening went with Billy and me to see Jean-Paul Belmondo in *Cartouche* in the Morrison Room of the Union. A couple of months later she called shortly before spring break to invite us to a party of poets in her Connecticut Avenue apartment. Her teenaged daughters would be home, she allowed. Billy and I accepted immediately.

As it happened, my sedate, already elderly parents—on their way to visit Tokyo friends who had settled in the area—gave Billy and me a ride in the comfortable back seat of my father's large Impala. My father drove; likely my mother, after years of being driven in Tokyo, was no longer able to drive herself. (And, though we'd come to know of it only later, already she may have been showing some signs of incipient Alzheimer's.) As we rode, they called each other "Mr Ball" and "Mrs Ball" as they chuckled lightly, reaffirming their relationship. It still makes me sad today.

They left us off on a corner in downtown Washington; Billy confided, "Your folks sure are burghers," as soon as they drove away. "Let's check out this place," he added, as we came upon a bar. After two bourbons (painless for Billy) my head was beginning to revolt. That evening, I spent much of the party lying in darkness in a quiet bedroom, closed off from chat and smoke and laugh. By morning I was fine—and in no mind to drink again.

That next afternoon Billy returned to North Carolina. Carolyn and I took the train to New York, sat in the bar car drinking (I had ginger ale). We weren't at all "involved," but as we rolled along, she—in all her big, blonde attractiveness—hugged me twice—when I declared John Kennedy "just another Harvard zero," and when I told her of her resemblance to Melina Mercouri.

In New York we stayed, in separate rooms, with her friend Panna Grady. Her enormous apartment with high ceilings and bare hardwood floors was number 52 at 1 West 72nd: the Dakota, the dark gray eighty-year-old German Renaissance castle-fortress designed by the architect of the Plaza Hotel for a Singer Sewing Machine heir. From one of Panna's white walls hung a framed black-and-white photograph of a bearded middle-aged man wearing horn-rimmed glasses. "Allen Ginsberg?" I asked our hostess. "No, Harry Smith." She was walking on air; she'd just returned from a weekend with Charles Olson.

Carolyn had left for a concert; it was ten at night, and Panna hadn't had dinner. We went to a nearby eatery—she kept almost no food at home—where we faced each other over a formica tabletop as she ate. She had lovely pale skin, slightly curled dark brown hair, high cheekbones, a broad smile. She spoke and smiled eagerly. "You young people and drugs," she looked at me, laughing, her eyes almost a twinkle.

"What do you mean?" I asked, affecting ingenuousness.

'66 Frames

We continued talking back at the oak table in the center of her quiet kitchen. I began to wonder what else might come of this moment, but my hopes were dashed by the midnight arrival of a short, quiet, ruggedly good-looking fellow with a plump moustache. He was the Austrian novelist Jaakov Lind, and he and Panna were close. Before Lind's appearance and the exit I made soon after it, I'd mentioned that I was bringing Jonas Mekas to campus in a few weeks. Panna volunteered, "Oh. I'm having two parties next week, and he'll be coming to one."

Three days later I met Jonas at the guardroom entrance to the Dakota, and we headed for the elevator. It would turn out to be scarcely more than a brief encounter—we simply talked a little and reaffirmed plans for his late April visit. Nonetheless something—it really amounted to no more than the smallest anecdote—struck me immediately, and has stayed with me ever since. Once we were on the elevator and had stopped at another floor below the fifth, another man got on, pressed the button for his floor, and became furious with the ancient hydraulic machine slowly transporting us. "Must you take all day!" he exclaimed, angry enough to kick it. Once our fellow passenger had exited, Jonas philosophized in his Lithuanian lilt, "Patience. Ve need patience today."

This stopped me in my tracks—though the door was now opening for us to get off. Mekas was working day and night toward a world-changing goal; the old virtue of patience seemed at a far remove, I thought. Yet in time I would see indeed how the values of Jonas—one of whose major works is a film called *Walden*—were indeed more traditional, more sacred than those of many others. Were his cherished solitude and reflection essentially different from Thoreau's contemplations amidst the din of the Gold Rush?

Indeed I believe the values of my new generation with all our apparently modish psychedelics were in fact older, more traditional, and far more time-tested than those of our immediate elders. It was *their* values which had gotten misaligned—we cherished older, perdurable values forgotten by our elders in their dance with the consuming monster of materialism and self.

This was a problem I'd grown aware of since coming to America—which, from the perspective of an uprooted child in a bombed and Occupied Tokyo, was like Paradise. From across the Pacific, America was a once- every-few years precious opportunity to return to the family,

people, and land of my life's first impressions. But on furlough to the
States at age thirteen—1958—I was doubly shocked: first, on a golden
Sunday afternoon under green boughs atwitter with birds, by the intru-
sion—for the remainder of the long radiant afternoon—of an electroni-
cally transmitted voice announcing every "event" in a game of a collision
sport; second, on a visit to another home, by the diffusive, wayward spec-
tacle of materialism—the centering heaps of television, toys, gadgets, shag
carpeting, toy guns and real ones, that dominated young and old alike.

③

Early on a sunny morning in late April 1966, two friends and I waited
before an approaching train as it hissed magisterially into the narrow
channel between cement platforms at the Charlotte station. Off stepped
a quick, tallish, elongated elf, a Giacometti-like figure with strong hands,
long dark hair pushed to one side of his high forehead, wearing a dark
suit, sweater vest, and tie. It was the constant play and twinkle of his
aspect, its oneness with his utter seriousness, that made the profound
mystery of Jonas Mekas.

A single dark green canvas dufflebag held his belongings, including
that evening's films. The lines of his extremely narrow, almost Asiatic
eyes closed their slight gap even more as he smiled. In one large peasant's
hand he extended toward me a small, heavy metallic cube. It was the
Revere 8 MM movie camera I later used to shoot *Georgia,* a magazine of film
inside. "Dis is for you," he said.

"Dis is how you single frame, dis is for continuous shooting, dis for
'normal'; here are de frames per second, dis is how to wind, and to super-
impose just reinsert de magazine" were essentially his instructions as
together we bent heads over this handsome, magical metal box set within
his expansive palm.

For the rest of the day this former Displaced Person from Lithuania
fitted his narrow, gangly frame into all we—our "gang," as he'd call us—
thought to do. As with certain others I'd meet—Corso, Ginsberg, for
instance—his sheer physical presence dominated. He simply seemed
more physically there, a power-laden three-dimensional intersection
of space and time, far different from those constrained by conventional

posture, politeness, grooming. Even were you blind, you could sense this difference. Here, I thought, was a human being!—large, life-sized, vulnerable. His coughs (he seemed to have a persistent tic in his throat or lungs), smells, gestures, his very voice with all its Lithuanian trills and embellishments, all were far more pronounced than the collective physical presence of his devoutly interested, politely muted hosts.

We went up the road for beer early in the afternoon, then took to the undeveloped edge of Lake Norman where the college owned property. Jonas hadn't finished his beer, and as he got out, his telephoto, eight-pound 16 MM Bolex in one hand, he held the green half-filled bottle in his teeth to close the car door. Riding back to Davidson in a convertible, we felt liberated. Jonas clicked single frames of the fresh green countryside, the sprouting hardwoods and the North Carolina pines that edged the now-alive tobacco, corn, and soybean. Against the stony bare April of Manhattan, all seemed to him green as if by magic. "Nort Karolina!" he exclaimed, "Nort Karolina!" and rewound his spring-driven Bolex.

On campus we parked near the old fraternity court, a handful of small and antiquated brick buildings kept largely for honorific purposes, and walked through a field of green freshly littered with bright white periwinkles. He did a dance among them, crouching down close with his lens just a foot above, single framing, then leaping back up. But under the large shading oaks a bit of dew remained, and as he ran to some flowering quince, he slipped and fell, skinning his hand. Immediately he picked himself up and continued. "It's nothing," he dismissed our concern.

Later, Eddie Rivers, my quiet and bookish friend who'd read everything I'd been able to assemble on Mekas and now had watched him film, volunteered, "He really is a poet!"

A midafternoon lounge discussion and press conference at the Union was attended by a dozen or two students and journalist Dick Banks from the *Charlotte Observer.* Banks's long article the next Sunday, headlined "'Underground Cinema' Will Help 'Revolution,'" would begin:

> The next five years will see the greatest change in human personality since the birth of Christ. . . .
>
> It's to be a change for the better. . . .
>
> "There are periods when there is a big difference between generation and generation," Mekas said. . . .

> ... the honesty of the "underground cinema"... will help
> bring about this revolution in taste.

With an accurate characterization of Jonas's "kind and somewhat amused eyes," it was decidedly favorable. Remarks on the evening films were generous.

In the afternoon discussion at the Union, Jonas, on a couch where I sat next to him, prefaced almost every spoken paragraph with "Real . . ." (for Jonas, the equivalent of "Really"). Raising one of his large open hands, he spoke of this revolution in art now taking place in America. Of the explosion in cinema, from Stan Brakhage moving the camera off the tripod and treating it as an extension of the human body, to Andy Warhol taking the cinema back to its beginnings in such movies as his six-hour *Sleep;* of the vast range of approaches represented in diaries, portraits, chronicles, and lyrics as in Baillie, Markopolous, Menken, Ron Rice, and Harry Smith and Jack Smith; even of the animated films of ten-year-old David Wise; of the new poetics of Ginsberg and others; of the Joffrey Ballet and other new dance forms; of Pop Art; of performance artists such as Tony Cox and Yoko Ono, of multimedia art, of happenings.

"But what of Hollywood?" asked someone with that year's Academy Award winner in mind. "What do you think of *Ship of Fools?"* And the answer came forthwith: "Surely that ship will sink." Dick Banks, sitting on the synthetic wall-to-wall grayish-green carpeting, asked, "How important is all of this compared to the Renaissance?"

"More important," Jonas answered quick as a whip, facial expression unchanged, a trill in both r's.

Unfortunately at one point I was summoned into the Union office by a secretary, who requested that I ask Jonas if he wanted his check now. I felt awkward about doing so, but evidently—they'd be closing up?—it was necessary. Hesitantly, I brought myself back to him on the couch.

"Excuse me, Mr Mekas." (Like nearly everyone else, I'd asked on first meeting, Is it Meh-kuss or Mee-kus? and even a fellow student with whom I didn't get along—the editor of the literary magazine, who'd wanted to ban *Flaming Creatures*—had rolled out the vowels in anticipation: "Jooh-nas Mee-kas. I like that name!")

"The Union wants to know if you want your check now." I asked.

"Vy? Do dey vont me to eat it?" he responded, testily.

④

That evening the film program was given in Hodson Hall, the carpeted, "woolly-seated" auditorium of the new Fine Arts Center, diagonally across campus from the student Union with its large Morrison Room and crowd-drawing fleshly fare. Jonas showed several recently made films, including Storm de Hirsch's prismatic, kaleidoscopic *Peyote Queen,* with its rapidly changing visual riffs geared to the rush of jazz on the soundtrack; Ed Emshwiller's *Totem,* a vivid, spider-webly precise rendition of a ballet by the Alwin Nikolais Company; and his own *The Brig.*

The circumstances under which Jonas had made *The Brig,* a filmed record of a Living Theater performance, set in a u.s. Marine prison, only added to the admiration I felt for him: police had closed the theater, but Jonas (with extremely heavy equipment) and the troupe shimmied down through a coal delivery chute for the sake of a special, recorded performance: for the sake of film.

Discussion followed screenings at a reception in the windowless room next to the auditorium, where some of the fifty or sixty attending helped themselves to highly sugared punch and highly sugared cookies under fluorescent light that made everyone vaguely green. After some minutes of talk, Jonas idly kicked an empty white styrofoam cup across the imitation marble floor as we began breaking up.

A handful of us retired with our guest to friend and classmate Rick Jensen's apartment. At Davidson—where that black-on-silver historical marker reminds you that Woodrow Wilson did attend three semesters before transferring to Princeton—we were insistently, almost desperately, reminded by the administration that Davidson in its own eyes was "the Princeton of the South." Having read of Jonas's appearances at Princeton and other Ivy League schools, one of us now asked him, "So how do the students here strike you compared to those at Princeton?"

Again Jonas answered immediately, without change of expression, quick as a whip: "Dey are brighter here." For an instant we looked around the room at each other, silently—a little stunned.

Before long it was time to go; Jonas was to get the midnight train in Charlotte. As we all rose to our feet, our host informed him, "Mr Mekas, your visit here has been a super imposition!" Everyone laughed; even

Jonas's narrow eyes, which angled slightly down toward his nose, narrowed further and the outer corners of his lips rose slightly.

Just after midnight we arrived at the station; Jonas settled onto a wooden bench and began pulling out sheafs of paper from that still full and upright dark green duffel bag. (What were they, I wondered? I imagined his *Flaming Creatures* defense, and other efforts to support filmmakers and fight censorship.) We exchanged thank yous; he told us we didn't need to stay, he had work. We—Billy, myself, and two others—returned to our car parked next to a laundry truck next to a utility plant under a starry sky in Charlotte, North Carolina, a trucking center of the South— and drove back to Davidson College.

ANNA MARIE

①

There'd been occasional intimations—seeing Joan Baez dance with blacks on stage at the Newport Folk Festival 1965; walking in the Village the same summer, as music and voices in French and Spanish kissed the streets. But now, through Jonas, I sensed, increasingly, something new and remarkable happening in our land. And by late spring and summer 1966 a series of small steps and tenuous connections—no stronger than a dew drop's to a grass blade—made up the tale of how I came to New York in September, seeking to work for him. Some few weeks after his Davidson visit he sent me an issue of *Floating Bear,* the mimeographed poetry newsletter-magazine then published by Diane DiPrima. Another few weeks later, having shot a sort of apprentice film of campus life with the Revere camera Jonas gave me, I was on my way north with Jon Mullis. We stopped in Richmond, where with my Revere I filmed his former wife, Georgia. Now a college graduate, bachelor's degree in English in hand, I was bound for upstate New York. A girlfriend there, Anna Marie Felner, had offered to arrange a computer programmer trainee position for me with the Traveler's Insurance Company, where she'd worked since dropping out of her first year at Syracuse University several months earlier.

It was late June 1966, the summer after passage of the 1965 Civil Rights Act, and as we drove through northeastern North Carolina one evening Jon and I stopped at a roadside diner and ordered two hot dogs. A black man entered behind us and started to join us at the counter, to place his order. The woman who'd just taken ours told him, "You go around to the rear, out back." Jon, a tallish man with a black page boy and a good build, told her, "Cancel our order," and we left.

Two days and a stop in Philadelphia later, front grille grinning, rear fins glaring, we rolled through the Holland Tunnel onto broad Sixth Avenue, cobbled on that lowest stretch. It was late on a warm Saturday afternoon, our windows were down, the boulevard was wide, it was quiet, there was no traffic and scarcely anyone was about. The entire city lay ahead of us. The orange of the dying sun illuminated the gray cobbles of the road and the flat warehouse windows and the sleek lines of the telephone posts, and I loved it.

②

Jon settled in to work at his new job, installing peepholes in apartment doors. I stayed overnight with him and his friends. Before it grew late, I looked up the number of the Cinematheque, called for Jonas, and was told he'd gone for dinner at "the Paradox." What, and where, I wondered, was that?

"Oh, that's easy—it's just two blocks from here," Jon's friend, a quite tall, large yet slim man, mustached and balding, volunteered. "It's the Zen Macrobiotic restaurant."

"Oh, Hello! Hello!" Jonas turned around in his seat in the small, rather dark restaurant, extending one large hand toward me, interrupting his close conversation with another gentleman seated across from him. His companion was dressed almost impeccably in a blue suit and white shirt and necktie. He had short light brown brassy hair all of a piece and was chubby with bright pink cheeks. "And dis is Peter Kubelka," he said, as we completed introductions.

Jon and I lingered only a couple of minutes, during which I mentioned my recent work with the Revere. But we didn't stay: they seemed engaged. Instead, we walked a few more steps through the Paradox and onto the outdoor patio at the rear. There, in a small enclosed space with a sky above and some strands of green grass at our feet, we sat at a large old-fashioned picnic table.

Two other men were already there, finishing their meal. One was short and slender with dark curly hair, a blue chambray shirt and jeans. We all talked together. When the two others rose to go the short one seized an abandoned umbrella and assumed the standard "on guard" fencing position, pointing his improvised foil at his friend as he shouted "Avant-Garde!" He was Paul Krassner, editor and publisher of the ribald, satirical review, *The Realist*.

By this time Lyndon Johnson's escalation of the American War against Vietnam had reached mammoth proportions; just three weeks earlier Secretary of Defense Robert S. McNamara had ordered our troop strength in the Republic of Vietnam raised to two hundred and eight-five thousand. Reportedly, over a dozen Americans—and over two hundred of "the enemy"—were dying daily. Our escalation was based on "the Tonkin

Gulf incident"—Lyndon Johnson's version of certain events in August
1964, about which many of us had been dubious. In two months the play
MacBird, likening Johnson to *Macbeth,* would be performed in the Village,
and next spring *The Realist's* "The Parts That Were Left Out of the Kennedy
Book" would depict Johnson inserting his erect member into the mouth
of the late president aboard Air Force One from Dallas to Washington.

Outrageous humor was indeed one way to respond to the outrage.
Krassner's grotesque vision was of course designed to draw urgent atten-
tion to a violation—a real, actual war—far more grotesque than his fictive
rendering. Now here I was in the company, momentarily, of one like-
minded politically, accomplished in satire, long in print. Now, I thought, I
could give voice to a small private fancy of my own. I sounded Krassner
out about making toilet paper that bore Johnson's image, but he told me
that had been done in World War II, with the Nazis and the Japanese.

③

The next afternoon, Anna Marie was out with someone else when I
arrived in Syracuse; the job I'd anticipated was nonexistent. Over the next
week—staying with Anna Marie and her mother—I visited the State
Employment Office and responded to newspaper classifieds. Quickly, I
began to sense the limitations of my college degree. I tried one odd job for
a day, then ended up working nights, midnight to 8:00 A.M., as a security
guard at a 25,000-square foot supermarket warehouse.

I held my guard job until just after a Davidson friend from out of town
visited me at work. When I took him on some of my rounds, we lifted sev-
eral cartons of cigarettes and some toothpaste. The next afternoon, I drove
out to pick up my paycheck—my first after two weeks' work—when my
supervisor asked to look at my car. "I always smoke Kools," I lied as he noted
the unopened carton in my glove compartment. We walked to the nearby
cubicle where I'd sat all night each night, except when making the rounds.
He and a quickly summoned coworker (who, like himself, was a good bit
larger than I) put me through the preparation of a confession. The confes-
sion included one of the worst things I've ever done: naming my friend.

While my supervisor asked me questions, his companion sat eyeing
me, ballpoint pen in hand, a clipboard bearing a report form on his knee.

When asked my educational background I answered "twelve years of school, and four years of college," and each looked at the other and gasped. As I signed the statement promising to never come near my former place of employment again, my now former supervisor held his massive doubled-up fist three inches from my eyes. His short-sleeved shirt exposed the bristly blond hairs on his large and long tanned forearm. "Just as a friend—just as a friend," he exclaimed, "I oughta beat you up for what you did."

I did indeed regret it, profoundly. And in spite of its generous monotony and routine, and my fairly frequent fatigue, I'd liked the work. At regular intervals I'd leave my perch in that parking lot cubicle and make my appointed rounds: I'd check on the refrigerator room, with its blast of cold enveloping fog whenever I opened its mighty wood and metal door; on the enormous space that housed thousands of dormant cartons of cigarettes; on the others with neat little mountains of boxed baby powder, villages of cooking oil, cities of brillo pads, canned vegetables. At each station I'd take from my pocket a large metal key which I'd insert in the clock on the door, recording my vigilance; each was a morgue by night.

I most enjoyed my visits to the nearby docks. Under grim yellow 2:00 A.M. lights (bugs were still visible within their halos), on a cement platform between columns of cardboard and wooden boxes heavy with food stacked as high as you or I, small men drove large yellow forklifts on which squatted fresh tomatoes in rough wooden housing, or cans of ham or beef or dessert pears or other enclosed delectables in cardboard cubes. Drivers would lower their loads onto the edge of a spit-and-gum-stained platform for trucks to pick up, then return for more, the now naked silver tongues of their lifts reflecting the yellow incandescence, while a transistor radio played the frantic insistences of a d.j. that it was 2:00 A.M. and the night had just begun.

(4)

I'd stolen once or twice before, in my last year and a half at Davidson. Among certain circles of middle-class teenagers at Charlotte's racy Garringer High, which Anna Marie was attending when I first met her, shoplifting was more or less par for the course. My English exchange student friend, Simon, became furious with Anna Marie when she lifted something at the Davidson student store only moments after he'd asked her not to. For me, it was a lark. I persuaded myself that taking something small from an institution (not from an individual) was okay, and tried it—but not at Davidson.

Only I did it differently from most. Instead of putting the object in my pocket, I thought, why not simply hold it visibly in my hand and slowly walk out? I did it twice like that—and then lifted several items at the warehouse that night.

My career as a graduate of an upper-crust Southern school was off to a disastrous start. Not only had the job I'd expected proven nonexistent; I'd lost the job I did get, and it was my own fault. While at the warehouse I'd arranged for an interview at Traveler's Insurance, and enjoyed with my interviewer a rather urbane discussion that included international politics based on national interests. (There was no mention of Vietnam.) Unfortunately the interview took place just a day before getting caught at the warehouse, and I'd identified my present employer on my application form.

Meanwhile personal problems were on the rise. One evening soon after I'd started the security work, Anna Marie and I had walked around the old green trees and frame houses of the hilly residential area immediately next to the university. During that twilight stroll, we happened to meet one of my former classmates from the American School in Japan (A.S.I.J.). A gathering-place of sons and daughters of international diplomats and businessmen, and some English-speaking Japanese, A.S.I.J. was for me the object of a profound affection that would only grow in time. Dave Seaton, with whom I'd graduated, was the son of an airlines executive. Tall and slender, he'd been popular with girls, and was called a "pansy" by the large and rather unattractive galoot on the basketball team. But he was artistic and bright, and the star of the show in our senior class play.

We ran into him in Syracuse in front of the two-story gray frame house where he lived, just as he was leaving. We spoke briefly and he invited us back. When he asked what I was doing, Anna Marie immediately answered, much to my regret, "He's a cop!" I was hurt, and felt absurd trying to explain that wasn't quite how it was.

My worst fears were realized when I did return, solo, a few nights later. Entering Dave's kitchen, where he sat at a small round wooden table, I breathed the friendly, familiar smell of marijuana smoke. I wasn't working that evening and so could turn on—if invited. The thought of the two of us, coming from a virtual "city on a hill" of privilege and distinction, having discovered independently one of life's forbidden joys, was cause for not merely fellowship but elation. But when I observed, "Gee, Dave, it smells nice in here," he refused to take my lead.

"What? I don't smell anything," he answered, dark eyes locked in puzzlement under frowning brows. Hopes dashed, depressed, and not knowing how to relieve his fears, I left quickly.

(5)

After another week or so, the rift would prove temporary: I'd return and find Dave amiable, our talk would be easy, and we'd turn on. The large old frame house on the ground floor where he had an apartment was divided into half a dozen or so others, all of which were rented to blacks, as was most of the residential area around the university. Dave and his neighbors seemed comfortable together.

I came for a visit just as a small party was revving upstairs. Over the noise Dave and I talked a good bit together. He'd just been listening to Bob Dylan's new *Blonde on Blonde* and showed me its double jacket cover, exclaiming again and again over "Sad Eyed Lady of the Lowlands," how its twelve-and-a-half minutes took up a whole side of this four-sided album, how Dylan used the title as a refrain. He also mentioned Allen Ginsberg's visit to Syracuse University the past year. I asked eagerly, "Oh, what happened?"

"Everyone wanted to know what LSD was like."

"Oh no," I responded, disappointed. I hadn't taken the hallucinogen yet. To me, at that time, its prominence in student questions seemed a sort of vulgarity.

I enjoyed seeing Dave and wanted to see more of him, and to meet others in the university area. But my yearnings weren't shared by Anna Marie, who responded "There's no one there worth meeting," when I suggested visiting again. The cause of many of her problems seemed to be her father, a laywer who had left years before—a psychic and economic devastation she and her mother seemed unable to repair. Unfortunately, even though I found myself in the midst of it, I had little appreciation then for such a condition. Had I the sense—had I been less self-absorbed—I might've seen how the disaster of her parents' relationship had shattered the wholeness in her soul. And I might've taken her charges of my selfishness, my childishness, seriously.

Likely, I found something in common with her confusion and pain, as we first spoke, perched together in a cranny of Crowder's Mountain outside Charlotte during a day-long hike one May afternoon in 1965. And certainly I was drawn to her light green wolf-like eyes, her pale skin, her long blonde hair. In the spring of 1965 I was still a virgin, and she offered to lay me.

When I knew her in Charlotte she'd played folk songs on acoustic guitar, listened to Dave Van Ronk, Tom Rush, Tom Paxton, and perhaps most of all Bob Dylan, whom she remembered socially from New Orleans the year before. Her ear for Dylan was more advanced than mine; when The Byrds' "Mr Tambourine Man" came out I couldn't understand, at first, how she could prefer his solo roughness to their ensemble glitter and spangle.

She did indeed seem crushed by her father's abandonment; one night at dinner with her mother and myself, she burst into tears, "I just want to die!" as I sat there stunned. She seemed eagerly to accept the nickname (and seemingly, almost a whole new identity) I gave her when I called her "Cat"; so she signed the daily special delivery letters I received at Harvard summer school, 1965. She called me "Dorgie" (for "Doggie").

She now lived with her gray-haired mom high on a hill far from the university, renting the upper story of a suburban, red brick and colonial house from the upper-middle-class family who lived on the first floor. I slept in a separate bed in her room and we left the door open and had no sex.

This was very much unlike the summer before in Charlotte, when I stayed with them a while before leaving for Harvard. Then, Anna Marie and I had separate beds in the same room, her mother was across the hall, and both doors were left open. We would wait a few minutes and then cupping a foiled Lubricated Trojan-Enz in one hand I would go to Anna Marie just a few light steps across the uncarpeted wooden floor, the oily rubber smell blending with the cricket-crazed summer night. We even had fun once in a while during the day when her mother wasn't there, and once when I got out of the bath Anna Marie came in and tied a red ribbon around my freshly cleaned cock, its skin soft and tender like a babe's.

But such playfulness was gone now, and differences had sharpened. In the fall of 1965 I'd written of my efforts to show *Flaming Creatures* at Davidson, and enclosed clippings on the film. After I'd bussed up eight hundred miles for Thanksgiving she characterized *Creatures* (which she hadn't seen) as "a worthless piece of celluloid." Now, in July 1966 I showed her my just-completed *Georgia,* which she seemed to like. But when viewing other rolls I'd shot diaristically—not "whole" films but everyday notations, impressions, experiments made spontaneously under a variety of circumstances—she became irritated. "Hold the camera still!" she scolded.

(6)

I hadn't appreciated Anna Marie's attitude from the start, and it seemed to grow worse and worse. Now it was just a few days after my security guard fiasco, and, jobless again, I moved into Dave's. As it happened, he was leaving the same day for Provincetown, and his roommate would still be away a while: I'd have the entire small apartment to myself.

One or two of my first evenings there I visited briefly with a few of the young black guys in the neighborhood, and with one, Ben, went out for a beer. My worries over Anna Marie, and the future of our relationship, began to recede slightly. But my first several nights turned into a sort of small horror, for in Dave's apartment hundreds of cockroaches came out after dark. Though of course I'd visited in New York before, and we'd had some roaches and water bugs in Tokyo, I'd never gone to sleep in a room full of hundreds of crisp-shelled brow-wiggling scurrying beasts the shape of flattened bullets. Vigorous spraying, I found, brought only laughable results, never denting their mighty numbers. For three nights I lay there in the dark, hearing them. I was sleepless much of the time.

On the fourth day I got a daytime job; that night I lay there listening once more, only knowing now that I had to get up at 6:00 A.M. for my first day's work, and had to get some sleep for it. Yet I couldn't sleep at all. Anna Marie and I had now begun to reconcile slightly; I became so desperately anxious at the prospect of a new job, another chance just hours away—and was so helpless—that I drove back to the home I'd left and asked her mother, then begged her in tears, for one of her Seconals.

⑦

My new job was carpenter's apprentice with a large firm run by two brothers who'd come to Syracuse from Sheffield, England a decade before. It was to be sort of ad hoc work, going here, going there, helping with this job and that, as needed. The company was highly organized and paid each Friday for the work done that week—and my first day of work, a Friday, would place bright green cash into my newly chafed, empty hands.

It was gruelling that day as a whole team of us tugged at the innards of an old house on the outskirts of town. Huge eight-by-four panels of heavy sheet rock: from rooms upstairs we pulled them out, hauled them downstairs, then made our weary way out through the front door and released them into the waiting upheld hands of others on the back of a truck. Having only watched a warehouse, bagged groceries, and bussed tables before, it was the hardest work I had ever done. My arms and shoulders ached as they supported the mighty panels of rock. The $13 and some odd change handed me in a small manila envelope just after 4:30 felt like a gift from the gods.

I came home and got out of my clothes and laid my wallet on the dresser and headed for the shower, happy and carefree. When I came out of the shower Ben and two other guys from the neighborhood were in the front room. I began talking with them as I dressed.

I picked up my wallet on the dresser and just before putting it into my pants pocket, I opened it. The day's green reward was gone. "Hey, y'all know how my money just disappeared from my wallet?" I asked my guests. "My first day's pay? It was all I had."

One of Ben's companions said no. Ben just stared back at me, then down at his feet.

I called on each of them by name and each denied any knowledge, even Ben, who looked me in the eye and said no. Watching all this from the hall—I hadn't seen her at first—was a young black woman named Gloria. "You all took it. Admit it. I know 'cause I was out here in the hall when he came, and when you came, and no one else has gone in that apartment. Admit it!"

They all looked down at their feet as they began filing out the door. "So this is what Black Power means!" Gloria shouted after them. None turned to answer.

(8)

Gloria had moved into the building just a day before. She was Dave's roommate's girlfriend and she'd stay part of the time in the other room in Dave's apartment but most of the time with other friends in the building. She was cute, bright, friendly, and vivacious, but I looked upon her as already committed romantically. She and I did go out once together—a black lounge with live soul-singing from a small stage—and I made casual friends with some of her friends in the building (she complained about having slept one night upstairs next to a fat fellow who farted all night) and we two were casually in and out of each other's lives.

One day not long after the confrontation that followed my shower, she came in while I was lying on the apartment's small couch. She came over onto me and stripped off my pants and unbuttoned her dress and pulled it off overhead and then teasingly lowered herself onto me, just a little at a time, just a little, just a little, then went back up and off, then back on and down and she giggled as she did it and her bright dark eyes reflected all the afternoon sunlight illuminating the room and she did it again and again, teasing but for real, giggling and intent, quiet yet almost jubilant, and I watched and watched, absorbed, captivated, my hands caressing her waist and front, and then I watched her more and more and she giggled and her eyes flashed and I came and we held each other close on the narrow couch next to the pale green wall.

9

Around this time I got to know a guy with whom I hung out for a while—though I always tried to keep a little distance. He was short and trim yet stocky, and somewhat older, with pale skin and short neat black hair and a wide thin mouth and square jaw. He'd been arrested for marijuana possession. Once, he removed and unfolded for me the news article from his wallet. How different the person in a narrow column of black ink—"Herbert Nadelman, 26"—from the poor, short fellow next to me, full of hopes and aspirations and a beating heart.

He'd also done a good bit of heroin, he said, and this made me cautious. We smoked grass together, and I visited his parents' middle-class suburban ranch home and met his two younger sisters and their boyfriends. They were fascinated by Bob Dylan and the whole question of his mysterious identity, and told of how once a young man had come among them pretending to be Bob Dylan and for a while had all of them fooled.

With Herbert, I had two important drug experiences. In my car we drove the seven hours to New York one weekend and looked up one or two of his friends and then Jon Mikul and Susan, whom I'd visited with Jon Mullis several weeks earlier. At our first stop, we sat in a third-story room that through the fire escape's black iron diagonals and horizontals overlooked St. Mark's Place. His friend produced a small jar of white crystalline powder and passed it to us and we began sniffing from it. It was pure methamphetamine and it jacked me up incredibly and made me feel great. There was no comparison to the little speckled diet capsules I'd taken in college. I'd never had this before and couldn't restrain my joy. "This is really good," I said, again and again, "Gee, this is really good," and then as I finally became a little self-conscious—my companions had remained entirely quiet—I added, "I-I'm sorry for being so . . . enthusiastic!—but this is really good!"

They stared at me, quiet and tolerant. In time I'd see people whose teeth had turned bad from shooting amphetamine, methedrine, or methamphetamine. People who seemed concerned with little outside their drug—except for the funny habit of unmethodically cleaning up (not necessarily their own person, but things around them). Many

A-Heads became known for their hyperness, paranoia, and constant monologues.

Herbert's friend gave us some to take with us and we went on to visit other friends, sniffing more every now and then. Soon after we arrived at Jon Mikul's and Susan's, Herbert began hyperventilating. He'd proposed we both try it as an experiment; then, after I stopped, he couldn't. He sat on the bed at Jon and Susan's, tore off his shirt and talked frantically—in between almost panicked gasps of air—of trouble with his parents. The three of us watched, exchanging glances with each other. In time Susan, a skilled and thoughtful counselor, calmed and relaxed him a little.

After we took some more Sunday morning before the drive back, I stopped taking it. But that night back in Syracuse, as I lay down to sleep, my heart pounded, pounded, pounded, and wouldn't slow. I tried and tried to sleep in my white sheeted single bed next to a wall of chipping green paint as cockroaches scurried and ambled across floor and table. Still my heart raced as one hour and then another passed and my heart still thudded with unremittant fury.

I drove to the emergency room of the hospital and said that my heart wouldn't stop racing. I was seated in a separate room and asked to wait.

After some pounding minutes, a doctor—young, no more than early thirties—came in. Besides my health worries—I had, after all, a rheumatic heart murmur—I feared that if I divulged the cause I could conceivably be arrested. But fortunately I decided to go on instinct, to trust this pleasant-looking man not many years older than myself. "Do you have any idea why your heart won't stop racing?"

"Yes—I took a lot of amphetamine this weekend."

"Why'd you do that?" he asked.

"I was curious."

⑩

In spite of my reaction to the bombarding of Ginsberg with questions about LSD (as Dave had told it), my curiosity about the psychedelic had grown in recent months—not only from popularizing articles in *Look* and other magazines. Bookstores in both the East Village and the West featured whole volumes to help prepare your mind for a trip: Alpert and

Cohen's *LSD* with essays and large photos both documentary and impressionistic (soft tones and diffracted light, a sense of awe and wonder); Masters and Houston's *Varieties of Psychedelic Experience;* even a long-playing record from Leary in which he explained his ideas. . . .

I'd learned that two morning glory seed varieties—Heavenly Blue and Pearly Gate—contained LSD-6. ("LSD," as customarily designated, is LSD-25.) One Saturday morning, at a quiet hardware store on the hill, I bought a pack of Heavenly Blue Morning Glory seeds; they weren't then coated, as they are now, with a poison. "Sprinkle half of it on a bowl of cereal," Herbie advised.

The next Friday afternoon I did just that—then went into my room, smoked a joint Herbert had left me like a bottle of champagne to open before the big ship set sail, and lay down. Inside my head I saw a silent Allen Ginsberg, in a dark shirt and jeans on a stationary grayish brown horse, his large dark eyes staring quietly, unblinking, in my general direction, against a landscape of trees and plains. I had no other visions or visitations, no hallucinations. As I think of it, I really don't know if I'd taken enough of the morning glory seeds for an effect. But the marijuana (if not the Heavenly Blue, or the two in combination) was strong and that night I was to learn, painfully, some constraints in using it.

I left for a movie date with Anna Marie feeling vaguely disoriented, as if there were a slight gap between myself and the world. As I drove to the theater in the early darkness we entered a traffic rotary. I came too close to its raised core and for an instant ran up onto its curb, then came back down, just as quick. With equal quickness Anna Marie—who one night the summer before had unzipped my jeans and begun jacking me off as I drove a quiet North Carolina blacktop—reprimanded, "Watch what you're doing!"

I could tell—though I couldn't correct it—that my perception of space had been altered. From this I learned never to drive on marijuana. But I still had to get us to the large old-fashioned theater way crosstown, then drive Anna Marie back home to the white suburbs, then return to my wooden frame apartment near the university.

Knowing Anna Marie's general disapproval of drugs except alcohol, and acutely aware of the tenuous nature of our relationship, I could see no way of telling her what was happening to me. I drove us safely to the theater, just by being extra careful and allowing for my depth perception

problem. But once inside the large dark chamber before a wall of flutter-
ing silver and black, things turned worse. On-screen was an interminable
British short which featured a character of highly dramatized facial ex-
pressions, given to speaking nonsense syllables. "I think chow han mufer
a wg un serry, von bly ak, chornten," might've been one of his many
dozen lines. And they were always delivered with considerable emphasis
and flourish, as if entirely to the point, logical, appropriate. All other
characters remained absolutely silent and straight-faced whenever he
spoke, letting his spat syllables from an imaginary linguistic universe hit
the audience with full impact. This disturbed and frightened me. What
horrible mess-up in the Cosmos was going on here? What paranoia be-
come president? This was a joke, or—? In some desperation (knowing her
attitude toward drugs, I tried to hide it), I whispered to Anna Marie
"What's going on?"

Not hearing a sympathetic response, not hearing anything other than
"Just watch the movie," and fearful of tipping my mitt, I sat there in tremu-
lous silence, telling myself to accept it—as comedy. I was no better suited
for this movie viewing than the jocks at our *Flaming Creatures* showing.

(11)

In the meantime, my carpenter's apprenticeship was to prove as short-
lived as my first pay. My employment experience with the English was no
happier than my cinematic experience. Monday, my second day at work
for the large firm run by two brothers, found me with a genial mason. A
cheery but otherwise quiet fellow in late middle age, he was completing
patchwork repair on the foundation of a white frame house under large
shading hardwoods in an old residential neighborhood. As he wrapped
things up there wasn't a great deal for me to do, but I did whatever he
asked, fetching a trowel, a bag of cement, copper tubing, providing a third
hand as he dabbed or measured or hammered crusty concrete and rough
red brick. Once in the afternoon, an old Italian man, with translucent
skin-colored glasses, strolled up, the smile of contented age on his face,
and talked with us. "Yup," he said before walking away, as if offering his
cachet for what he took to be my work, "Learn a craft. Learn a craft. Then
you're set for life."

No less than an hour later I was sitting on the ground near the mason when another fellow, white shirt open at the neck above brown dress pants, pulled up in a car, got out, and walked over—with authority. Dispensing with any introduction, he asked "Are you sick?" There was haughtiness, anger in his tone.

Tuesday I was with two carpenters in their early fifties, restoring and renovating a garage attached to a suburban home. The garage had been partly destroyed by fire.

This would be my final day as a carpenter's apprentice. When one of the two carpenters gave me a task involving an "outlet," I stood there a moment, stupefied—as he saw. Although I was a college graduate, my childhood in Japan had left significant gaps in my knowledge of ordinary words and phrases. There were several such instances; I tried desperately to be of help, to compensate for the basic background and smarts that I lacked; yet the only way that I could respond at all was on a personal level. When using a device I didn't know the name for, one of the men sliced a sliver of skin off his finger; I inquired most solicitously and offered to help, and asked again, later in the afternoon, the condition of his wound.

The following morning I went to the office to inquire about my work for the day, and the woman buckling papers at the counter told me I'd have none.

⑫

I'd heard that the extremely large candle manufacturer, Meunch-Kreuzer, often had openings at some of its plants. I went there the next day, a gray overcast afternoon. In their quiet office the balding brown-haired manager with modest sideburns and his older, graying assistant listened as I told them I wanted a year of physical labor to get in shape.

They hired me to work the dock at Plant Three—to assemble orders for all of their products (secular candles; votive candles for Catholics; Christmas candles; candles for Hannukah and many other Hebrew holi-days) inside the huge, dimly lit, several-storied warehouse; then to load all these boxed candles onto shiny dollies and push them to the pick-up area at the end of a concrete platform where the dark, cavernous rears of large trucks would push right up to the dock's metal rim.

After I'd been several weeks at Plant Three, a letter—which survived multiple delays due to forwarding—finally reached me. Not long after my brief visit with him at the Paradox Macrobiotic Restaurant, Jonas had written in elegant blue fountain pen:

July 9, 1966

Dear Gordon:
Forgive me that because of my Austrian guest, Peter Kubelka, who came that day to N.Y., I could not spend much time—or no time at all—with your friends during your visit to N.Y. But I had no choice. I had promised Kubelka to meet him there that evening. I hope during your next visit to N.Y. I'll be more free. And bring your movies with you, when you come . . .

Best to you & your friends—
Jonas

I wanted to go, to offer to work for him. What would I do? Would he have anything? Since he obviously lived on very little, and his whole cause was, seemingly, supported not even by half of the proverbial shoestring, could he possibly pay anyone anything? I was willing to put up posters, were any to be posted. I'd call people on the phone. I'd carry film and equipment. I'd project. I'd . . . I didn't know what, but I'd help any way I could: I wanted my life to be meaningful. After all, what about a vow I'd made only five months earlier, after Stephen Daedalus, "to forge in the smithy of my soul the uncreated conscience of my race"?

My alternative was to stay where I was. Had Jonas not written, and had his letter not survived the relay from college address to family home to upstate New York, I might have well remained in Syracuse, docking candles for Meunch-Kreuzer. For a week or more, I thought it over. There were all my immediate, personal problems with Anna Marie—and larger issues and differences as well. One example, as we watched the 6:30 news: in close-up a Vietnamese woman wept profusely at what we were told was the death of her son; Anna Marie insisted "She's faking it! She's just doing it because the camera's on her!"

And though I didn't use such a term, there was the broader cultural difference I found myself confronting in Syracuse, New York, August 1966. It was expressed, in part, over hair; almost overnight, just as in North Carolina, hair had become some great index to values and attitudes.

When I began growing my hair long (merely down to my ears, not shoulder length) at Davidson College early in the fall of 1965, no one else in that Presbyterian enclave of one thousand men did the same. Why'd I do it? I didn't know, exactly. It felt good. It looked good and felt sensual. The Beatles in *Help!* and *A Hard Day's Night* had longish hair. Among the small "handful" of girls I was sleeping with, each one, I found very quickly, liked it—as I liked their running their fingers through its long light brown softness.

Nevertheless my hair—not to mention my efforts to bring *Flaming Creatures* to an historically Calvinist college—upset members of the community. A sign was posted in the student Union, with an envelope attached, "To Raise Money to Get Gordon Ball a Haircut." It was the inspiration of a classmate, Jack Martens, and though he told me later his plan was to use the money—several dollars in small change and a dollar bill accumulated—for a party, it never materialized (or I wasn't invited!). Many months later, late in the spring of my senior year, I came back to my single room one night and found a note on my door:

> Mr Ball
> While I deplore your judgement and taste, I cannot but admire your courage. Therefore, I feel compelled to issue this warning: If you do not take steps to have your unsightly locks shorn by Friday next, I fear that a group of rather amateurish barbers will correct your negligence. Since I am certain that Mr Johnson or even Mr Norton would perform this service in a much more satisfactory manner than would these fellows, I am hopeful that you will heed this message.

It was typed on a half-sheet of erasable bond stationery. The Johnson and Norton referred to were of course the town's two barbers, black men both, whose Main Street shops served all the young white Davidson men and their professors. Beneath the message I responded in black magic marker:

> Mr "X"
> While I deplore your arrogant and pompous style, I cannot but admire the courage shown by you and your fellows in hiding behind your mask of anonymity and in refusing to accept any variation from the noble view of life which you intend to so intelligently support. Anyway, boys, don't let me kid you—

I will soon obtain a bottle of black hair dye and other materials to sport my new "Afro" look.

Yours for God, Mom, & Conformity,
G.V.B.

Beyond the area of its university in those days, Syracuse, New York was not largely different from Davidson. When during our half-hour Meunch-Kreuzer lunch break I passed by some middle-aged women workers at a snack bar table dominated by machines housing illuminated artificial food, I heard a shocked if not wholly unfriendly reaction: "It looks like one of the Beatles!" Mouths hung open. Sometime later, after working one Saturday morning for overtime at another Meunch-Kreuzer plant, my short-haired coworkers and I passed a bar. In its door stood a middle-aged man, pot-bellied under a long white T-shirt hanging out over creased pants; a cigarette dangled at his side between two fingers of one bare hand. "Isn't that sick, isn't that sick," he pronounced authoritatively in a loud voice.

Of course in my considering leaving Syracuse, hair wasn't directly the issue. What was I actually thinking?

I was of course disaffected with Anna Marie, and did indeed want Jonas to see *Georgia.* Could I work for him in the New York—his New York—that I wanted to see more of? Though it had developed unconsciously at first, for a year now I'd felt a sense of hope, of chance, of youth, of imagination and possibility in America. And its focus lay no more in Syracuse than Davidson.

(13)

Not long after Jonas's letter reached me in Syracuse in August 1966, I ran into another graduate of the American School in Japan. Don Stanford had entered midyear when he was a freshman and I a junior. A diplomat's son, he was the only African American in our school. We got together several times and smoked grass. Then one quiet Saturday morning ten days later, we headed out of town. I had six dollars in my pocket, enough to refill my V-8 Chevrolet on its way to New York.

As we left, I thought to stop by Anna Marie's and say good-bye face-to-face. She wasn't home, but her mother was. We spoke a few moments and I explained I had to go . . . a friend was waiting. "Oh, bring your friend in," she said. She was a small woman with a large forehead and gray hair and glasses.

Don came back in with me and we talked another few minutes and then he got up and left. Once he was out the door Anna Marie's mother looked directly at me, her eyes spitting fury. "Gordon!" she shouted. "You didn't tell me your friend was a nigger!" It was time to go.

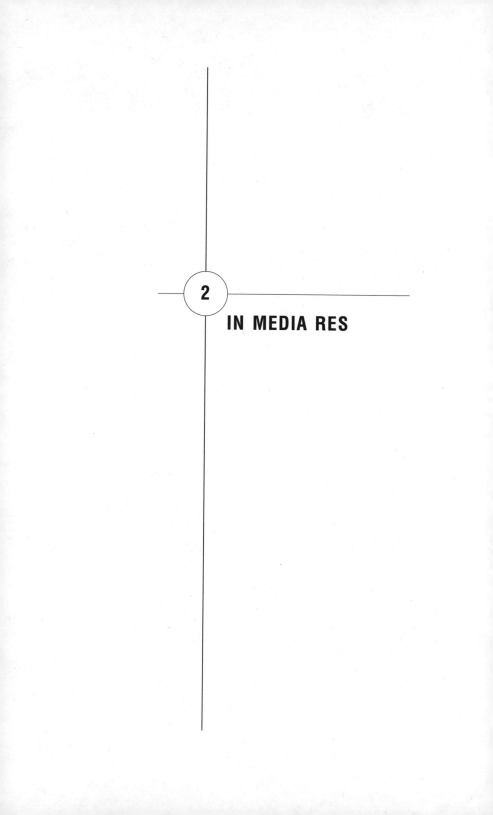

2

IN MEDIA RES

JONAS

①

The comfortable auditorium of the Library-Museum of the Performing Arts at Lincoln Center was well-appointed: two hundred padded seats; bountiful, acoustics-enhancing carpet; yellowish gold wall and stage curtains; a large stage and recessed screen. From my seat halfway back on the ascending floor, I saw Jonas Mekas, in a brown corduroy suit, down in the very front of the audience, rising to speak. On stage above him, at a table behind a small array of microphones, were Andrew Sarris, heavyset in a fine gray suit, and two fellow film critics, James Stoller and Roger Greenspun.

Sarris had begun the discussion with an anecdote illustrating what for him was key to cinema: the principle of amplification. As he told it, he'd attended a morning presentation elsewhere that was to have been given by Timothy Leary; Leary was sick and an assistant—a small man—took his place. Unknown to the assistant, a band of light was escaping from a slide projector some seats in front of him, magnifying his form several times behind him, echoing him in huge projected shadow—like a movie.

Now mise-en-scene had become the subject of discussion; someone in the audience asked for clarification, and suddenly Jonas became visible as he joined the exchange. From that first row he raised one large hand, then his whole long angular body, as he began to speak, without electric amplification, in a voice which I could easily hear from my distance. His unadorned, passionate and less "civilized"—"un-naturalized!"—tone clashed with the vestige of mellifluous, softened sounds from Sarris above him. "De term mise-en-scene," Jonas began, gesturing with his large raised hand, "comes from teater. In teater, in Europe particularly, it has very specific meaning. In de Stanislavsky teater . . ."

"Oh, oh! Oh, hello! Hello!" Jonas said, as at the program's end I went down front. He shook my hand, asked what brought me there, and "How's de rest of your gang?" I explained I had just come to the city and offered, "Do you need any help with anything?"

'66 Frames

He reached into his corduroy pocket and wrote briefly on a strip of paper. "Real, I'll be gone for two days, but you can come on Thursday. Call me dat morning. Don't give dis to anyone," he cautioned, handing me the strip.

For the first time the Lincoln Center Film Festival featured—likely because Jonas pressed for it—a program of independent, "experimental" films: Harry Smith's dental chair nightmare in black and white, *Heaven and Earth Magic Feature,* with animated skeletons of mandalas and disappearing and reappearing dismembered body parts; Peter Goldman's humble, nearly un-funded New York Neo-Realist feature, *Echoes of Silence;* several from the cinéma vérité Maysles Brothers; Ed Emshwiller's most recent film, *Relativity;* and the extraordinary *Flicker* by Tony Conrad. When projected—amplified—at 24 frames per second, *Flicker*'s alternating black-and-white frames filled a silver plane with rapidly pulsating rhythms of nearly pure light and nearly pure dark: and it was sixty minutes long. The audience had been "warned" about it through a brief introduction: anyone liable to epileptic seizures was not to watch it. I found that its extremely rapid alternation of black and white generated colors, arcs of red, yellow, purple. Sometimes a sort of swirling rainbow after-image effect triggered "representational" shapes, as when the likeness of an army appeared to be marching on screen. By its end—a good portion of the audience had exited the auditorium—I was one of the dozen or so who clapped.

②

Louise Matthewson—with whom I was then living—cautioned me the next afternoon as I drove my large green Chevrolet up Fourth Avenue into Union Square. Off to the right above us, under the overcast sky, we'd just noticed part of a signboard for "Jonas," in large vermillion lettering. What "Jonas" was, neither of us could see or figure. "Oh, wow," I said, taking it as a good omen. The next day was Thursday.

"Don't build it up too much," Louise said. She looked out for me; I never returned her generosity. Already in the week since I arrived in New York, I'd gotten two letters from Anna Marie. We'd had sex only once that summer: she returned late one night, came to my bed as I lay on my back asleep, and began kissing me as she never had before, digging her front teeth into the inside of my lower lip. But now in her first letter she complained of feeling sick in the morning, and closed by suggesting that I come back and help her raise a little boy named "Domani." When a second came with the same import, Louise counseled: "Call her up and ask her to go to any drug store and ask for a rabbit or a frog test—tell her you'll pay. Ask her to send you the results."

"You know," she added, "it's very unlikely a woman will get pregnant when she's on top." My afternoon with Gloria came to mind.

Later that same day I somehow found a working public phone (I hadn't wanted to use Louise's) on a corner in front of a Rexall's. I did precisely as Louise had advised, and didn't hear from Anna Marie again—for another eight weeks.

③

Jonas's home and workspace was a small loft at 316 Third Avenue, between Twenty-Third and Twenty-Fourth, above a dark and dusky bar, where I'd sometimes peer inside to see the shades of a few individuals, standing or sitting, as if stranded in two-dimensionality. The weary wooden stairs leading up to Jonas's reeked from the whiskey below. The end of the loft that overlooked Third Avenue, hanging over those tired stairs and that dim bar, consisted of a narrow room with a window but without a door; two single beds sat across from each other. Within the rather dark main room it adjoined, two work desks pressed against the south wall: one, an upturned door on two squat file cabinets, solid and spacious enough for paper and typewriter as well as film editing equipment; another, two feet away, was likewise an upturned door, but rested on two sawhorses, with 16 MM rewinds attached to its surface. I would work at the former, Jonas at the latter. Against the opposite (the north) wall of this main room, sat a somewhat worn dark nappy—piled—Danish Modern couch with wooden frame; a telephone with a long cord could reach either desk and the couch. There was no television.

At the far end of my desk, books and journals on film (Eisenstein, Godard, Münsterberg, issues of Jonas's *Film Culture,* among many others) as well as battleship gray 16 MM film cans stacked one on top of the other, filled two bookcases. Opposite the narrow room with the window, across a dark and partially carpeted hardwood floor, stood a small bathroom unit with a plastic-curtained shower stall at the west wall. A layering of white powder littered the toilet and sink and floor area erratically.

A young woman lived with Jonas. Ronna Page was half as old as Jonas—and had long shiny black hair with neatly trimmed bangs, large glistening black eyes, and flawless fair skin covering high cheekbones. Her small, chubby, inquisitive rosebud lips were like a baby's. An actress, her stage name separated her from her Brooklyn origins in a family of Schwarzes. She was in Andy Warhol's just-released *Chelsea Girls,* his first split-screen movie, and Ronna's only Warhol film with sound. In fact, I later learned, she'd just dropped by the Factory, not intending to appear on camera.

Late into the four-hour epic she has an interview—a confession—with the Pope of the Underground played by the actor Ondine. It's a two-shot from a stationary camera with Ronna on the left edge of the frame, on one half of the "confessional" couch, a sectional sofa with the two halves placed back-to-back. Ondine, on the other half of the sofa, is at the center and right edge of the frame, which is lit radically from the left in harsh black and white. Some minutes into the confession, the Pope, having counseled Ronna to "go up to the nearest image of Christ, kneel down and then peel away the loincloth in your mind," and blow him, suddenly explodes and slaps her: she's stunned, and the tears she sheds are real.

She'd made the error of calling him a phony after he'd declared "The mind is all," and "The soul is the mind," after she'd expressed her skepticism toward him, after he'd tossed "Popesi-cola" in her face, after he'd urged her to "Leave the confessional."

He slaps her not once but several times, with one hand and then the other, jumping from his side of the couch to hers to strike in both directions in split-second fury. After the first slap she pitifully raises an index finger and shouts "Stop it! Get your hands off me!" before taking more hits and being shunted off the couch, out of the frame. He spends most of the next twenty minutes justifying his actions, threatening her with more as she sobs and shouts off-screen, bragging that what everyone just witnessed "may be a historical document," lambasting her as "Hoah!" and "Cunt!" His late and brief apology to the camera ("I hope once I can say to her in honesty, 'I'm sorry for attacking you. If I can, I'll feel better about it.'") is negligible.

Gordon Ball

Was it, as some would later suggest, simply that Ronna had failed to adapt to the essential "ironic mode" assumed by virtually all the film's performers? That she'd failed to stay in or fully get into character, and it was therefore she who was remiss? Yet Ondine had shot up on screen minutes before his scene with Ronna, and his performance after his attack seems an exhibition of raving egoism and methedrine psychosis. He brags, "I hit you with my festered hand, you dumb bitch," and even takes on the absent Jonas:

> I don't know if it even is the same girl . . . but I think it's the Saint's wife. And the Saint, who's supposed to know a lot about movies, had better be sharp! I'll bring you to court! I'll sue you and your filthy husband! Now shuddup!

Occasionally when I was at Jonas's and didn't have work to be done immediately, Ronna and I would talk. I'd love listening to her low, soothing voice: once she was like a Jewish mother to me, telling me I'd never have to do factory work (like at Meunch-Kreuzer that summer) again. Occasionally we'd go out in the evening to Max's Kansas City—on Park Avenue between Sixteenth and Seventeeth, a ten minute walk from Jonas's—and a couple of times Andy and others would be there, always at a red-clothed table in the very back of that rather small and usually quiet back room, and we'd join them. A year later, when Candy and I moved into the loft briefly before leaving for Mexico, Ronna—and sometimes another young woman staying there—would delight in going out late at night for little plastic bedded packs of chocolate pudding at the deli across the street.

In the fall of 1966 she talked a lot about "vibes" and "auras." After meeting Ronna, Louise pronounced her "affected," but for me she was a good companion. I was puzzled a little by her relationship with Jonas, since I didn't really see them together physically, but that was not my affair.

I was there to work. "Come in any time during the day you want, vork as long as you want," Jonas said, handing me the key. "Den I vill give you twenty-five dollars each week." His Olympia manual typewriter just to my left, his cream-and-silver Wollensak reel-to-reel tape recorder to my right, I transcribed two panel discussions from the Lincoln Center Film Festival: one on *Cinematic Style,* the other featuring new, young film critics of the day.

Included on the second panel were the balding Ken Kelman, who was perhaps twenty-five; Toby Mussman, who'd graduated Yale three years earlier; and Sheldon Renan, who was writing a book on American underground film. The fourth "young critic" was orange-bearded P. Adams Sitney, who was my age, though I didn't learn that until decades later. Given his name, his vest, his suit, and his minute rimless spectacles, he seemed from the nineteenth century, vaguely resembling Chekhov.

Sitney's presentation was the most concentrated. It propounded a belief in "the secret diamond": a vision-expanding response to a work of art involving as much effort on the part of the critic as on the artist. Ezra Pound's *Cantos*, Stan Brakhage's *Metaphors on Vision,* and other books illustrated his point. Jonas's own appreciation of demanding, perhaps rarefied works of art seemed parallel.

While I'd work at his loft, Jonas would often be busy at the other desk. For lunch he'd buy a baguette and cream cheese, and would offer me a cup of hot tea. Inspired by his asceticism, I'd take the same sort of meal myself. The work he proposed to me that fall was varied. Besides the festival transcriptions, he suggested I interview any of several artists for a special mixed media issue of *Film Culture:* Richard Aldcroft, La Monte Young, and Yoko Ono.

Preparing for my interview with Aldcroft, I'd examined the recent September 9, 1966 *Life* magazine, starting with the cover—blazing in a rush of red and yellow was a medium close-up of Aldcroft, a slender man in his early thirties, a few lines of gray in his brown beard, seated in a director's chair, his hands dangling from its arms. Except for some large goggles over his eyes, he was naked, bony, all the way up from the beltless jeans that hurried out-of-frame below his waist. Like the wall behind him, he was bathed in projected image, color and form.

The cover heralded "New Experience That Bombards the Senses: LSD ART." Inside, the contents page explained: "Psychedelic artist Richard Aldcroft, wearing plastic goggles which force each eye to see independently and thus disorient his brain, takes a psychedelic trip—without the help of LSD. . . ."

On the same page George P. Hunt's "Editor's Note" reported on the photo shoot for "The Air War," a much longer article preceding "LSD ART." The purpose, Hunt explained, was "to put the viewer in the place of a combat pilot in action": tentacles of phosphoric light burst over tiny villages; clouds of tracer fire exploded in air (intended or not, they

counterpointed the vivid light shows of consciousness in the article fol-
lowing). The photographer had "his neck a long way out," Hunt said, "He
was right up there with the pilots." But no word for life below, under
falling bombs. Any question of bravery, pain, suffering, innocence, right-
eousness, fearfulness, fearlessness—or sacredness—of the lives that were
taken, wasn't raised. And the article itself even celebrated a DC-3 called
"Puff the Magic Dragon," a name that a new generation associated with a
beneficent, in-expensive, easily available herb which could relax, heighten
sensory awareness, and induce aesthetic and spiritual insight. The herb,
not the aircraft, was illegal.

I visited Aldcroft for the interview. He was quiet, thoughtful, accessi-
ble, friendly, a little spacy. He offered me DMT. We smoked it—I for the
first time—as we talked, as I recorded. And as, with goggles on and off my
eyes, I beheld the workings of his marvelous Proleidoscope—the "Infinity
Machine"—a smallish metal box with a projecting lens in front of sus-
pended celluloid particles moving, in a gel, in endless permutation.

I returned, more than once, for parties. In the midst of one gathering
the phone rang. "Oh, hi, Mom," Aldcroft answered in nonchalance, then
sat at his round blond oak table, black bakelite receiver to his ear, elec-
tronically engaged with his mother. At all angles from him younger
people laughed, talked, kissed, smoked—students, heads, fellow artists
from Manhattan, teenyboppers from Queens. In one dark end of the loft,
a small huddle of guests on mats and blankets gazed up toward the mov-
ing wonder on the opposite wall. . . .

I transcribed our interview, and Jonas took it for *Film Culture.*

(4)

On a summer visit with Howard Nadelman, I'd gone to Yoko Ono's
"Black Box" installation at the Paradox. It was a six-foot by four by six
cardboard and wood construction covered in black paper and cloth—you
pushed aside hanging black cloth to enter and exit. A kind of meditation
piece, I thought, strangely, sitting in it. Its creator had a Second Avenue
apartment with Tony Cox, but by the time Jonas asked me to look her up,
I discovered, she'd already left for London and the opening of her
"Unfinished Paintings and Objects"—where she'd meet John Lennon.

I don't believe I ever found La Monte Young, who was (as I'd later learn) a male composer of some reputation in avant-garde circles, and a collaborator with Tony Conrad and the Velvet Underground's John Cale—but I set out seeking a female. My background on some of my subjects was nonexistent, my vocabulary almost as limited as it was in carpentry, and my research, when I did some, as haphazard as any beginner's. Mainly, I depended on Jonas's files. (After all, there was no "Aldcroft, Richard" listing in encyclopedias.) If I thought of asking Jonas personally for information beyond his files, for his own impressions and experiences, I may not have followed through for fear not only of interrupting his work but of exposing my ignorance—and by so doing, arousing the suspicion that I might not belong, socially or aesthetically, in this whole concern. I found myself at the center of an unknown sea just learning how to swim.

Within Jonas's materials was an article on a large mixed media light show group, which I had trouble fully visualizing. Though the word "light" might be heard fairly often at mandatory vespers, I never heard mention of (let alone saw) a "light show" in my four years at Davidson. And though I knew Aldcroft's single work and had read of others in that "LSD ART" issue of *Life* with him on the cover, I had no concrete, first hand sense of a "light show" as a large scale mixed media event; in those first days, I hadn't even been to Warhol's "Exploding Plastic Inevitable" and Velvet Underground, let alone Leary's simulations of the psychedelic experience. I didn't know how to ask—or was embarrassed for my ignorance—or it didn't occur to me to ask—for more information. Though light shows would soon become as familiar as newspapers, in my first days in New York they were scarcely more than words.

Back in June 1966, at a wealthy uncle's car dealership in tiny Madison, West Virginia, my parents' graduation gift was a hundred-dollar down payment on a year-old, dark green v-8 Chevrolet—I was to provide the monthly payments. Now in the fall, whenever needed, evenings and days alike, my Chevy was at Jonas's disposal, but he didn't drive. Parking in Manhattan was so inconvenient that I seldom used my car for myself, more often for transporting "ekipment," as Jonas called it. Several times in the fall, for a nominal twenty dollars, Jonas's brother Adolfas and his wife Pola used it for the weekend.

Once as I drove us past the Murray Hill Theatre on Thirty-Fourth Street where I'd recently seen *What's Up, Tiger Lily?*, I volunteered that

Woody Allen's film was funny. Jonas didn't respond: I knew he wanted
more than just that sort of high jinks and hilarity—as ultimately I did
too, I said to myself, completing what had become an entirely imaginary
conversation.

On another occasion, at his loft, Jonas was out when the bare over-
head lightbulb blew out. "I'll get you a new one," I offered somewhat
apologetically when he returned. I not only felt responsible; I thought
that offering to replace it might bridge some of the gap I felt between us
as well. But Jonas brought me back to earth:

"Vot? Vot are you?! Some kind of a nut?"

From my end, much of my relationship with Jonas consisted of trying
to figure out someone far distant and different from myself. Occasionally,
little revelations of surface bits and pieces of his character would mani-
fest, as if the vast depth remained unfathomably hidden, encased far
beneath the harsh accent and clipped phrasing, a sudden elfish delight
opening up, then suddenly closing off. And as we'd set out on our drives,
I—who grew up in a banker's household where personal data seemed
vaulted away—would often show my admiration for him in a way that
only someone raised in the foreign community of 1950s Tokyo might—
approaching my parked car, I'd unlock and open his door first, then run
around the front to my own.

ANDY

"So you've left Virginia?"

"Yes—North Carolina—graduated. Done with all that!"

Following one of the first showings of *Chelsea Girls,* Jonas and I lingered a moment to talk with Andy, who, as I was beginning to see, always asked about something you said the last time you met.

Jonas had just proclaimed to him, "You've taken cinema back to zero point, back to de beginning, Andy," as Warhol sat there quietly looking up at him, allowing just one single, shy "Oh."

I'd first learned of Andy in a History of Western Art class, taught by a man ill at ease with Davidson College faculty sanctions then in place: no drinking, and a required loyalty oath not to teach anything contrary to the teachings of Jesus Christ. Doug Houchens was an artist, an old family Virginian with a broad and bony upper body, a red face and vigorous close-cropped white hair. He spoke emphatically, huskily, but haltingly; once he volunteered to our class, "Well, you know they say . . . that if an administrator at Davidson College . . . asks a faculty member to spit . . . the faculty member answers 'How fah?'"

Another day in class he presented a series of color slides, one of which was of a white-haired young man in a blue-and-white broad-striped jersey—a "surfer's shirt"—making hundreds of cardboard boxes that pronounced "Brillo" in cheery red-and-blue lettering, just like the "real ones" in the stores. How funny, I thought. How interesting!

Then I heard more of him through Jonas's writings. I enjoyed how Jonas attacked pomposity in film and elsewhere through his words on Andy's *Eat,* the forty-five minute close-up of a man (painter Robert Indiana) eating:

> A man is eating a mushroom. . . . He does nothing else, and why should he? He just eats. There are thoughts and reveries appearing on his face, and disappearing again, as he continues eating. No hurry, nowhere to hurry. He likes what he is eating, and his eating could last one million years. His unpretentiousness amazes us. Why doesn't he think of something else to do; why doesn't he want anything else? Doesn't he seek anything important? Does his world end with the mushroom? Doesn't he read books, perhaps? Yes, he disappoints us, because he just eats his

mushroom. We are not—or are no longer—familiar with such humility of existence; happiness looks suspicious to us.

What pompous asses we are!

Even *Esquire* magazine had given some attention to Andy's eight-hour *Empire,* which Jonas shot with a stationary camera on the forty-first floor of Time-Life, framing the upper portion of the Empire State Building eighteen blocks away; filming began at dusk and ended a couple hours after midnight. People ridiculed the film for its length, and for being about "nothing." But I thought its length not much greater than some all-afternoon Kabuki programs I saw with my mother, father, brother, sister at the Kabuki-za in Occupied Tokyo when I was very young. The Japanese brought box lunches and came in and out quietly as necessary. And as it would happen, I did see several hours of *Empire* at the Cinematheque in the fall of 1966, and it was more or less as Jonas had said: after you've watched the first half hour, itself quite a length of time given gradations of light on an unmoving subject, suddenly against a now fully darkened sky the floodlights pointed at its pinnacle are turned on, and it's like a moment of illumination within you; it's a "meditation film," Jonas said.

Of course it's also thumbing one's nose at middle-class expectations. But in his comment about Andy's taking cinema back to zero, Jonas was alluding to his original stationary camera, single shot, single long take, silent film approach. In later (or "later early") works, drama was heightened, sound was introduced. *The Chelsea Girls* was an early Warhol film to use color—and far more camera movement than usual: so in that sense his oeuvre became a sort of technical recapitulation of film history.

Back at Panna Grady's in April 1966, Andy and I had gotten in just a few moments of conversation—who I was, where from, what doing— before Norman Mailer intruded, accosting Andy with his "A real movie directah!" routine. But it was long enough for him to have issued an invitation in his soft voice: "Why don't you come down to the Factory tomorrow. Would you like to?"

The Factory then was at 231 East Forty-Seventh, near the U.N. I took the service elevator four flights up to a large loft about forty by eighty feet, walled and ceilinged with silver foil and silver paint. Andy showed me around, then others came up to talk with him. At Panna's the night before, I'd gazed upon Mary Woronov, who had come with Gerard

Malanga. She was wondrously beautiful, but I hadn't had the nerve to speak to her. Then I hoped she'd be at the Factory—but there wasn't a sign of her. Instead, I found myself staring at the striking Neapolitan profile of Gerard Malanga as he sat typing at a black manual near the door. Would she show up? Perhaps I could communicate with Gerard, establish some however tenuous relationship. "How late did you stay last night," I found myself asking him, and embarrassed at my own woodenness, I left.

Now, September 1966, before Jonas and I headed for the stairs of the Cinematheque, Andy asked me to the Factory again. When I arrived late the next afternoon, they were about to start shooting a movie on Bob Dylan.

"Here, why don't you be the microphone man," Andy said, handing me the mike.

He went behind his 16 MM Auricon. I held the mike on a boom arm over a central, illuminated area of the concrete floor, as a small crowd of Factory people gathered round. Suddenly a short curly haired fellow roared up on a noisy Harley Davidson. It was a parody of Dylan (who unfortunately had been seriously injured on his Triumph motorcycle less than three months before) and the young man playing him was loud and obnoxious. With lots of challenge and defiance and put-down he engaged in rapid give-and-take with the others there: it was a caricature of the Dylan as interviewed by *Time* magazine in D.A. Pennebaker's *Don't Look Back.*

After some minutes the tension dissolved. All the assembled turned to me, as mike in hand I stood silent in pale shirt, leather belt, boots, and tight, low-rise gray-and-black striped bell-bottoms that showed off what a friend once called my "nigger ass." "Mr Microphone Man," someone shouted, and started taking off his shirt, which he threw at my feet. Others did likewise, with shouts in my direction, as they stood there offering to me what a moment ago had pressed close against their flesh. I stood there silent, unsure, a little paranoid, guarded, holding the mike, as Andy swiveled the Auricon in my direction, and still I stood there silent, the torn-off clothes piling up, in almost a circle, at my unmoving boots.

Gordon Ball

LOUISE

My relationship with Louise Matthewson—I'd moved in right after our first night together—was my first time living with a woman. Though I'd become pretty active sexually once it did finally happen, I hadn't lost my cherry until late in the spring of 1965, when I was twenty: after nearly a decade of silent yearning. During the next fifteen months or so I enjoyed a number of relationships, but they typically involved repeated overnights, afternoons, weekends (or, in the case of Anna Marie, staying for a short period with her and her mother): no real experience living one-to-one with another person.

Louise and I soon ran into problems. Her son, David, had been kept by friends that first night. Only six months old, he bawled his head off quite early every morning, almost driving me crazy. I'd complain to Louise, "Make him stop it!" and did little or nothing myself. A small child, even a loved one's, was simply not, so to speak, in my program.

What was, I'm not sure I could say. Some evenings Louise and I went to see her friends, most of whom were, as was she, four or five years older than I; some seemed a decade older (that meant, of course, not simply thirty or thirty-one, but half my own lifetime older). Even the age of twenty-five seemed so old that at twenty I'd resolved to kill myself if I hadn't done what I wanted to by then. Exactly what that was remained unspecified beyond some sense of immortal aesthetic accomplishment, perhaps a little like Rimbaud's—to be young and possessed of a triumphant mortal gesture!

One such evening, as Louise and I walked home to Perry Street, I began filming, using the heavy but compact box-shaped regular 8 MM Revere movie camera Jonas had given me. As she watched me and my Revere at work—or play—with streetlight, storelight, window, and the reflections and superimpositions of each, she seemed to sense what I was doing. "You're a good filmmaker," she offered. I can't remember saying anything similarly appreciative about any aspect of her life or work.

Although I was self-absorbed and inconsiderate at times, I was made to feel that her quiet apartment, far on the west side of the Village, near the docks looking over the Hudson to New Jersey, was mine to make myself at home in. I set her typewriter on her round oak table and, inspired, wrote my younger friend Jake Floran, still at Davidson College, about my

'66 Frames

work just begun with Jonas: "This great man . . ." I typed, thinking of his dedication, his vision, his saintliness. I wrote a short essay on aesthetics, about how an artist's or poet's vision couldn't manifest only in a spiritual or refined aesthetic realm but must embody itself in earthly form too. For example, Walt Whitman had to love boys. "You're a genius," Louise told me, reading it. She was a painter, and though she tried to show me how to paint with acrylics—I had in mind to do something expressionistic—I resisted, preferring to try my own ideas instead. Eager for the execution, I was impatient with the instruction, even though I'd asked for it.

And as we continued together we fell apart. My lack of interest in David remained fixed. My work with Jonas, the *Film Culture* work I was starting with Richard Aldcroft and others, the excitement of simply walking among hundreds of people, real as my own thoughts, on the fast, bright, and dark streets of New York, absorbed and uplifted me. Even things as simple as walking into a delicatessen and getting a ham sandwich, sixty-nine cents, biting into its soft pink meat and pale bread as I walked, sneakers on pavement, in light chinos, windbreaker. Some of the time, walking around buoyant, in my head I'd hear (when it didn't jump from stores, apartment windows, or cars) Paul McCartney's "Good Day Sun-shine." Its rolling blues piano seemed almost to propel me, driving my celebration of being young and in the city. Sometimes, I'd hear his equally forceful "Got to Get You Into My Life." But I never applied its message to my relationship.

"My friends say you don't love me," Louise reported in a soft voice one night after we returned to Perry Street. The next day when I came back at dusk she asked "Have you made any new friends in your work?" I left the following morning.

JACK SMITH—AND JONAS'S CINEMATHEQUE

Though at his suggestion I'd work later in the fall at the Cinematheque and then in January start at Filmmakers' Cooperative, I continued helping Jonas with the two issues of *Film Culture,* and doing a variety of other work as well. My friend Billy wrote a Davidson chum, "Gordon's his chief cook and bottlewasher."

One of the first filmmakers I visited at Jonas's request was Jack Smith, the maker of *Flaming Creatures* and other works. On a golden day in late September I entered his loft at 186 Grand Street near Greene Street, with its view of congested traffic beneath tall hardware district windows. Entering, I maneuvered my way around one object and another: a wheelchair evidently used as a dolly in shooting film, a human skull, a toy green alligator in a curving blue plastic pool. All seemed emblems or extensions of Smith himself, a tall, slender, and broad shouldered man who always seemed to be looking elsewhere, absorbed in thought—thought that often had immediate inspiration or application. His blond hair was very short, a "lie-down" crew cut, though the image associated with the "crew cut" seems inappropriate to Jack Smith. He had a striking, pirate's profile —above a large hooked nose two small, deeply set blue eyes squinted in the shadow of a large frowning brow. In his strange voice that seemed to moan its way from some well within, he worried a lot about the poor, who were "forced to live in apartments with low ceilings." (Oh, so that's it! I said to myself: that's what makes those places so depressing.) Before him I always felt paltry, middle-class, philistine, simpering, trivial. It wasn't until years later that I wondered if that were a desired effect.

A little later in the fall, on assignment from Jonas, I helped him repaint the ceiling and walls of the Cinematheque lobby. In those days the Cinematheque—virtually the only regular showcase in New York for independently made film, and the site of my first viewings of many significant works—was in the basement of the Wurlitzer office building on Forty-First Street, not far from Bryant Park and the New York Public Library. Its first incarnation had been at the New Yorker Theater late in 1964, but even before then Jonas's impressario efforts were impeded by three difficulties very much present 1966 – 67: financial needs, building codes, and, perhaps most frustrating, censorship. His 1964 arrests for showing *Flaming Creatures* and *Un Chant d'Amour* (shown soon afterward to raise money to defend *Creatures*) came at the New Bowery Theater and the Writers' Stage, about half a year before the Cinematheque was started. In the intervening months, "clandestine" showings were held at the Coop—which was then part of his own small apartment—until it was raided, and police were stationed across the street.

One evening on Forty-First Street city inspectors suddenly appeared, issuing an ultimatum, threatening to close us down unless certain technicalities were addressed. "What's wrong with these guys, anyway?" Ed Emswhiller asked after they left, as he and I took a leak in the john. Later, a friend named Barbara Rubin told how Jonas always had to pay off city officials. That a Cinematheque had now lasted two years—even if in different locations—seemed only because Jonas had managed, from the bowels of utter precariousness, to put together funds—and remain watchful in all directions.

Now we were to improve on its dismal subterranean looks, transforming stained green walls from stairwell through lobby into a cheerier creamy white. Jonas put out a call, two weeks running, in the *Village Voice*:

VOLUNTEERS
wanted
to work with
JACK SMITH
painting Cinematheque ceiling
125 W. 41 564-3818
after 3

Though film showings began at 8:00, this starting time was apparently convenient for Smith. Jonas had gotten funds for paint; I'd show up and follow Smith's instructions for the rest of the afternoon until close to show time. Sometimes Billy Trotter and others came too, for several hours of dipping fuzzy cylindrical rollers in globby aluminum trays, running them across wall or ceiling. While we were so involved one day, a small middle-aged man in an unzipped dark blue nylon jacket appeared on the stairwell and offered to work:

"I can sweep the floor. I can do anything you ask."

But he needed to be paid . . . we couldn't help him.

———

The Cinematheque was managed by Tom Chomont, a slender young filmmaker with dark curly hair and a surprised look in his eyes. He'd started a film series in Cambridge, Massachusetts which ran successfully (with cop "chaperones" at each showing)—until the police closed it down for a movie they considered obscene, Bill Vehr's *Brothel.* Tom was earnest, hardworking, dedicated. Helping him some of the time was a short Jewish girl named Yvette, who was so fat she was shaped like a bell; she'd sit in our little cubicle in her shapeless dark blue gabardine overcoat and eat potato salad from a Forty-First Street carry-out deli box. I came there one night to help out and she instructed, "Pretend I'm not here, Gordon."

Through a door at the opposite end of the lobby from the office lay the auditorium: nearly two hundred wooden chairs bolted to the slightly tilting floor afront a small stage and recessed screen. It was here that I'd first shown *Georgia,* getting that uplifting immediate response from Jonas. At the same "Open House" evening, Billy had shown his *The Battle of Goat Island,* a parody of *Alexander Nevsky* which we shot at the end of May at Davidson. Tilting his head from side to side, smiling wryly, Jonas had proclaimed Billy's film "fun." Bruce Byron, the cinéma vérité protagonist of Kenneth Anger's *Scorpio Rising,* also admired it.

Likewise, it was at the Cinematheque in the fall of 1966 that I first saw some of the early works of Stan Brakhage (we'd seen only *Dog Star Man* at Davidson). They included the rather embarrassing educational film he made in 1960 with science fiction writer George Gamow, *Mr Thompkins Inside Himself;* his striking psychodramas *In Between, Reflections on Black,* and *The Way to Shadow Garden;* the exquisite *Window Water Baby Moving;* and obscure early work like the vivid *Ballad of the Colorado Ute.* Here I first saw works by Bruce Baillie, George and Mike Kuchar, and Kenneth Anger (including *Scorpio Rising,* at last!); here I saw Warren Sonbert's *Hall of Mirrors* with a lanky blond boy (René Ricard) sitting alone in a room, weeping as if from lost love, while *What Becomes of the Brokenhearted?* and *Walk Away Renée* sound their sadness. And of course, here at the Cinematheque Andy Warhol's *The Chelsea Girls* premiered soon after I arrived in New York: playing to packed houses, it would change the showcasing of underground films.

A December 29 program of films by Jerry Joffen attracted Allen Ginsberg and a lady companion, as well as many others. She was silent, slim, blond, and high-cheekboned, a small wool cap on her head, a big dark heavy coat from neck down. Lips tightly closed, head and back erect, she moved slowly, deliberately, quietly, sternly, a crane among ostriches. She was Maretta Greer, back from many months among saddhus in India, Pakistan, Tibet. Someone in the crowded linoleum-floored lobby whispered, "She knows Tibetan!"

And though a sexual—and perhaps spiritual—revolution was taking place, and the young were living it, occasionally a lonely older man might attend a program that included "offbeat" sex, hoping to meet a favoring stranger. I encountered such a man one night after everyone else filed out. "I'm lonely," he explained. He was determined that the kinds of films we showed meant that those who came to them, or worked here, might be inclined to gratify him.

Of course some Cinematheque programs included sexuality—along with many other aspects of life and art. One night in February, cellist Charlotte Moorman performed, as she often did in those days, with video-maker Nam June Paik. This time, she was topless, wearing nothing above her waist but a series of hats and masks. Below, as she played two arias from Paik's *Opera Sextronique,* she first wore a lightbulb-lit bikini, and then a formal gown with its top down (at one point, her breasts sported battery-operated propellers). In the midst of Max Matthews's "Interrational Lullaby," playing bare-breasted with a mask, she was apprehended by men who suddenly appeared on stage in dark blue clothing with double-breasted, gold-buttoned jackets. Next week *Village Voice* society columnist Howard Smith, displaying a photo of her performance, observed that she "attracted a large, appreciative crowd of two types of people who came for two different reasons."

CANDY, APARTMENT B, AND RICK & CHRISTINE

Sexually, personally, my life continued to enjoy new ground, fall and winter 1966 – 67. Once I'd moved in with Candy in late October we found satisfaction and excitement not only with ourselves but many others. To a degree, my tale of a year in New York is set in three sometimes overlapping milieus: sex, psychedelics, and avant-garde film.

At fifteen, Candy had reacted to her Catholic upbringing—kissing a boy, she'd been told, could send her straight to hell—by vowing to sleep with a hundred men before marrying. Profoundly curious about the electric lure and bonding in sex, she began her investigative crusade without waiting for anyone's permission. Her husband Bill O'Brien—whom she now intended to divorce—was number eighty-two, and "a mistake," she told me.

At twenty-three, though sixteen months older, she was still closer to my age than Louise. And unlike Louise, she was neither artist nor mother. She was practical, quick, down to earth, unrestrainedly energetic. And almost unconstrainedly expressive, sensuous, and "garrulous to the end" —like Walt Whitman. She had a knack for figurative expressions: "Drinking Coke puts a sweater on your teeth"; "When I graduated high school I said 'Don't tell me anything more—I know where the library is.'"

I was brooding, slow, quiet, unconfident. I needed—I used—the bravura or bluster with which Candy met a world I still found confusing, fearsome. And evidently, I was cute and needy enough for her to take me in. She never asked that I stay; after our first night we were simply together.

Her apartment—it soon began to feel "ours"—was rich with drop-in friends and, not infrequently, strangers, friends-to-be. Until spring, Candy would be away till 5:30 weekdays as secretary-clerk at Aycock Enterprises, an advertising agency where she filled out orders, typed letters, made logos and imprints. Our evenings, when not Jonas or Cinematheque-centered, were often social, and often sexual, too. Starting in late October or early November, we devoted most Saturdays to taking LSD.

We had just one room, basically. Beneath a ten-foot-high ceiling, most of the eleven by eleven foot floor space was covered with six mattresses, which were covered with sheets and topped here and there with a pillow. Two steps up from this "living room" lay the short narrow (and much lower-ceilinged) kitchen, with the door to the hallway at one side, and a tiny bathroom at the end. Masking-taped to one of the cream-colored walls of the main room was a large black-and-white rice paper woodblock print—made by a friend of Candy's—of a couple on the edge of a bed, naked, in contemplation and reflection—despairing over their relationship? Having broken some sacred innocent trust? The woman sat at the very edge, the man had partially risen, on one upright arm, close behind her. Were they satiated after strenuous intercourse, seeking a second wind—or resisting the need to rise from their garden of delights and face the world of Order and Form?

In a nearby corner of our living room-bedroom, Candy's radio, a big old upright mahogany-colored Phillips with tubes inside, loomed imposingly. When turned on, the broad dial near its waist-high top glowed amber. On the other side of a barred window that looked out onto an airshaft stood Candy's dresser, on top of which sat a small portable LP record player. Miss Lyn, Candy's silvery, satiny gray cat—named after Candy's nail polish remover—rested or played somewhere about.

Sometimes we had sex with our guests, sometimes not. Some visitors appeared but once, some many times; most, at first, were Candy's friends. Philip was a short, stocky, well-muscled gay fellow in a gray polo shirt with narrow black stripes and (even though the weather was cold) short sleeves: they showed off his biceps. He had dark blond hair and he hung around one evening (never to return) with tears running down his cheeks. Everyone else who was there that night just kind of squeezed around him, ignoring his response to my not welcoming his desire.

From time to time we were called on by granny-spectacled "Dylanologist" A.J. Weberman—he'd given Candy her first mescaline—and Ann, his tall blonde girlfriend or "old lady," as he sometimes called her. Occasionally, there might be a sort of wandering bikkhu kind of figure, a stranger to us both moments before we encountered him on the street, accepting our offer of food or warmth or company, telling his story of sights seen. Such was a large red-headed fellow in his late forties or early fifties, with long red hair and beard, and a mighty oaken walking stick, who was making his way on foot across America. He spoke with great admiration of Allen Ginsberg, but took exception to, as he put it, his "sickness" of homosexuality.

Once in a while, friends from out of town might call. Rick Jensen, my classmate from Davidson College, was one. Tallish, attractive, with short blond hair and a piercing look, he was the son of a Presbyterian minister with large congregations and a "big rep." His wife Christine was the granddaughter of a distinguished botanist. Rick and I had become friends after I won the creative writing prize the spring of my freshman year. He fit in socially—he was an "SAE," a brother in the most prestigious fraternity—in ways I (a "God-Damned Independent," kicked out of Sigma Nu the end of my freshman year) did not. Nonetheless, he too felt alienated by an essentially provincial environment. His dorm room was across the hall from the new single I took in January; we bummed cigarettes from each other frequently. "Reynolds Price says you're talented," he told me one afternoon after the visiting author had lunched at his frat house. Our relationship was underway.

By our senior year Rick was married, lived in an apartment: the second floor of the small white frame house of a widow who never made a sound. (Christine, now at "the girls' school" in Greensboro, drove down for weekends.) Occasionally I'd join him there for a meal, and he'd make hamburgers: "If you cook them slow they cook in their own juice," he said, laying the red meat speckled with white onto its black iron bed.

Christine's good looks were model: large head, strong cheekbones, graceful nose, clear complexion. She smiled easily; her modest-bosomed figure was trim. When I'd first gazed upon her a few years earlier in the Davidson guest house, she seemed an "older woman," a "grown-up," one of long evening gowns, dignity, expense: the kind Gregory Corso imagines with cigarette holder in penthouse near the end of his poem "Marriage." But she always seemed—in the presence of Rick or almost anyone else—a little nervous.

One Saturday afternoon in late November 1966, Candy and I were in the midst of an LSD trip when the phone rang. I always found it difficult dealing with the telephone while tripping. It wasn't simply its jarring, imperious ring but the need to disengage abruptly from myriad phenomena and focus suddenly on the poor little verbal electronic squawk from the round black box at my ear, and the linear information it would fire at me—and expect back.

Rick was on the other end, proposing that the two of them take a day from their their upper-crust, Old Family Thanksgiving week and visit us. I may have responded somewhat tremulously, but I managed to utter the syllables, "We're tripping," and to say they'd be welcome.

Two mornings after the phone call Candy and I slept late, waking only when Miss Lyn began nuzzling our faces. Neither of us had to work that day. My fingers idled their way through Candy's bountiful auburn hair and I nudged my face across her breast. After some sweaty sex, we both slipped back into lavish sleep. Later in the morning I fell awake and became immensely aroused all over again—and then came a knock on the door.

At first we intended to ignore it, then remembered Rick and Christine. With sighs we disengaged; I rose naked from the bed, springing up the two steps to the door. Both guests seemed to stop midbreath as they looked at me, looked down at their feet, then back up at me. I stood there inches before them with a wet hard-on, inviting them in.

As her black pumps hit the yellow linoleum on her first steps inside, Christine looked up at the low kitchen ceiling; Rick seemed already to have focused on Candy—rising from the bedsheets—and the waves of auburn that caressed her large bare breasts.

We settled back into the one main room of our apartment, Rick and Christine side-by-side on sheet-covered mattresses, their backs against the wall, facing us. At the foot of the two steps down from the kitchen, his burnished weejuns sat next to her dark low pumps, next to the sheeted bedding.

Candy offered, "Would you like some acid?"

Rick looked at Candy's breasts. Christine answered, "I shouldn't—I may be pregnant."

"Oh, really?" Candy responded, interested, reaching for her Camel Filters, offering them to everyone, lighting one. "How much pregnant?"

Moments later Candy's suggestion—declined—that they too take off their clothes, that we have an orgy, led to a debate of lifestyles. The Jensens sat there shoulder-to-shoulder, clothed from head to toe. Rick, on vacation from graduate school in the midwest, wore dark sharkskin pants and a yellow oxford cloth dress shirt with button down collar. Christine, on leave from teaching certification studies, a demure dark blue sack. From the wall the naked couple in the woodblock print gazed down upon them as a live naked couple faced them one mattress away. Rick and Christine argued—he, in clipped, sharp, vaguely New Yorkerish speech, she in softer but rushed, anxious tones—on behalf of a lifestyle devoted to hard work and responsibility, as they attacked their conception of ours.

Gordon Ball

The battle raged. Rick, a well-muscled former discus thrower, alternated with Christine in espousing their better way of life, throwing charges and counter-charges as if performing athletically. His voice was slightly loud naturally, and he sometimes rolled up his eyes rather than looking at us directly, as if addressing a superior, unseen presence. Meantime Candy, vigorous of speech from the start, was holding her own, animatedly advancing a way of life in which we could do as we pleased. The silver East Indian bracelets on her left hand jangled with her every point and whenever she rhythmically tapped cigarette ash into the glass bowl next to her bare knee on the mattress. I wondered what Rick really thought, and what Christine thought Rick thought, as he heard Candy's ardent words and gazed upon her rich hair and flesh, clothed only by a ringing bracelet, six feet away from him on a white sheet.

"But we can go to Europe," asserted Christine. "If you work hard and save—"

"And get a little family help," Rick inserted wryly.

"—you can go on interesting trips," Christine finished.

"So can we," returned Candy; "we can just get up and go!" She tapped her Camel Filter rapidly against the rim of amber glass. Soon, dispute unresolved (all of us were coming to see its futility), Candy and I put on clothing, and the four of us went off—to the Cinematheque, to some places uptown, and then to the Chelsea, for a gathering at Shirley Clarke's. Our guests had survived their reluctant baptism inviolate. Our friendship, for all its incongruities, seemed intact.

JONAS, *GEORGIA*, AND MYSELF

When I'd entered his loft for work on October 19, the day after the Cinematheque open house premiere of *Georgia,* Jonas greeted me with, "You should put your film in the Coop for it to be listed in de next catalog. And tell your friend to put his in, too," he added. In a few weeks' time, Leslie Trumbull, secretary of the Coop, would read me the generous blurb Jonas had written:

> *Georgia* is a good example of a new genre of film that has been developing lately, and that is, a portrait film. In some cases, like those of Brakhage, Warhol, or Markopoulos, there is an attempt at an objective portrait of a man or woman; in other cases, like in the case of *Georgia*, the portrait becomes completely personalized, poetically transposed; it may not be as multi-faced, as say, Brakhage's portrait of McClure, but an inspired portrait nevertheless, in the vein of a single-minded lyrical love poem.

I appreciated Jonas's words enormously; I was moved by them. Yet I was slow to act on some of his advice. Since *Georgia* was shot in regular 8 MM, he recommended having it blown up to 16 MM, a much more accessible format. Storm De Hirsch, whose *Peyote Queen* Jonas had brought to Davidson, would know where to go for that, he said.

Nearly everyone, even in avant-garde film—excepting Stan Brakhage —associated "motion picture" with "sound." For a possible track for *Georgia,* Billy had offered a 45 RPM record which he'd picked up his junior year in Finland: a song without words played on the Finnish kantile, whose evocative quality worked well with the film. Had I the money (and it never occurred to me to ask Jonas for funds in this whole effort), I could've had the song optically printed onto the film (the usual procedure)—but that would have required projection at 24 frames per second rather than 16; the images, already quick to appear and disappear, would move too rapidly for this dream-like movie. Had I even more money (and had I known of the process), I might have had it step-printed, with every other frame printed twice, to eliminate the added speed at 24 FPS projection. But step-printing was never mentioned in the discussions I had. Instead, I transferred the song to reel-to-reel tape. Though it could sometimes make for awkward logistics, it wasn't then uncommon for a projection booth to connect a tape-recorder to the sound system to accommodate such films.

I talked with Storm, a small woman with intent dark eyes and dyed blonde hair—a medium, a shaman, as well as a filmmaker. She recommended the u.s. Photographic Equipment Corporation in Corona, and all seemed set. Except I delayed. Finally after several more weeks Jonas asked, "Real, vot is de problem getting dat print? I have four or five bookings waiting I can use it for."

What was I afraid of, why did I delay? Was I unconsciously worried about cost, and didn't want to ask Jonas? I wasn't sure myself. In spite of being near the midst of much activity, there was an impulse within me which I did not understand—and still do not, fully, today—to withdraw, to retract from exposure or perhaps even a goal or achievement I thought I'd sought. Did I want to extend the excessively sheltered experience of my earlier years? After my early writing success at Davidson, I couldn't stand it when people would ask me later, "What have you been writing, Gordon?" I didn't like what I took to be typecasting, and though I too maintained the fantasy or notion of myself as a writer, I didn't know what to do next.

In the case of making the blow-up of *Georgia,* part of my delay had to do with feeling it ought to have something in the way of credits. As it was, it was virtually how it had come out of the camera, with just a few splices. One evening late in the fall, I laboriously cut through black poster paper the words "Georgia" and "by gordon" (as if I still saw, or wanted to see, myself as diminutive and my "public" as family that knew me by first name). Then I shone a light behind the paper and filmed it, so that from out of darkness the names were diffracted, golden, like the film. Then, just before turning it in to the Coop a few weeks later, (and almost as if to ruin it aesthetically), I shot by light of day a length of footage with "by Gordon Ball" in red magic marker block lettering on white poster paper, which I spliced on after the end. It was ungainly aesthetically, but it was a formal, more objective identification which the opening credit lacked. Perhaps the two titles referred to two selves: the child, the playful being, wanting to be known to everyone by first name; the aspiring adult, bracing to meet the world even as his block lettering betrayed his origins as sober banker's son.

MORE ON FRIENDS AND VISITORS—AND LSD

(1)

Sometime after my first few trips on LSD, I attended a presentation by Timothy Leary called, after Herman Hesse's *Steppenwolf,* "The Death of the Mind," at the Village Theater on Second Avenue, two blocks south of Gem Spa. Its huge auditorium gathered together over 1,000 youthful folk, nearly all longhaired, many males with beards, at a time when, as my English exchange student friend Simon at Davidson had sworn to me in great earnestness, "If you wear a beard, Gordon, everyone thinks you're homosexual." Many, male and female alike, wore bright, natural colors, making their own shifts and shapes with large volumes and bulks of cloth, not bothering to consult the overground dictates of "fashion"; many came with bells, or buckskin, or cape, even a feather. They seemed possessed of a singular, secret, and forbidden knowledge: as if they'd discovered the shape of the universe, held it in their hands, examined closely, beheld in unmitigated joy the stuff of which it was built! In clothes and affect they stood apart from the many thousands more who also walked the streets to which they'd return at evening's end.

And as I continued my experiments with LSD, I got into an argument with almost everyone. Already I'd argued with Billy, soon after my first trip with Robert: he'd cut into my rhapsody about the new phenomenon I was beholding with "C'mon, Gordon, I knew a guy in high school who could talk to trees!" For him it was risky, it was crazy; it threatened the fundamental order of things. One evening at Beverly and Rachel's (friends I met through Billy), I argued that LSD could revolutionize our conception of humanity, change the way we lived toward the older, more perdurable. Unlike Billy I wasn't a student of history but was reacting to the materialistic horror of our civilization, its work ethic, its aggression in Vietnam. I continued to hope for something more spiritual, cooperative, personal, aesthetic.

"I know a young man who wants to be a doctor. Are you saying he shouldn't be—that he should just drop out?" Rachel, dark eyed, curly haired and chubby, challenged me in their narrow white kitchen. Like most everyone else there except me, she had a mixed drink in hand. "I don't know," I answered.

"Yeah, and what about, say, mathematicians—and other professional people?!" She was picking up steam, and Billy joined her in eyeing me, waiting for my response.

"Well—" I began, then faltered. Moments later, I thought, "If it's for the health and happiness of humanity." But I didn't speak it; that moment had passed.

Speechless though I was, perhaps I had the last word. Another month passed, and Rachel's roommate Beverly came to our apartment at 57 Thompson Street one Saturday morning for her first LSD trip.

(2)

And there were others who came, once or many times. There was the young filmmaker John Cavanaugh; Johnny Carson, a sixteen-year old runaway; Tuli Kupferberg from the Fugs; even, eventually, from Syracuse, Anna Marie. Even later, there was Gail Samuelson, an Ohio State student whom Candy came upon in flagrante as she was sucking my cock. With both hands she pushed us apart, shouting "I told you she's got crabs, even on her eyelids!"

Not all were friends. One visitor—I was out—was Candy's ex-husband. They'd broken up just under a year earlier, but hadn't separated or divorced. Thinking Candy available at his pleasure, he'd dropped by the apartment (which had been his, originally) a few times before I'd moved in, then on this last visit discovered that Candy had changed the lock. Angered, he'd tried to hit her; she blocked his blows, and made him leave. He did so in fury, punching his bare hand through the thick glass of the building's front door. When I returned that night I saw shiny shards and dark blood stains on the small dusty black-and-white porcelain hallway tiles. A still angered Candy told me the story.

Candy's friend Dave stopped by a few times, then did not return. He was an older man who lived farther west than we, but on our latitude. (Our neighborhood at the bottom of Little Italy—with small stores, four- and five-story apartment houses of brick and stucco, Italian grandmothers on stoops, occasional groups of tough kids in tight black pants and pointed shoes—was too far east and south to be associated with the West Village, too far west for the Lower East Side. A decade later, the area would be known as SoHo.)

Dave was short, slender, pale, and acne-scarred, with horn-rimmed glasses, and full-length (in the older, 1950s sense) black hair, parted and combed neatly with oil. He liked to wear dark sweaters and a big black belt over thin blue jeans. A truck driver, he sold amphetamine and once left a jar half-full of its white crystals with us for safekeeping and occasional use. From midwinter on I parked my large green Chevrolet near Dave's: though a dozen blocks west of our apartment, it was the only place I could find where I didn't have to move it every day. When in the spring it was vandalized, Candy, doubtless grasping at straws, wondered out loud if Dave—whom we then seldom saw anymore—had anything to do with it.

And there was also Candy's friend A.J. Weberman, and his girlfriend, Ann. A.J., or "Weberman," as he was often called, was a slender young man perhaps a year or two older than I and an inch or two taller, with brown curly hair and mutton chop sideburns to go with his granny glasses. He often wore a somewhat Spanish-style broad flat-brimmed hat with flat top and strings that tied under the chin. He was on occasion our source for LSD. With his longish curly brown hair and pale skin, Weberman vaguely resembled Bob Dylan, but his cheeks were too pudgy (perhaps his muttonchops were an intended distraction) and his lips a little too chubby. His manner of speaking was assertive and frequently exclamatory with many "Man!"s and pointed index fingers making numerous points, narrating strange histories, explaining Dylan lyrics that were otherwise fascinating. Ann, tall as A.J., pretty and quiet, would usually sit or lie there on one of our sheeted mattresses, seldom speaking, sometimes echoing A.J.

An only child, Weberman seemed to have a mother fixation. One evening he went on at length in his charged voice with its emphatic hard consonants about how his mother used to gossip "all the time" with her friends at Schrafft's as they clinked long-necked spoons into splayed-top glasses full of parfaits. Yet his solemn fixation on Dylan was perhaps far greater.

Dylan—his life and his lyrics—was at the center of much of Weberman's conversation; in a few months, he proudly announced one evening, he'd be giving a course in "Dylanology." A few years later—well after Candy and I had left New York—he began delving into Dylan's garbage can at his MacDougal Street home, for further clues, and writing his conclusions. His investigation reached such a pitch that—so Ginsberg later told me—when he was once in the presence of his exasperated subject he grabbed Weberman by the collar with both hands, pushed him against a wall, and shouted into his face, "You're Dylan! You're Dylan!"

Dylan's lyrics circa 1966—*Bringing it all Back Home* (with "Bob Dylan's 115th Dream," "Subterranean Homesick Blues," and other synaesthetic anthems) as well as *Highway 61 Revisited* and *Blonde on Blonde*—were richly symbolic, Rimbaudian. At home on the ground floor of 57 Thompson, I listened to Weberman's assertions that this meant that and that meant this, as we passed the small brass pipe rich with harsh hash. I inhaled the charge from its small reddening coal deep within, and ignoring Weberman's illuminations, I reveled in the beginning of "Just Like a Woman" that came from Candy's small LP player:

> Nobody feels any pain
> Tonight as I stand inside the rain . . .

I thought it as richly suggestive of an entire social setting as the opening sentence of Chekhov's "The Lady with a Dog." And it was a setting with which I could identify. Other songs on *Blonde on Blonde* gave more details—of scenes that were much like my own at that time:

> Lights flicker from the opposite loft
> In this room the heat pipes just cough
> The country music station plays soft
> But there's nothing, really nothing to turn off
> Just Louise and her lover so entwined
> And these visions of Johanna that conquer my mind.

For all his notion-taking, theorizing, and formulating, Weberman could also be entirely resistant—a Doubting Thomas, not unlike Carl Jung's fellow medical school students who categorically, on principle, denied anything "occult." Once when the three of us were on acid together, Candy and I mentioned the psychic energy we'd discovered. As we placed our fingertips near his to demonstrate, he denied—before it could happen—that such an event could take place. Yet moments earlier he'd spoken of the amazing power of the "mere chemical" LSD.

(3)

Since Candy and I took acid most Saturdays, it was in a sense our regular—our most regular—weekend guest. Because I'd had psychic energy experiences with Candy as well as Robert, and because I'd levitated the hand of an interested and willing Davidson College visitor as well, I knew such phenomena weren't taking place exclusively in my own mind, but I knew that some sort of openness and interest were necessary for such moments to occur.

I spoke openly of the power of LSD whenever someone seemed interested and I thought it safe—even though armed men employed by the state were empowered to make arrests for personal use, and informers were materially rewarded. In those days even to discuss acid without clear condemnation suggested that you used it, inviting an unsympathetic, uncomprehending, or ambitious listener—or eavesdropper—to report you to the authorities. More often, when I did speak of it to people unfamiliar with the experience, it would be hard for them to understand "mere" verbal representations. A young Norwegian journalist—Gunnar Magnus from Hvalstad—came to our apartment to continue an interview begun at the Filmmakers' Cooperative. When he asked "But do you need LSD?" I felt he'd missed the point.

You didn't—in the sense of needing a scale to weigh vegetables at the grocer's, or a particular educational degree to land a certain kind of job. For those open to receiving it, LSD was an insight, an offering, a gift. Its ultimate demonstration (as I'd begun to realize on that first trip with Louise) was that all forms of existence were interconnected—that what was called "Gordon" and what was called "potted plant" or "cat" or "Candy" or "Italian grocer" did not necessarily end in the hard formal dimensions we may see every day, but merged fluidly with all other identities we're accustomed to seeing as separate. For myself this was of great interest not only from the perspective of metaphysics and aesthetics, but also within the context of a society bent on private accumulation of wealth, alienation of large groups of humanity, estrangement of individuals from within and without, demarcation of humankind from nature.

When Paul McCartney declared in 1967, "If the politicians would take LSD, there wouldn't be any more war, poverty, or famine," I felt he was largely correct. Of course, looking, let's say, at a sunset—available to all women and men—it's a wonder how anyone can fight. But even those things in life most widely appreciated are limited in their good effects. I wondered how judicious use of psychedelics along the lines Leary laid out would hurt; and if well-funded research might reduce or eliminate difficulties and hazards. Meanwhile Leary had already entered upon what would be decades of persecution, including his Harvard expulsion, and a thirty-year sentence for less than half an ounce of marijuana.

After several months I became uncertain where to go with my own "home research" with our weekend guest, particularly with the psychic energy use I'd learned from Robert and re-applied with Candy and one or two others. It was marvelous—but what to do with it now? Try raising whole bodies? And then what to do with them?! And when Candy once told me she was starting to feel I was losing her—mentally—as her hand, suspended in the air, followed mine, I stopped. It was marvelous—but I didn't seem to be able to develop this particular feature appreciably beyond the level of a toy—a toy with some risk.

My decision to stop using this form of psychic energy would come some weeks after a night at a friend's. One early winter evening Candy and I, having taken acid, attended an inexpensive preview performance of Norman Mailer's play *The Deer Park* at the Theatre de Lys on Christopher Street. The play was hard to follow in any linear fashion, presumably because of the acid. A stock Jewish Hollywood producer appeared on stage recurrently, but to what end? What was the real drama? I couldn't quite tell, and I hadn't read the 1955 novel from which it was adapted. But there were lots of pretty bands of color illuminating, halo-ing figures and props. Yet given all the possibilities with LSD, it wasn't a "rich" scene in terms of such psychedelic embellishments, not to mention deeper enrichments. Considering acid's potential, it was cramped, it was wasted, it wasn't time well spent.

But things became much worse afterward as Candy and I went to see nearby friends, Stanley and Carri. Though we had been visiting them so frequently that their apartment almost felt like our own, evenings there weren't without unpleasantness. On this occasion we took off our coats, joined several others on the hardwood floor, and listened as Stanley Fisher, a blue-eyed older man with a neatly trimmed beard, continued speaking to the group. After a few minutes I began using psychic energy

—showing it off—with my hand to Candy's. Stanley saw hers rise in response and was unimpressed. He remonstrated: "The value of that kind of communication will never be any greater than what you bring to bear in your everyday communication. What matters is what's actually communicated, Gordon." He then proceeded to lecture us and the rest of the group.

"What?! And he knew you both were on acid?!" Robert almost screamed when I told him of it.

STANLEY FISHER

Who was Stanley Fisher? Soon after I moved in with her, Candy told me of a friend named Stanley who with his friend Carri was "into" orgies. She asked was I interested? "Yeah, sure."

Candy arranged a visit. I invited Billy who, ever since coming to town in August to devote a year to seeking publishing contacts as he continued his considerable writing projects, had remained loveless. Stanley suggested we meet near his home, at the bar and restaurant at 72 Grove Street, on the east end of Sheridan Square. Shortly Candy and I were sitting with Billy in a wooden booth across the table from this broad-faced man of average height, small penetrating blue eyes, and a slightly dark yet ruddy complexion. From his thin lips words came with an unabashed, quiet force, a little throaty yet crisp. He had a vaguely Mephistopholean cut to his short beard. Next to him sat a quiet, pretty woman with long straight black hair that nearly reached the tail of the large loose blue corduroy shirt hanging over the belt of her jeans. She had pale skin and modest breasts; when she spoke or smiled she'd brush her hand across her mouth, gaze slightly downward.

"What sort of person do I look like to you, Gordon? How do I strike you?" He looked directly, intently, at me, rolling back just slightly one of the sleeves of his open-necked gray velour shirt.

"Oh, you look very distinguished," I answered freely, eagerly, almost joyfully, pleased to be part of his company. I considered his sculpted beard. "You look like maybe you're a painter."

Stanley indeed had painted, I learned much later, but he never let on that my surmise was accurate. He simply nodded slightly and asked me about myself. I told him I was working for Jonas Mekas, that I was a filmmaker, that I'd made one short film.

"What's it like?"

"It's sort of a hymn to a woman in the night, in water, in light, gossamer, impressionistic—the way I shot it." I sensed I wasn't communicating well. Two blue eyes, commanding, discriminating, relentless, above a rather handsomely hooked nose, remained unblinking.

"It's very kinetic," I said, giving up, but hoping to explain why it was hard to explain.

"You sound like a dilettante," he responded immediately.

I sat there silent, hurt, when suddenly I heard another voice. "I've seen his film and it's really good." Billy, loyal as ever, broke in from his end of the table. "It's beautiful, it shows something we've all felt about women, about the mystique of women."

"Uh-huh. And what do you do?" Stanley nodded tentatively and asked.

"I write—"

"Poetry?"

"Prose—fiction, nonfiction, drama. A long novel—a bildungsroman, about—"

"A love story?"

"Yes—"

"Based on yourself and someone you knew?"

"And loved. And she, me. But it didn't work, she rejected me even though—"

"Did you ever think she was leading you on?"

"No."

Neither Billy nor I were prepared for Stanley's blunt, disarming abruptness. It came, I'd soon learn, from a belief that the solution to our ills depended on being entirely honest with ourselves—and with each other. Months later, he shared with Candy and me and several friends gathered at his and Carri's the origin of his recognition: when after several years of marriage his wife asked him "What would you really like for your birthday?" he thought and said "Another woman." Now he no longer had a wife.

By day, Stanley Fisher was a substitute schoolteacher with a B.S. in psychology, but what distinguished him in our eyes was that he acted on his conviction that most men were desirous of other women in addition to their wives, and that the converse applied to women. Candor was the only way to address the conflict that would inevitably result. The primary source of our unhappiness, he felt, was our repression of our desires. His proposal, though he granted that it could involve great pain, was to acknowledge desires to each other, and to work together to follow them —openly. At his home, much of the talk which sometimes preceded or followed sex consisted of Stanley's assertions regarding someone's sexual attractions or intentions, followed by frequent protestations otherwise. Stanley might claim, "Mike, I think you're attracted to Helen, and you don't want Sherri to know it"—and Mike would labor to correct or challenge his insistent host: "No, that's not really the case, it doesn't mean that . . ." Or, "What is this, group therapy?"

"You're not leveling with us, Mike," Stanley might counter, cold blue eyes under large forehead challenging all resistance. Though Stanley might have overdone his disarming critiques, I never thought him mean-spirited, and never saw him violently aggressive. His persona was one of unflappability, leavened, at times, with humor.

Contrary to much of the discussion preceding it, the sex that usually followed wouldn't be contentious or didactic, would involve most of those present, and would often be unpredictably, profoundly enjoyable—so I found it at any rate. For Candy, Stanley's "power-tripping" could lessen the sexual enjoyment, but she went for the intellectual stimulation too. Stanley, it seemed, had some special insight into human beings.

The locus of this effort at honesty with ourselves and others was 521 Hudson Street, third flight up, often on weekends but on occasional weeknights too. It would involve a handful of guests, having sex, or watching, or talking, on the several sheeted mattresses on the dark wood floor of the main room. The apartment, altogether twice the size of Candy's and mine, included a narrow kitchen, at one end of which was a small room with two bunk beds, but no door. The guests were usually from age seventeen or eighteen to their late twenties; Carri was twenty-two or twenty-three. Stanley—I was surprised when I first heard it—was forty-one. His posture was good, his voice and presence not only "presiding" but intriguing; naked, he seemed Pan-like, as if, cloven-hoofed and pointed-eared, he were piping the flute of Eros and absolute honesty. Morally, was he good? Was he bad? Time and again he'd cut through the protective coating of many a guest—sometimes, perhaps, cruelly. Often he'd give us new thoughts about human motive and possibility. Much later on, after my sister visited and after we'd taken her to Stanley's, she volunteered, "He shouldn't be so hard on people."

Our first night there we five (Candy, Billy, Carri, Stanley, and I) were joined later by another couple. They were slightly older, quieter, and stayed to the rear of the circle, holding back, with all their clothes on, coats still draped over shoulders, while several of us engaged in what was my first experience with group sex.

I began kissing Carri and running my fingers through her long dark shiny hair. I got hard immediately. I unbuttoned her heavy shirt and

'66 Frames

licked and sucked at her small bare breasts, her pale skin pretty under the single bare bulb hanging over us like a blessing. Her affection—her touch, her kiss, her skill—was so welcoming and expert I felt free to do all I wanted. Up and down and across my back I recognized Candy's fingertips and polished nails tingling glissandos, adding to my delight. With one free hand I reached for Candy and caressed her shoulder and breasts. I looked up at Carri's face and caught her smile as she reached for the vertical row of buttons on my bell-bottoms, just under the large leather belt that Candy had given me. She undid them and through the slit in my white jockies pulled out my cock and brought her face to it and sucked in long, graceful and generous strokes, her cheeks contracting in rhythm. I managed somehow—Candy helped—to wriggle my pants down, then swerved around underneath Carri, tugging from below at her jeans . . .

As Carri and I made love, I felt rich and varied caresses all over me. When I'd look up, all I could see was human flesh, oceans, plains, mountains of it, pale, vaguely pink, lightly haired human flesh, vivid to the quick. Stanley had joined Candy in stroking the lovers (I was sure Billy hadn't) and they took their own delights doing so. What I'd see whenever looking up was like a geography of bodies, an extreme close-up celebration of fleshly hill and dale, in all directions, on all planes. Did it matter which part was whose? An arm there, lips here, finger right there, the tremulous lips of love kissing all?

Then Candy and I started making love. As we began rocking in joy, I heard sounds of involvement to one side of us; opening my eyes I could see just enough to sense, peripherally, what was going on. At long last, the quiet withdrawn couple, after witnessing (perhaps they were student observers) numerous configurations of ecstasy and wheezes and poundings of the back and gaspings of delight, had given a nod to Billy. Like them, he'd stayed on the sidelines, only, eager trooper that he was, he'd taken off his clothes. Now he was joining them in the back room. My friend had lamented his two months in New York without love; I was happy for him.

Gordon Ball

THE CHELSEA GIRLS, BILLY, and RENÉ

(1)

Though Jonas had looked for it earlier, by the time I turned in my 16 MM print of *Georgia* to the Coop it was late fall, early winter. And it had a couple of bookings right away, just as he'd promised.

Several months earlier—four days after I'd arrived in town—Andy's *The Chelsea Girls*, three and a half hours long in split screen, had premiered at the Cinematheque, and played there through November. Once or twice I projected it while we tried to accommodate the unusual crowds. That phenomenon—the sudden, unexpected and overwhelming popular interest in an avant-garde film, and the virtual dilemma it created for this small subterranean exhibition space—was the subject of a letter to the *Village Voice* in early December 1966 by music critic Robert Christgau. He was, of course, presenting himself as Straight Man Out:

> Dear Sir:
>
> This is a story about me and *The Chelsea Girls*.
>
> Everybody said *The Chelsea Girls* was great . . . Plan to go in late October with friends. Arrive 7:55, sold out, fair enough. View *Cast a Giant Shadow* from the balcony of the Victory. It's terrible . . . Plan for a recent Saturday with some friends. Cagily arrive at 7:30 to beat the rush and learn, via a sign in the lobby, that now reservations are required. I am slightly pissed because it seems to me the ad could have mentioned this peculiar desideratum. *The Fortune Cookie,* from third row right at the Selwyn, assuages me somewhat.
>
> The following Tuesday, determined though without my friends, I make reservations and enter the enormous, shapeless crowd in the Cinematheque lobby at 7:40. After five minutes I manage to obtain my tickets and am directed to a line by someone in the lobby. No Cinematheque functionaries visible for more than a second, audible at all. After half an hour I realize my mistake and charge for the auditorium. I complain, loudly, to a film votary [Gordon Ball] who promises to get chairs for me and my date. Doesn't. [I couldn't find any!] I

'66 Frames

demand refund, get it, but *Khartoum* does not ease my spirit. I will see *The Chelsea Girls* all right—at the Cinema Rendezvous [the spiffy midtown theater it moved to December 1].

Underground film buffs have been putting up with broken seats and inadequate projection for years, but this is different. Mekas likes to pule about the dangers of selling out to material success. Now it is clear he is sincere, for he can't really cope with it. His inability to handle large numbers of people is symptomatic of his contempt for them. . . .

A technical feature of the film itself was generally "poor" sound quality, which for some critics reflected a lack of concern for viewers (rather than lack of means or skill). To other critics, it even showed hostility—of the sort Christgau attributed to Jonas. Still others complained of the evidently random switching from one screen to the other, which they associated with an overall pointlessness to the film. Yet Jonas was scarcely the film's only enthusiast: many praised it for its unaffected brilliance, its revelations of our world, its ambiguity between life and art. For Shirley Clarke, "Anyone seriously interested in films must see Warhol's new movie because it takes us into a whole new dimension." In *Newsweek*, Jack Kroll rhapsodized upon this "fascinating and significant movie event":

> The underground cinema is the natural expression of a class; the young American dropouts who call all others dropouts . . . that cadre of bizarre haberdashers who make far-out threads to replace the emperor's new clothes. *The Chelsea Girls* is the testament of that class, the *Iliad* of the Underground. And Andy Warhol, that smiling, alfalfa-haired, infant-eyed, no-aged Peter Pan of pop art, is an appropriate Homer for such an epic . . .
>
> Now Warhol has turned his baleful, catatonic camera on the dropout generation and asked them to show how they drop. . . . There [at the Chelsea Hotel, "the historic Waldorf of New York's Bohemia"] Warhol peeps into eight different rooms to give us eight gamy hours of . . . life. But in a masterstroke, he splits his screen to show two peeps simultaneously. The resulting nearly four-hour film sets the eyes on alert, the teeth on edge and the heart on trial. . . .The fact is that in today's splintered world, Warhol's split-screen people are just as meaningful as Jack Gelber's garrulous junkies, Edward Albee's spiteful comedians, John Updike's poetic suburbanites.

> . . . Film societies and universities should have a look at this
> movie, which touches more nerves than a multifariously per-
> verse world will ever admit.

It begins with a mostly silent reel of Nico in a kitchen cutting her
bangs and, in the adjoining frame, an interview—confession—of Ingrid
Superstar with Pope Ondine on the confessional couch. Much of the film
is a bouquet of interpersonal eruptions: early on, filmmaker and *Time*
staffer Marie Menken loudly confronts her real-life friend Gerard
Malanga. Given recording quality and the rather frequent loud, staccato,
violent registers of ambient noise clunkily dominating some of the
soundtrack, a good part of it is indeed hard to hear—or was at the Cin-
ematheque. To Jonas such things may have been merely part of the point;
in his celebratory review he claimed that *The Chelsea Girls* was about us,
about Vietnam and other horrors of our civilization. For Jonas it was "the
first time that I see in cinema an interesting solution of narrative tech-
niques that enable cinema to present life in the complexity and richness
achieved by modern literature." Not only did it have "a classical grandeur
about it, something from Victor Hugo," but

> . . . it is a tragic film . . . in black on white before our eyes, this
> collection of desperate creatures, the desperate part of our
> being, the avant-garde of our being . . . the people in it are not
> really actors; or if they are acting, their acting becomes unim-
> portant, it becomes part of their personalities, and there they
> are, totally real, with their transformed, intensified selves.
> The screen acting is expanded by an ambiguity between real
> and unreal . . .
>
> The terror and desperation of *The Chelsea Girls* is a holy ter-
> ror. . . . It's our godless civilization approaching the zero point.
> It's not homosexuality, it's not lesbianism, it's not heterosexu-
> ality. The terror and hardness that we see in *The Chelsea Girls* is
> the same terror and hardness that is burning Vietnam; and it's
> the essence and blood of our culture, of our ways of living:
> This is the Great Society. . . .
>
> It's not the artist that is failing today. It's the critics that are
> failing by not being able to explain the real meaning of art
> to man. These works, once understood and embraced, would
> become rituals of holy terror, they would exorcise us from
> terror.

My friend Billy, whose wealthy grandfather in Charlotte was enabling him to spend a year or more in New York to make a go of it with his writing, deeply resented Andy and his work. He never met the man, but evidently felt his contact with this one film—and the way its maker appeared from afar—was sufficient. "Tell that Warhol to take off his sunglasses sometime!" he once ordered me after having just seen Andy, in black leather jacket and black jeans and shades, speaking to me quietly, inquisitively in the lobby of the Cinematheque. And once after Billy came to meet Candy and me at the end of a *Chelsea Girls* screening, I watched as he completed one of the comment sheets that were available in the lobby, attacking the movie for its moral and aesthetic "corruption." Sometimes our disagreements would be strong—he'd turn quite bitter and almost violent-edged—but one Sunday afternoon in his Twenty-Seventh Street living room when we did finally talk directly, at some length, about *Chelsea Girls,* he was willing to grant it status as "document"—not film, not work of art.

Nevertheless we'd still enjoy some of our same repartee and roustabouting as in college—at least on occasion—and his spirit remained in many important ways comradely and generous. One fall evening he came with me to help as I made a walking tour of the wooden telephone poles of lower Manhattan, carrying *Chelsea Girls* posters, a brush, and a large bucket of paste, putting up flyers, wedging them in between those for *Man of La Mancha* at the Anta Washington Square Theatre, Eric Andersen at the Gaslight Cafe, and *Gigi* at the Beekman, side by side with mimeographed statements of wisdom by Benedict Schwarzberg.

Schwarzberg? Who was he? I never met him, only saw him—and his work: a tallish God-looking Jew in rumpled gray hair, beard, and horn-rimmed glasses; each of his single-spaced typed statements filled several legal-sized white sheets of paper. They were mimeoed on both sides and when not posted were stapled together, offered for free at the East Side and one or two other bookstores. Rich with unrestricted metaphysical punning, they used any popular or personal event or reference as starting point. Example:

> *Cat Ballou* is playing at the St. Marks, 2 Ave. & 8th St., Thurs. June 6 (40-65¢). *Cat Ballou* is KABALLAH, & is not a you-man production. Kaballah is the teaching behind Youish-Trustin'-Muzzle'im Trinity of Religions. Kaballah is letters & numbers

(the ad features the capital ("Capitalism") A, "Silent Aleph" (Silent Life/Laugh/Love): mountain peak with snow line: Mt.: Empty (o), with its point Cat's vagina (Kab.: "The highest mystery is sexual in nature"). B: 1 & 3 joined: "My Story/Mystery of the Trinity," The 1 is many and the many 1: "be."

Send name for free classes Friday sundowns, Benedict Schwartz-berg, 610 E. 13 (3C). Financial support appreciated.

Such then were a few of the pieces already claiming precious eye-level phone pole space. It was a warm night in early October and we were having a ball, goofing with our charge, playing with the paste and paper, bandying the brush on our shoulders, singing loudly as we tramped down the street: we were those two rogues from childhood comics days, the Fox and the Crow. Then a police car pulled up and enacted a drama that never could've taken place in the South we knew in 1966.

"What're you boys doing?" asked a large, heavy, mustached black man in uniform through his open driver's window. His white partner sat stoically to his side.

"Puttin' up posters." I had my squeegee in one hand and my bucket of gobby paste in the other; Billy stood next to me with the roll of posters.

"That's against the law. Post no bills. We could have you arrested for this."

"Oh, I didn't know. I'm sorry."

"Don't let me catch you doin' that again."

"Yessir," I answered, impressed with his mercifulness.

②

Our high spirits disintegrated, of course. After a few furtive postings, we retired for the night. Our sudden mood swing after the encounter with the cops was as dramatic as the difference in the ways the two of us adapted to New York. For myself, being there was almost as if I were back "home," living once more in a city of 8,000,000. Billy, on the other hand, was in a place which in its very largeness was "crazy"—as he so often repeated. Not only that, but he suspected that now that we were within this enormous center of change and transformation, I'd become too involved with those who were socially or artistically "In," as he put it. I listened quietly, thinking that

'66 Frames

I was interested in people I found interesting: certainly Warhol was far
more interesting—and funnier!—than any Davidson faculty member;
Jonas far more inspired and visionary. . . . I didn't know if Billy's worries
might or might not have some validity, but I felt slightly insulted by
them—and almost embarrassed for him. But I never said so.

This lingering unease between us expressed itself oddly and intermit-
tently while we continued to see each other, fall and winter, perhaps sev-
eral times a month. One cold Sunday night he became quite upset by
something I did. *Newsweek* magazine, considering an article on under-
ground films, was coming to Jonas's loft that evening for a showing. Jonas
had invited me to come and bring *Georgia*; I stuck my neck out and asked
if Candy might come with me. Knowing how remote he could be, how
he prized privacy, I'd never before asked to bring someone. En route to
Jonas's, I thought to bring Billy into it in some fashion. While Candy
waited downstairs, I ran up to his apartment and asked to borrow his
Nevsky film for possible showing to *Newsweek* that night. He was hurt and
angry that I wasn't inviting him in person—it was a further sign of my
exclusive "In"-ness—but he let me take it. As it happened, few films were
shown for *Newsweek*'s Jack Kroll and companion, and in the pages of their
magazine two months later little attention was given any of the few
young filmmakers at Jonas's that evening, other than Barbara Rubin.

Once Billy—with whom I'd often looked for girls when we were at
Davidson—and I went to see a new Godard movie, *Masculine Feminine,* at
the comfortable midtown Carnegie Cinema. Before the showing began, I
picked up a young woman in the lobby, so that when we settled into seats
my two companions, old and new, male and female, were on either side
of me. The instant Godard vanished from the screen, Billy, his chin jut-
ting forward, wordlessly pushed off in the other direction, leaving my
new companion and me alone. When I saw him next he declaimed "I dare
say the only reason I went was for the pleasure of your company. I don't
like French movies and I think Godard is an over-rated fraud!" But his
turmoil then was nothing like what it was when I introduced him to a
new acquaintance, René Ricard.

One fall evening I was at the Factory when time approached for Andy
to take a reel from *The Chelsea Girls* to show and discuss at New York
University. He didn't want to; looking at me he said, "Oh, why don't you
go? You go and say you're Andy." Several of us (excluding Andy) did leave

the Factory in a cab, bringing a forty-minute reel. I was intrigued by Andy's proposition. I might've assumed (as I'd later learn) that he made such suggestions to others as well, but in any case I didn't see how I could act on it, outrageous as it was. And foolish as it was, I was on some level flattered. But there was no need to fear, for among us was a tall, slender, long-legged and bony young man with long fingers, blue eyes, dark brows, and shortish blond hair—and a hyperexpressive inclination toward campy and outrageous exercises in faggotry.

In a silent reel René Ricard appears in *The Chelsea Girls*—in seersucker suit and open neck shirt, he joins two other males sitting up in bed in varying degrees of undress, and eats an orange. At NYU's Loeb Student Center—a hundred or more people in molded plastic chairs awaiting us, or awaiting Andy—René had no trouble taking charge. Standing center stage before the screening, he spat out the briefest of introductions, this time being heard as he was not in the movie.

After the showing, a perplexed voice from the audience asked, "What's this film about?" René returned, "It's about nuuuuthing, it's about boo-ooredom," drawing out the long vowels excessively, as long as he could, as he camped his way to an answer. "What do you waaaaant it to be about?"

One mild late October evening a little later I was out walking with René near Billy's neighborhood (Twenty-Seventh Street between Second and Third), and we stopped in to see him. With Billy was his friend, Rachel, who lived nearby. René camped his way in, I made introductions, then he proceeded to dominate the conversation. His gratuitous references to the wealthy and famous weren't fully convincing but were sometimes quite funny, as he stood and strode about the small, rather narrow apartment, collapsing long bones into a helpless overstuffed chair, thrusting big slender fingers into the air like a referee signaling on a playing field, blinking his blue eyes, proclaiming himself in outrageous, triumphant camp. I was interested and amused, fascinated, even—though I wondered how our host and his invited guest were taking it. A few minutes passed, and an extremely nervous sinking feeling displaced my initial levity. When René stepped into the john, Billy hurried to me: "Get him outta here!"

When René returned, I proposed that we go out for food, and tried to nudge him toward the door. But there was no leaving until, as if to claim victory, he sat down at the phone at one end of the living room and tried to reach—first asking for his number through information—an acquaintance whose name was easily heard by all: André Segovia.

René's outrageousness would, in its own way, get the best of me as well. One evening at the Cinematheque, not long before that night's showing of *The Chelsea Girls* before a packed house, the phone was ringing with requests for information about showtimes, future play dates, and location (for most callers, the Filmmakers' Cinematheque was obscure). As in much of Warhol, and as with much middle-class interest in the "underground" in general, part of the curiosity was voyeuristic—people felt they'd see something which the everyday routines and sanctions of their own lives (which they themselves ritualistically condoned and enforced) kept them from seeing.

René entered the office as I was on the phone. He shut the door and announced, as I stood there, receiver to ear, "You look like you need a blow job." He bent his angular body down and undid my belt and unzipped my pants and took my cock into his mouth and began sucking in wholehearted commitment and dedication as I managed to conclude, "Yes, at 8:00 tonight . . . Maybe—through—all—of—next—week."

He sucked and sucked and I came vigorously and it felt good and he sucked it all up and just as I was starting to put my cock back into my jockeys and pull up my pants the phone rang again and René got it, first ring. "I've just *buh-loan* the manager of the Cinematheque," he tittered. "And *what* can I do for *you?*"

LEFT TO OUR OWN DEVICES

Over the coming months, Candy and I might visit Stanley Fisher and Carri once a week, but almost never when tripping. On many Saturday mornings we'd place on our tongues a tiny piece of blotting paper or cellophane or capsule or "sunshine" tablet, and wait twenty minutes for that characteristic slight "kick" or little sense of pressure in the back of the neck, telling us that the LSD was taking hold.

Weekends and weeknights when we weren't tripping or involved with Stanley or Jonas or their realms, we would often rest and reflect, play with each other, experiment with the Swedish back massage device Weberman's companion Ann had just given Candy, or play with Miss Lyn and her five kittens who came in January. Or go out after dark with nothing planned. Briskly our boot heels pounded the pavement through West Village throngs: first-time youngsters from Queens with Italian or Dominican voices; old denizens of the neighborhoods; policemen (every now and then, a pair on horseback); tourists in button-down collars and crisp above-the-neckline haircuts, or makeup, sprayed hair and heels; and others like us only in long military overcoats or furs or caftans or ponchos, perhaps from Limbo, the newly opened secondhand store on St. Mark's Place, the street where Richard Aldcroft and W.H. Auden lived. Onto the charged blocks above Houston, Candy and I would go, down MacDougal, past the Cafe Wha?, past Manny Roth's Cock-n-Bull II, past where the Village Blimpie's would open, with Gerard Malanga reading his poetry.

Or we'd simply enjoy the quiet in our apartment (a family immediately above sometimes fought, with loud epithets hurtling, children rumbling). During the week, evenings at home would go quickly, with friends, with just ourselves, with film work, sex, smoking, listening to music, a little reading. Once Miss Lyn had her five kitties—I filmed their wet entrance into this uncertain world—we could join them whenever we wanted for endless play as they scampered, seriously, boldly, comically, across sheets onto hardwood; up toward the small stereo or looming radio beneath frosted-glass window; into a parked shoe; up a silent stair; onto the shiny linoleum.

Through John Cavanaugh, a young filmmaker friend, I bought a single lens reflex regular 8 MM Bolex whose viewfinder frame was accurate where the Revere's was not. The Revere viewfinder area was approximate:

I always had to point the camera slightly above and to the right of a subject that was at all close to me. But I never stopped using the Revere, which sits in a drawer inches from my hand at this moment.

Besides shooting new life, I sought the "romance" of the city: lights at night in several layers, glassy jeweled images of the sort I'd begun filming when walking with Louise Matthewson. It was perhaps archetypal filming for many lyrically-minded young filmmakers in New York in those days— almost all of us did it. "You have the best lights at night," one of them, twenty-five-year-old Matt Hoffman, offered generously after I'd projected some recent footage for him at 57 Thompson. I regret not seeing his.

With razor blades, Candy and I scratched on film (to remove emulsion) and painted on it: enjoyable, absorbing work, but for myself not profoundly involving like making *Georgia.* And the results showed it, for they were inferior, I felt, not only to a master like Harry Smith, but to many others. Later in the year I'd take my new Bolex and two rolls with us on a nudist camp picnic with people from a studio Candy would work for; in the fall, when we left the city for good, I'd store that footage, along with others, in Shirley Clarke's penthouse attic—and never retrieve it.

At one point I became curious about black and white. In regular 8 MM it was much harder to get than color, but Berkey Photo near Fourteenth Street got some for me. I took some everyday shots, indoors and out, of filmmaker Barbara Rubin and other friends. But I was never satisfied with the often milky results.

Nonetheless, one little black-and-white project, even though a joke, was successful. One afternoon in spring Candy and I stripped naked; I placed the Bolex on a tripod as far as possible from the white sheets where she lay, focused it on the length of her odalisque, wound the spring-driven camera, pressed "Continuous," and ran to her as the Bolex rolled, pouncing upon her as we giggled and fucked, through the end of the uninterrupted twenty-second run of film. Rather than pay a lab to print and reprint this single shot, we shot and re-shot it again and again, to the end of the three-and-a-half-minute reel. When it was processed I intercut it with some found footage titles that announced: "What to Do In Case of Nuclear Attack." It was corny, silly, fun—my only work in black and white that pleased me at all.

Naturally, we didn't usually film ourselves when having sex. Just lounging about, Candy could be quite playful, as for instance, one evening when we lay completely clothed on a mattress. In blouse and full skirt she climbed on top of me, spreading the cotton cloth in all directions over my midriff, chuckling in a lilting voice, bright dark eyes spark-ling as she unzipped me, "This is how girls in the olden days would do it, so no one would see."

The music we listened to was of course Dylan. The Stones' new *Between the Buttons,* with its imperative "Let's Spend the Night Together," stretched the boundaries of what could be said on the airwaves (on Ed Sullivan, it became "Let's Spend Some Time Together"); there was Ali Akbar Khan and Ravi Shankar, as well as WBAI and other radio. Sometimes, smoking grass or hash, or even coming down from LSD, I'd try (usually in futility— or by kidding myself) to see that the pounding beat of the music was syn-chronized with the flicker of the candle at which I stared.

Candy did all the cooking, and was very good at it. Though we both took a look at George Ohsawa's book on macrobiotics, we ate basically stan-dard fare and rarely experimented. She did most of the housework, and together we made the six beds.

She was reading a lot of Zen Buddhism; her main question was "Could women become enlightened?" (Looking back, one might wonder if the same question might not better be asked about men.) When once she asked me about it, I answered, "Oh, sure. It's silly to make such distinctions!"

What did I read? Though now I might study several books simultane-ously, in those days—beginning well before New York—I seldom read seriously. ("Ve all develop at our own pace," Jonas once said.) I would often resist knowing, resist reading. In high school, words on a page sometimes appeared double; highly referential reading assumed a discouragingly greater cultural knowledge than I had. In eight semesters of college, I read only one book through: Sinclair Lewis's *Babbitt.* Yet the summer between my sophomore and junior years, returning home from bagging groceries, I read, on my own, every word of James Joyce's *Ulysses.* Too often, however, I seemed satisfied with merely knowing author, title, and what I took to be the basic concept of a work. During my senior year I identified with Norman O. Brown's *Life Against Death,* thinking I was "for" life and my par-ents "for" death, leaving it at that, with scarcely a word read.

In New York I'd look at occasional pages here and there, but that was usually it; often my mind would wander before becoming engaged. Soon after I arrived in the city, the summer 1966 *Film Culture* appeared, its cover the famous close-up of the mule's slivered eye in *Un Chien andalou*. Inside were several articles on Tony Conrad and his *Flicker*, as well as Stan Brakhage's *A Moving Picture Giving and Taking Book*. The latter presented various kinds of homemade magic available to everyone with a few lengths of film: making patterns of illumination by moving a flashlight over unprocessed film; scratching on emulsion; making everyone's first movie, a flip book like Pathé's early projection of seashore waves for Melies in 1895. But I didn't read most of the issue at length, not even the Brakhage piece, not even as much as my novelist friend Billy. Excited, he exclaimed about it to me, after he read it through.

Coming a little later was the fall issue, its cover photo a long shot centered at crotch level of Pier Paolo Pasolini, Andrew Sarris, Agnes Varda, and Annette Michaelson in panel discussion, with stockinged knees, metal folding table legs, wires and outlets. Inside, there were my transcriptions from Lincoln Center as well as numerous festival-related articles on Godard, Emshwiller, and many others (even a photo of the audience, including myself, watching *Flicker*). But outside of the material I'd worked on, I believe I read little.

After winter's dark and cold had set in came the uplifting, twenty-five cent, fifty-two page issue of the spectra-colored San Francisco *Oracle*. Its cover reproducing multiple likenesses of the four prophets, it featured "Changes," a lengthy discussion by Alan Watts, Gary Snyder, Ginsberg, and Leary at Watts's Sausalito houseboat before a question-asking audience. Snyder suggested that historically, dropouts have been necessary to healthy societies; longshoremen who'd been laid off, he claimed, eventually switched from "driving around boats that were just like cars," to taking up sailing. Likewise, those who wanted to spend all their leisure time hunting and fishing eventually made their own arrowheads: TV watching and beer drinking were only "what the working man laid off does for the first two weeks."

After Leary discussed dropping out historically, in terms of the development of small tribes, Ginsberg pointedly asked him, "Precisely what do you mean by drop out . . . for the millionth time?" Then with remarkable sympathy he argued that Leary himself, though "dropped out" of Harvard, was not dropped out; that he was lecturing, planning the Be-In, defending himself legally, providing for Millbrook, involving himself in a larger community: "So you can't drop out, like DROP OUT, 'cause you haven't."

Gordon Ball

Earlier in the fall, I'd purchased Leary's *Psychedelic Prayers,* with its pinkish acid art nouveau cover with snake, phallus, breast, and horse's head. Of sixty some decoratively embossed poems modeled after the *Tao Te Ching* and dedicated to Aurora and William Hitchcock, the one remaining in my mind was:

> Please Do Not Clutch at the Gossamer Web
> All in Heaven
> and
> on Earth below
> Is a crystal fabric
> Delicate sacred gossamer web
> Grabbing hands shatter it
> Watch closely this shimmering mosaic
> Silent . . .
> Glide in
> Harmony

Among other books gracing our apartment was the hardbound *The Psychedelic Experience: A Manual Based on the Tibetan Book of the Dead,* by Leary, Ralph Metzner, and Richard Alpert; it was a running analogy between the loss of ego potentiated on psychedelic trips and the loss of body/ego at the time of death. I never looked at it in great detail; after Candy and I visited Millbrook later in the spring, however, I began to read the Tibetan original, as translated by W.Y. Evans-Wentz.

From A.J. Weberman we had on long-term loan a copy of the galleys for Bob Dylan's *Tarantula,* though I'm not sure either of us read it through. Candy had the new Grove Press paperback *Naked Lunch,* but I didn't seriously read it.

I doubt I completed a book in my year in New York; on the other hand, I was trying to penetrate several mysteries, several mystical "books" that not everyone was examining in depth or detail. Perhaps out of fear of entry into a world more complex than I wanted it to be, or fear of being too dumb, I often allowed my own general impression to substitute for detail and accuracy.

JONAS AND ADOLFAS AND POLA

"I want you in my rogue's gallery," she said, her large dark eyes twinkling. Dark-haired, pretty, she sat several feet from me in her small living room on the Upper West Side, a 35 MM single lens reflex poised between both thumbs and index fingers. She was Pola, Jonas Mekas' sister-in-law of just over a year.

In the summer of 1965, Pola Chapelle, Italian American chanteuse and lover of cats, had married Adolfas, Jonas's junior by three years. At the Third Avenue loft, I'd seen some of Jonas's color footage of the wedding. As his older brother's accordion-playing and singing sound plaintively, Adol-fas appears in dark velour-necked Western suit and large white cowboy hat; in photograph only, we see Mekas's parents, Povilas (barefoot in a plowed field) and Elzbieta (in scarf). Pola is in wedding dress, veil and train.

The two brothers had escaped the Nazis at home in Lithuania, only to fall into German hands as they attempted to make their way to Vienna mid-1944. For much of the war's final year they were interned by the Nazis, but made two escapes and worked several months as farm laborers in a spot so distant that word of the war's end came two weeks late. With the Soviet Union taking their homeland, they spent the rest of the decade drifting and on occasion nearly starving through defeated Germany, camp to camp and city to city, until landing in America, "Displaced."

Now, nearly twenty years later, Adolfas and Pola were established in a small comfortable apartment on West 89th. The two brothers remained in fairly frequent communication with each other. In fact, when phoning Jonas (who was often beleaguered by dozens of calls a day), Adolfas had his own signal: two rings only. His older brother would then know to ring up "Fuss," as photographer Peter Beard had christened him.

Adolfas had worked with Jonas on a number of film and publishing projects in the 1950s and early 1960s—still worked with him on *Film Culture*—and most notably had directed (Jonas assisted) an important new work in American narrative film in 1963, *Hallelujah the Hills.* In the fall of 1966 I'd been invited to see *Hallelujah* in a cozy, comfortable, and classy midtown screening room. Presumably Adolfas was raising funds for a new film (he said to me that day in his apartment, "We'll be going into production in January, I'll be calling you"), showing the best of his previous work to potential producers, patrons. There weren't many people there that day, maybe two dozen, but it befitted the size and the quiet comfort of the place. I remember the physical circumstance because turning down the aisle before the film began, I saw Shirley Clarke, who introduced me to the quiet, bearded, gray-suited black gentleman at her side. "This is Ornette Coleman."

Hallelujah the Hills had become known as a kind of filmic romp by "the Mekas brothers," but many critics had given more recognition to Adolfas. This was only just—it was more Adolfas's film. Articles on Jonas mentioned it, but that was usually all. Jonas was there, in the movie's spirit, its anarchic and poetic inspiration—but as I saw that day in the screening room, *Hallelujah* was ultimately a kind of American nouvelle vague film, a sort of American *Shoot the Piano Player,* a narrative film that was playful and self-conscious but still essentially a narrative. It was very different, for example, from Jonas's single night shoot with everyone descending the coal chute to re-enact *The Brig;* or his lyrical, personal diaristic works with their hurried single-framing of everyday New York.

Hallelujah featured Peter Beard, Sheila Finn, Martin Greenbaum, and Taylor Mead on screen, but for me its most delightful moment had nothing to do with actors, actresses, or action. Snow starting to fall, the camera tilts up from foreground campfire and smoke to distant field and pine forest and a farther line of mountains in mist; what looks like kanji appears at the right margin of the frame, and that snowy, misty landscape suddenly becomes a woodblock print: Hiroshige on celluloid.

So that was Adolfas's finest, and it was as different from Jonas's as the brothers in person differed one from the other. Adolfas was almost as good-looking as his new wife; he was handsome to Jonas's exotic, almost otherworldly, Giacometti look. Adolfas in manner and spirit was urbane, worldly. I sometimes remember—or imagine—him with a cigarette holder, for it seems in character, though I'm not certain I ever saw him with one. I can conjure him in his home (much smaller and more "sociable" than Jonas's) offering me a drink; I note his zippy manner, his bent for satire, his clothes finer than the corduroy of his monk-like, ascetic brother. Next to Jonas, he was a dandy.

"Cinema is all technique," he told me as he and Pola and I sat and talked. He admired Ed Emshwiller, his cameraman for *Hallelujah.* I never got to know him and Pola—particularly Pola—well, though they used my car for a few weekend trips that fall. All went well—until early

November when he collided with another vehicle. No one was really hurt, and my large green Chevrolet still ran, though it picked up a sizable dent on one side near the front. From Peekskill, New York he phoned me about it soon afterward ("I'm in Peegskeel," his voice sounded over the phone, as if part of some Adolfan satire) and on letterhead stationery sent me a statement for my insurance company:

> Adolfas Mekas, 29 W 89 Street, New York, N.Y. 10024 TEL.: 787-2468
> November 7, 1966
> To Whom it May Concern
> Re: Accident on the road.
>
> Time: November 6, 1966; about 1 P.M.
> Place: So. Londonderry, VT.
> Car damaged: Chevy 1963, 31III F237267
> LIC.: EC 8048 N.C.
>
> Car causing accident: LIC.: TRKC 896 VT.
> Driver: Mr Albert Barnes
> Place: So. Londonderry, VT.
>
> Explanation
> In So. Londonderry there is one (and only) four corner inter-section. I approached the intersection from the West. Though I had the right of way, I did come to a full stop before crossing the intersection. Then, as I was crossing the intersection, there came, from my right, a small pickup truck. The truck had a STOP sign, but it did not come to a complete full stop until it hit the car driven by me. I, seeing the truck approaching, made a sharp left turn and thus avoided a more serious dam-age to the car.
>
> There was a witness to the accident, Miss Pola Chapelle, who sat in my car and who observed the entire incident and heard everything that was said afterwards.
>
> The above driver, Mr Albert Barnes, freely admitted to me his fault.
>
> The above is a true and correct statement.
>
> [signed]
> Adolfas Mekas

Gordon Ball

I appreciated Adolfas's writing this. But in my shyness, my fear of entanglement or rejection (or my lack of interest, since the car still functioned), I never sought repairs—or the insurance company's help in getting them.

STANLEY AND HIS EFFECTS

Every week or so Candy and I would walk the dozen blocks north and west for an evening at Stanley and Carri's. On two occasions, eight or ten mostly naked people seated in a circle on the floor, Stanley happened to ask everyone, one-by-one, whom they most wanted to make love to. When on both nights nearly all the women answered "Gordon," I began to consider the possibility of my own attractiveness and worth; that I might not be as bad as I sometimes thought, or as I sometimes thought others thought.

But around the same time, as if to hold me in check, Stanley offered his own assessment. I'd just started to elaborate on something I'd said—not by offering specifics but generalizing and repeating myself, becoming nervous and unsure—when Stanley interrupted me before the whole group: "Gordon's intelligence seems to just fritter away."

I wasn't very smart, was I? I wondered. Or, to hear Stanley say it on another occasion—totally honest?

I was left with one certainty, which was not much consolation: I scarcely knew how to speak with others. At twenty-two, with that light brown hair and those large impressionable eyes, I was immensely curious—and immensely shy. I once sat alone on the sofa at Art and Richie's with Richie's attractive girlfriend. She did all the talking for some minutes. Finally she offered, "You don't talk much"—and still I just sat there, smiling briefly, worried by my being drawn to her. I was Richie's friend—though I didn't know him well. Should I, shouldn't I? I just sat there, still and mute. Years later, Candy would recall, "You'd just let your beautiful lips hang out."

Of course sometimes I did speak more easily once I felt I knew someone or sensed some beginning intimacy. Needless to say, visits to Stanley's were opportunities not only for verbal communication but expanded ones for the nonverbal.

Though Stanley would trip me, make me think about myself and my motives in ways I hadn't before, there were numerous occasions of unmitigated, unsolitary, wordless delight. One came with Libby, a seventeen-year-old high school girl who lived in the West Village with her parents and was studying with a musician of some reputation. She was outrageously, overwhelmingly, profoundly sexy: tallish, slim, with thick,

Gordon Ball

brushy honey-blonde hair, blue eyes, broad nostrils, and big thick lips that jutted out boldly and unashamedly. We—Stanley and Candy and Carri and I—met her one evening at the Staten Island Ferry terminal, at the end of a Public Parks arts presentation. When we got into a cab for Stanley's she sat inside, in the back, next to me: Candy was in front next to Stanley; Carri on the other side of Libby. She had on a tight black sweater and her breasts pushed straight out as if trying to break free from her brassiere and she wore a brown miniskirt and black tights. I couldn't believe my good fortune: as I closed the cab door, I had the chance to make out with someone of such commanding sexual beauty. I kissed her hard and mean and she held me fast. At Stanley's I screwed her hard as I could and she made me come again and again. But when we spoke of going to Stanley's next, Candy said "You just want to screw Libby again."

So the delight was sometimes colored by jealousy, and our ways of dealing with it weren't always aided by sessions at Stanley's. One Saturday morning in spring, Candy had gone to her new job, modeling at a photographic studio. I dropped by the grocer's, where I ran into a young Italian girl whom I'd met once before. She wasn't a hippie; she was more rooted in her own culture, which only made me all the more curious. And she was young and energetic and inquisitive and pretty. We went into 57-B, took off each other's clothes, and made love.

Afterward, at her suggestion, we went to a florist, bought a bouquet for Candy, and kissed good-bye. Later that afternoon, when Candy returned, I handed her the long green stems enclosed in crinkly green paper, bursts of white and pink at their heads. She hurled them in fury onto our defenseless yellow speckled kitchen linoleum.

Nor was such jealousy one-sided. One afternoon in the fall I'd been present when Marvin, a West Village filmmaker, gave a pretty young woman a "screen test" which consisted of her wearing a slight, almost translucent mint green negligee and assuming various poses in the bed of his large loft. While she did so, he shot her with the 16 MM Bolex he held alternately in one or both hands. At times, he joined her on his knees in the bed.

Marvin's hair was dark, oily, and he was swarthy. I didn't like him and fancied myself much purer—in both sexual and aesthetic motivation. Yet one afternoon several months later I came home and found Candy sitting there with him. By some previous sign, indirect or otherwise—a word, a gesture, a shrug—I'd indicated my acceptance of their being together, at

'66 Frames

least for a visit. When they began making out I assumed they'd make love and that would be that—or they'd invite me to join them.

Instead, they made love and they made love and they made love and they remained very self-contained and displayed no intention of extending any invitations. Steamed, I left the apartment and walked the block —then returned and found the same. Again I left—and again I came back to the same. On my third return they continued as a whole round organism, curled up within each other, slurping and squishing oceanically. By this time I was so hurt, angry, and exasperated—although on another level I was aroused—that I went to the grocer's to call Stanley, to ask what to do. . . .

Moments like those weren't common, but they did occur.

Though over time Candy would become disillusioned with his mind games, we generally continued to enjoy Stanley's, and to bring others to our home in some sort of spirit of togetherness. An example of pure sweetness was Tuli Kupferberg, who came back with us late one warm evening in 1967. We'd gone to see the Fugs at the Players Theatre on MacDougal, where the tattooed biceps of their big-armed T-shirted drummer Ken Weaver had rolled and flexed as he drummed and shouted "I couldn't get high!"

Tuli brought us his *Kill for Peace,* an inexpensively printed eight and a half by eleven pamphlet of his musical parody of the official rationale for our war in Vietnam. He had a vaguely sallow complexion, dark hair, scraggly beard, and a deep rich voice. After he'd made love to Candy, we three lay side by side on our backs. I asked, "How old are you?"

"Forty," was the number I heard, and I didn't believe it; it was beyond all thought here in this room of sheets and pillows and mattresses and Miss Lyn and kitties and rock 'n' roll.

At one point we discussed Allen Ginsberg's *Howl.* I knew enough to know—or he told me enough for me to infer—that he was the "who" who jumped off the Brooklyn Bridge. "What did you think as you went down to the water?" I asked. "What were your last thoughts?"

"Now I'll see if there's a god."

An hour or two later, it was nearly 4:00 A.M. "Candy loves Gordon and Gordon loves Candy," Tuli pronounced as he got ready to leave. I didn't know if it was true.

Needless to say, for most group sex, some degree of easygoingness was a necessity—and at Stanley's, a healthy coat of heavy armor was helpful, too. From midautumn onward, over the course of nearly a year we had many interesting evenings with Stanley and Carri (always at their place, not ours), but when someone couldn't roll with punches or Stanley was too harsh, it could make the evening feel as empty as a dry well.

Considered a generation later, questions about the "open" sex of those days are complicated. Today, given the wide range of sexually transmitted diseases, some fatal, that were then unknown or nonexistent, such sexual practices are almost unthinkable.

We sought pleasure, certainly, but also honesty in expressing feelings: we hoped for new possibilities in human relationships. Yet jealousy and other problems intervened. Within two years, Candy and I would split up, though we have remained friends.

Today, I find myself frequently disturbed by attitudes—male and female alike—within my daughter's teenage society. Stereotypes persist. Yet in general the recognition that women, like men, have sexual desires is far more prevalent than it was in the sixties. Could sexual experimentation have contributed to that? Perhaps.

Thirty years removed, the "open" sex of my day seems in part an unsurprising alternative to what we saw as a "closed" society in which sexual feeling was tied to shame and embarrassment. In the late 1990s, people talk about sex more freely, but are they more honest in expressing emotions? Noble aspirations notwithstanding, as I look back I see simple enjoyment of sex as a dominant motive on my part, for which Stanley's provided a framework. I believed that one could feel not only attraction, but affection for more than one person at a time, and express it through sex. For years after last seeing Stanley and Carri around 1970, I continued to have multiple partners, hoping the inevitable problems could be solved. But over time I came to realize that I couldn't make it work. As for sex itself? Why, in 1966, that was the Great Thing.

BARBARA—AND MEL'S

In the fall and winter of 1966 – 67, not all the young women I met were through Stanley and Carri's—nor did I think of sleeping with every one of them. I first heard of Barbara Rubin one night leaving the Cinematheque as several of us came up the stairs together from the subterranean theater. A friend—filmmaker Ken Jacobs—challenged Jonas, "All this talk of flowers and butterflies and angels and saintliness—what is it, anyway? None of us—admit it, Jonas—would bring in a bum from off the street and care for him."

At the ground floor corridor we paused. As Jonas cocked his head slightly to one side, a wry, slightly amused expression seized his face. "R"s trilling as always, Jonas responded unhesitant, assured: "Barbara Rubin would."

One December afternoon just a few weeks later, in a coffee shop facing the Filmmakers' Cooperative, I sat across from Barbara in a booth. We were discussing—or rather she was informing me of—her ideas for a Cinematheque program. It was to be called *Creeping Kreplach;* later, it became *Caterpillar Changes.* As she spoke, her face glowed; hearing something funny, her head would tilt back with giggly abandon—before she quickly thrust, like a javelin, her next point. About the same age as I, she was radiantly rich with ideas. And pretty: generous smile, gentle white skin with dimpled cheeks; she looked into your eyes, intimately, as she spoke. Torrents of excited words could tumble from her mouth, and if you asked her to clarify apparent vagueness she might become irritated.

But this afternoon her notions for a multimedia film event came briskly and directly, as if taking me in as confidant, collaborator, friend. Best of all, I discovered, was that for all of her bright-eyed, intriguing beauty there was no sex—the game, the lure, the pull, the tug, all that play and tension wasn't there for the two of us. It was a great relief.

And it only intrigued me about her all the more. Who was she, really? What was the history of such a young woman to whom Jonas attributed a kind of saintliness? I heard (was it partly apocryphal?) that at fourteen she'd run from her middle-class New York home for California, where she took LSD—with Aldous Huxley. Back home, following some confinement to a hospital (frustrated parents hoped to reform or "conform" her), she was released in Jonas's care: he accepted a request of her uncle, who owned the showcase Jonas then used, to take her as an assistant. And so early on she became a friend of Jonas and was close to the great tide of optimistic belief in human potential expressing itself in New York in the early and mid-1960s in a multitude of ways, from antinuclear demonstrations to Andy Warhol's early films to Naomi Levine's film *Yes*. She was there in the springtime of Jonas's Filmmakers' Cooperative when it took up the front area of his small apartment. In 1963 she made a movie of her own in 16 MM, her own *Flaming Creatures*, so to speak. Earlier titled *Cocks and Cunts*, it had become by the time I met her, *Christmas on Earth*, after Rimbaud. A superimposed silent black-and-white orgy of faces and naked bodies, some in white grease paint, many in close-up, some in negative, it was, as Candy would write in a blurb, "a study in genital differentiation and psychic tumult." Getting into trouble with police in Rome 1964 for some apparent misbehavior, Barbara's head was shaved just before her return to the U.S.—thus her extremely short hair in the photo taken some weeks later, reproduced on the back of Dylan's 1965 album *Bringing It All Back Home*, as she massages his tired head. After he saw her film, Allen Ginsberg made love to Barbara on the dark green carpeted floor of the Coop/Jonas's apartment— "She was just this groovy girl who'd made this groovy film," he told me a few years later when I asked.

With Jonas she'd gone in 1963 to Knokke-Le-Zoute, where she'd met Roman Polanski. Some months after our meeting she showed me Polanski's magic marker cartoon portrait of her, sucking a popsicle—(She was how old at that time? Eighteen?) its "pop" portion was an erect male member.

Now, over a coffee shop's dark plastic-topped table, she and I discussed her grandly conceived show at the Cinematheque. And we planned a quick trip to Boston as well—a new Cinematheque was opening, and Jonas had asked us to go in support.

It was cold the day we left and by the time we reached Boston it was dark. As we headed toward the place we'd stay, we saw few people on lonely streets bracketed by quiet buildings under occasional pale, chilled lights. We were going to Roxbury, a ghetto-like section of town.

We stayed in an old Victorian frame house atop a hill with ten or so people in their late teens, early twenties. They were led—if that's the right word—by a man who seemed older, more seasoned than everyone else— a quiet man, a musician and prophet with combed blond hair very slightly long, upright posture, and a straight-ahead look to his clear green eyes: self-enclosed—yet with some kind of power, apparently, over others.

Soon Jonas would publish Mel Lyman's small book, *Autobiography of a World Saviour,* in which he told of having been selected to come to earth from another planet in order to raise the earth's lower vibrations. He told of the painfulness of his mission, the closeness of his relationship with his mother on earth. Copyrighted "Jonas Press," it was a small paperback of 82 pages, virtually unparagraphed, with numerous words in capitals, two uncredited close-up photographic portraits of the author framing the text, and an astrological dedication to the reader.

Years later, long after an *Esquire* magazine article on Lyman ("God is Back," with a full-page portrait by Diane Arbus that made a dark halo of the banjo case propped behind his head) I'd hear disturbing stories. But before catching what was an overnight glimpse in December 1966, I hadn't heard a word about him, nor seen any of his writing. Of Mel Lyman the man I had little decisive sense, except to be impressed by his utter quiet and self-composure. During my one night at their cold dark house he scarcely spoke; he seemed oracular, remote, impenetrable. After we returned from the program at the Cinematheque, a few young men sat on chairs in a dark room, talking a little before it got still colder. "I guess it's just more signs of destruction, of breaking apart," one of them remarked about a film by Brakhage which we'd seen; perhaps he was alluding to our era's being known as Kali Yuga, or Age of Destruction in the Hindu system. "I felt a lot of positive things there, a lot of putting together," I proposed in response, but the discussion was no more animated than I was as a speaker.

It was late, and we visitors were to be up early. I slept in the same place as one of the young men of the commune: outdoors in a Volkswagen bus. It was where this young man had been sleeping for two months already, as if it were part of his spiritual practice to sleep with no heat whatsoever. On this night under a clear and starry sky over the old framed houses and gabled roofs of Roxbury, it was nineteen degrees and yet I slept easily in the blankets and sleeping bag given me. Drifting off, I thought of the strange new, curious, impressive woman with whom I'd come to Roxbury. And I thought of the young longhaired and blue-jeaned Cinematheque people moving all the chairs and sweeping the floor clean at the end of the program. I felt there was hope.

Gordon Ball

MAILING *FILM CULTURE*

Unfortunately, soon after our Roxbury trip my work seemed to take a bad turn. The fall 1966 issue of *Film Culture* was coming off the press the morning I was to meet Jonas and Adolfas at the entrance to David Stone's apartment building on West Eighty-Sixth Street—that looming gothic affair where Stone and family lived in an exquisitely large, high-ceilinged, hardwood-floored apartment. Stone, a generous friend in film production, had funded *The Brig* and helped with numerous other projects; he was also an editor of *Film Culture*. At 8:00 A.M. we were to load large, heavy mail bags full of the new issue into my green Chevrolet, then drive them to the post office.

I was worried about making the trip of nearly one hundred city blocks, all the way uptown from our apartment below Houston in early morning traffic, possibly getting stuck in rush hour—I didn't want to take a chance of being late. I arranged with Billy to sleep on his couch, and brought my electric alarm. It woke me the next morning at 7:00, just as I'd planned, leaving twenty minutes to dress and eat breakfast, and forty to cover the remaining five dozen blocks.

Starting out, I got the 8:00 news on the car radio—I was already late. I had no idea what the problem was at the time; only afterward did I realize there must have been a power failure in Billy's building or neighborhood overnight: as I later discovered, his clock was forty minutes behind.

I drove as fast as I could through several miles of rush hour traffic and by the time I pulled into the 86th street entrance area it was 8:30. Adolfas and Jonas and David Stone, a small man with an oval face and glasses, were all standing at the ready, grim-faced to a man, half a dozen or more stuffed, large, gray mailbags at their knees. Only Stone spoke—icily. "Good morning, Gordon."

I knew no way of explaining what I didn't understand myself. I said nothing, other than returning Stone's greeting. Then some weeks later I came to Jonas's one day and he greeted me, "Now ve have completed our projects and I don't have other projects for you to vork on."

"Oh, okay," I answered. Had I done something wrong? If so, what? What was going on? Had there been a theft at Jonas's? (He'd also asked for my copy of his key.) My lateness that earlier morning wasn't connected in my mind, but was it in Jonas's? Of course we had finished the mixed media issue of *Film Culture,* and I'd completed my transcriptions of the Lincoln Center tapes. And he'd never proposed an endless work relationship. But this felt sudden.

Likely, it was purely Jonas. I never heard—and never asked—for a reason (and that, of course, was purely Gordon). Perhaps it was simply as he said, or he wanted to change his own work habits, but its suddenness was baffling. And intimidated as I was by Jonas's remoteness, plus my own shyness and complete sense of guilt which invariably held me at fault whenever something went wrong, I didn't ask.

CENSORSHIP AND OTHER PROBLEMS

My work continued meanwhile at the Cinematheque, and shortly I'd be
asked to work at the Coop too. (And as it happened, I'd go back to Jonas's
a number of times, as well.) Besides serving as Cinematheque assistant
manager ("Are you de mouse of de house?" Jonas asked as he walked into
the yellow-walled office one evening) I came a few afternoons to project
for visiting filmmakers. It was on one such occasion that I first saw
Kenneth Anger's *Scorpio Rising,* from behind the warm illuminated machine
inside the glassy-eyed booth. On another, I stopped projecting momentar-
ily when the film came out of register in the gate. The great Austrian film-
maker Peter Kubelka, who was viewing the films within the auditorium,
became alarmed. He moved to the edge of his seat, turned toward me as I
stood at the Bell and Howell 1000 within the booth. "Did you stop the pro-
jector?" He called. "Never stop a projector with film running!"

Often for evening—public—programs we'd have a professional (union
member) projectionist who'd appear when he should and project compe-
tently and then disappear. Sometimes filmmaker Bob Cowan, always capa-
ble, did the job. But Jonas himself was never averse to doing whatever might
be necessary. Once as some of us were conjuring up a highly specialized
future program (perhaps Barbara Rubin's *Caterpillar Changes*) we volunteered
our respective duties, when someone remembered the most essential task:
"But who will project?" Jonas answered immediately, "I vill project."

In fact, I first saw Jonas's newest film, the three-minute *Hare Krishna,*
when he himself held a wobbly telephoto lens immediately in front of the
projector's regular one. An overly large and bluish Ektachrome image—
of Barbara Rubin, Allen Ginsberg, Peter Orlovsky, and many others mov-
ing joyfully down the street in a peace march procession—spilled beyond
the borders of the screen, onto curtain, ceiling, stage.

How did Jonas do all that he did? Keep the Cinematheque living?
(Though it helped significantly during a relatively short period of time,
Andy's *Chelsea Girls* didn't secure it eternal life.) Support filmmakers and
their visions of new art to come, if only they had financial and technical
means? Bring them together for the common good, despite the great
(perhaps excessive) individualism of each? Nourish the Coop? Protect all
the "ekipment"? Deal with police, fire, and other bureaucracies? Fight the

obsessive grip of censorship? (Among those who appeared most ardently interested in the Cinematheque, of course, were the police.) Make his own movies? Publish *Film Culture* (obviously, like all of Jonas's other efforts, not a money-making venture)?

Jonas was Shiva-like, only his many arms moved not for destruction but for asking and making (as well as, at times, for fighting). I had an impression of his trying here, trying there, eventually putting enough financial resources together to keep operations going, all from the inspired center of his frenetic life. I'm not certain if he could identify Billy by name, but he knew him as familiar, friendly, one of the "gang." As we were walking out of the Cinematheque one evening, he asked him out of the blue, "Do you want to manage de Cinematheque?"

The plague of censorship: it hadn't ended with Jonas's 1964 arrests for showing *Un Chant d'Amour* and *Flaming Creatures,* as numerous other instances show. A few of them: in the spring of 1966, a short scene in a work by José Rodriguez-Soltero where a man dances naked to the accompaniment of "The Ballad of the Green Berets" had contributed to a threatened closure of the Cinematheque; around the same time, Tom Chomont's Boston film series was closed down; in early 1967, Charlotte Moorman was arrested. A few months later, the Supreme Court would refuse to reverse Jonas's *Flaming Creatures* conviction, thus giving him a "criminal" record. (In related arts, things were hardly better: in the same year—1966—that poets DiPrima, Orlovsky, and Ginsberg read in Washington Square Park to celebrate a court decision that poets could do so without prior approval of manuscripts, police broke into Ed Sanders's Peace Eye Bookstore in the middle of the night "on suspicion of burglary," ransacked it, seized books and periodicals, and arrested the alarmed Sanders when he appeared.)

And censorship continued in almost endless variety as institutions and offices themselves took up the policing of films: as Burroughs's Dr Benway recognizes, "A well-functioning police state needs no police." The *Village Voice*—with Jonas's columns, virtually the only review and advertising space given films that weren't made with considerable financial backings and large casts and crews and sets—had refused to print one title within a weekly Cinematheque program notice. According to the *Voice,* the night of Wednesday, December 28, featured such works as *Anthony* by Tom Chomont, *The Kiss* by Carla Liss, *Madonna* by Mike Kuchar, and A Film by Al Rose.

Gordon Ball

The title of Rose's film, as submitted to the *Voice's* Display Advertising Department, was *Penis*. On another occasion, a line which noted that Stan Brakhage's *Flesh of Morning* was a "psychodrama on masturbation" was deleted, as was the last word in Ben Van Meter's *Up-Tight, L.A. Is Burning, Shit*.

Nor was print media the only area of difficulty. Only a few weeks after Barbara and I had attended its opening, the fledgling Boston Cinematheque was forced to vacate and look for a new home, when their landlord objected to the title of George Kuchar's *Hold Me While I'm Naked*. Charlotte Moorman's February arrest would be favorably resolved in May, but the threat that police could suddenly disrupt any performance or showing remained a constant in everyone's consciousness.

And Du Art, the film lab most frequently used by independents (how ironic that word, since everyone had to use labs!), had turned over to the police some footage it had processed, and the filmmaker was put on trial. At his eventual acquittal, he was finally able to get his film back. In another instance Du Art refused to complete the processing of an order—and held on to the negative—because it had discovered "dirty" pictures within. And after leaving some footage for processing at another lab, a friend of mine received:

Notice
Peerless
Date 2/24/67
Dealer No. 2 19 27   Order No. 24638
Customer: Criterion Film Labs, Inc.
Amount Withheld: approx 85 feet 16 MM KIIA (from 400 foot roll)

This order was found to contain pictures that cannot legally be delivered to you in person, or to any person representing you, or by any means of transportation.

Please give us permission to destroy them by signing and returning this notice to the address below. If permission is not received from you, they will be held for two years, then destroyed.

EASTMAN KODAK COMPANY
Color Print and Processing Sales & Services
16-31 Route No. 208
Fair Lawn, New Jersey 07410

Date

The pictures described are my property, and I hereby authorize you to destroy them.

Signed

Discussing the lab situation and possible responses one night with several of us in the Cinematheque lobby, Jonas suddenly turned to me: "Perhaps you can do something. You have some imagination."

Gordon Ball as Shane,
Tokyo 1954.

Haneda Airport (Tokyo) with Mother and Father,
July 17, 1962.

College freshman ID card, 1962.

Outside Duke Dormitory at Davidson College,
Revere in hand. Photo by Eddie Rivers © 1966.

Jonas Mekas filming at Davidson College
April 20, 1966. Photo by Eddie Rivers © 1966.

Jonas Mekas discusses films with moderator Gordon Ball,
Davidson College Union April 20, 1966. Photo by Bill Olson, *Davidsonian.*

Frames from *Prunes* (Gordon Ball and Jonas Mekas.)

Prunes poster by Billy Trotter and William Walker.

Billy Trotter at Eddie Rivers's desk, Duke
Dormitory. Photo by Eddie Rivers © 1966.

Frames from *Georgia*.

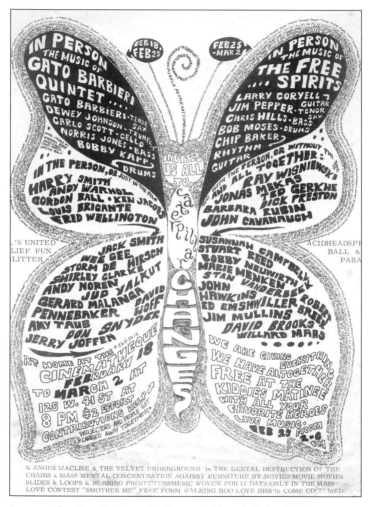

Poster art for *Caterpillar Changes* by Susannah Campbell, Candy O'Brien, Barbara Rubin, and Gordon Ball, 1967.

Tatouages « psychedelic ».

Gordon and Candy, faces painted,
at the Central Park Be-In, 1967.

Gordon and Candy
near Filmmakers' Cooperative, summer 1967.
Photo by Wheeler Dixon

Gordon and Candy
in photo booth,
circa 1967.

Gordon Ball at 12 St. Mark's Place (Richard Aldcroft's),
June 1995. Photo: Allen Ginsberg.

LESLIE

I continued doing one thing and another for Jonas, often ad hoc. Some time in January I began working with Barbara Rubin on that gala mixed media (film, music, and multiple projection surfaces) program she had in mind for the Cinematheque. *Caterpillar Changes* would be an aesthetic event in itself, but would also boost the Cinematheque financially and spiritually—or so we all hoped. By the end of November, *The Chelsea Girls* moved uptown from the Cinematheque, whose two hundred seats had been unable to accommodate the crowds, to the much larger Cinema Rendezvous ("a theater with carpets," complained the *Times'* staid Bosley Crowther). The first night, after the large crowds left, the business-suited Rendezvous manager said to thirty-eight-year-old Andy—in shades and jeans and black leather jacket and motorcycle boots—"You've certainly accomplished quite a lot for such a young man, Mr Warhol." Andy answered, "Oh."

Now we were back to programs that might typically bring in fifteen or thirty to forty people per night, at $1.50 admission. (For *The Chelsea Girls* it had gone up to $2; the Rendezvous showed its matinees for $2, evenings for $3). From the Cinematheque office I telephoned, somewhat leerily, a range of filmmakers and friends of the Cinematheque, asking for their participation in Barbara's program. As I did so I explained, through almost gritted teeth, "The Cinematheque is trying to make a new image for itself." (It was my own awkward, embarrassed phrasing.) I even called Norman Mailer to ask him to read, but he explained that he couldn't do anything until after *The Deer Park* got through its early weeks of performance.

Then one night, Jonas and I were having dinner together at a small restaurant. Sitting across from me as we ate our modest, brief meal, he volunteered out of the blue, "Leslie at de Coop says he needs someone to work with him and dat person should be you."

Who was Leslie Trumbull?

I didn't learn his story till later, but my version of it began when from Davidson College in the fall of 1965 I first telephoned Filmmakers' Cooperative about *Flaming Creatures*. We'd just received the Coop's catalog, with entries for several dozen other films as well, including Andy Warhol's *Blow Job* ("A passionate matter handled with restraint and good taste."). Leslie was, as he'd often be, quite helpful.

But between our actual private *Creatures* showing and Jonas's visit I talked several times again with Leslie Trumbull, and we came to be on somewhat familiar terms. Soon after arriving in New York in September 1966, I went by the Coop, several flights up at 414 Park Avenue South. A few years earlier this had been Jonas's living space, which he shared with the Coop. In the evening many filmmakers (Jack Smith and his "creatures"; Barbara Rubin; and Andy Warhol, who saw his first underground films here) would drop in for impromptu screenings.

I introduced myself to a man in his early thirties with short wavy dark hair combed and parted on the right, dark horn-rimmed glasses, high cheekbones, an unassertive broad and rather flat nose, lively dark eyes, and an eager smile framed within wide thin lips. He was rather broad-shouldered, stood posture-perfect, and smoked Philip Morrises that he lit with a small red cylindrical lighter he kept on his dark desktop.

Leslie explained that the Coop was moving to a larger space on the ground floor at Lexington and Thirty-First. (The Filmmakers' Distribution Center, which shared the Park Avenue South Office, would soon follow, to a separate space in the rear of the building.) The next couple of days, I made numerous trips hauling filmmakers' cans of films (all works distributed by the Coop belonged to the filmmaker) to the new site in my large green Chevrolet. I also went with Leslie to the extreme west end and down to the Ennis Commercial Furniture Company on the Bowery to look for used office desks. I was just starting to get to know New York. Looking at the workaday street out Leslie's window, I remarked, "I thought Park Avenue was ritzy," and he corrected, "Yes, it is—this is Park Avenue South." He motioned toward the window and the tall broad building that swallowed the north end of the street. "Above the Pan Am Building, that's Park Avenue." High in the Pan Am Building loomed the home office of my father's First National City Bank.

Five years earlier, Leslie Trumbull had come to New York from a town near Toledo, Ohio. Discovering he was gay, he'd cut hometown ties and left for the city.

In New York he found work through a personnel agency at a Wall Street stock firm, proofing the day's transactions, correlating handslips (the handwritten records of brokers) and computer printouts. But Leslie aspired to something more literary, and so turned to an editorship at Prentice Hall, where he and a fellow editor decided to go into business for themselves as consultants; an agreeable manager laid them off to receive unemployment.

One unemployed evening in 1963 he saw a movie called *Twice a Man* by Gregory Markopoulos, one of the few avant-garde filmmakers making feature-length narrative films. Just a few nights later, he saw it a second time. He was captivated by this exquisite exploration of identity and sexuality, with its brilliant intercutting of single frames. He had read in Jonas's *Voice* column that the film was filling the Bridge Theater, but both times he found himself in a tiny audience. After his second viewing, he asked the cashier "What's with this crazy guy in the *Voice* writing that this film's filling the theater? It's gonna scare people away!"

The cashier was Flo Jacobs, who in 1966 would help her husband Ken found Millennium Film Workshop. "Talk to the filmmaker," she responded, and Leslie turned to shake the hand of a natty gentleman with dark wavy hair.

"Jonas is trying to help, to arouse interest," he explained to Leslie. "Would you like to help?"

Markopolous later took Leslie to the Coop, and following a meeting with Jonas, he began work—for free—by running the Coop. He'd volunteered to work without pay till his unemployment ran out; when it did, two months later, David Stone suggested that Leslie be paid.

Very early on he started working five days a week and, by choice, weekends too, so that, as he once said, "Mondays wouldn't be so hellish." By the time I met Leslie, he'd been the Coop's secretary for nearly three years, in charge of all operations including the renting, shipping, and return of films, and the maintenance of filmmakers' accounts. There was a board of directors in charge, but the actual hands-on work and office management, fifty hours and more per week, was Leslie's. Starting sometime in late January 1967, I began keeping filmmakers' accounts, making bookings for renters on the phone, filling out rental order forms, carrying prints to the post office at the Murray Hill station near Park and Thirty-Fourth. . . .

Eight to ten feet from his I had a large heavy secondhand wooden desk with manual typewriter and a telephone. I sat in one of those straddle-legged office chairs on wheels, with a soft seat and a single pad for a backrest. I would move my typewriter's little metal left and right margin-setters to their farthest position, and insert around the black roller large red-and-blue columned white sheets bearing the filmmakers' accounts. For a few filmmakers, like Stan Brakhage, accounts ran several filled-in pages; for others, younger and much less well-known like myself, there were only a few lines of activity on the whole large gridded page.

The office was high-ceilinged, white-walled. In an adjoining room the film cans were kept on metal shelving, and Jeffrey Childress, a brooding, hulking filmmaker (and in his own way a friend), hunched on his spindly stool and cleaned film prints with Carbona—it smelled like formaldehyde—as his ashy Camel dangled from its insert at one corner of his mouth.

I worked from ten to six, with a half hour for lunch, for $68 a week, an amount so large—compared to my previous part-time pay—that Candy soon quit her nine-to-five secretarial job to work fewer hours as an artists' model.

Leslie lived somewhat reclusively in a sizable loft, seventy-five feet by twenty-five, on Pitt Street in the Lower East Side. There he had a very fine stereo system in the service of his large classic music collection; an aquarium of guppies and blue-and-red neon tetras; and more than a few shelves of books stuffed with much science fiction (Roger Zelazny was a favorite).

Though withdrawn, Leslie seemed to enjoy having young people over from time to time, hearing about their lives (his own, outside of work, seemed very much an interior affair). One evening I listened to him tell of a woman who could summon at will visions from her LSD trips; on another, of his reaction the one and only time he tried smoking marijuana. A friend brought some over, he tried it, and soon was at an open window, vomiting.

At work, he was driven by a quiet and complete commitment. Not to say he couldn't be affable: but his quick telling-off or turning-off of someone when he saw the need—a renter casually returns a film two days late, a filmmaker asks for an "advance" of rental income—seemed a matter of reflex. And his relationship with Jonas was somewhat adversarial. Often Jonas would come rushing in on his long brisk legs, full of ideas and plans—expansive and joyful, or anxious and demanding—and Leslie would feel compelled to utter, from between thin, straight lips as he eyed him head-on, "No. No, Jonas. No."

Leslie carried out to the letter the Coop policy of not recommending any particular film, as I discovered on reporting that a university group was on the phone asking for suggestions. And some of my own hopes of bridging gaps within what I saw as a new, emerging culture were doused with cold water when I once reported to him that Bob Dylan's office was on the line, asking to screen some films—at no cost. To me it was a possible breakthrough opportunity; to Leslie it was business as usual. He responded much as he did to Jonas, tight-lipped and firm: "No. They can pay to look at films, unless the filmmaker gives them permission. Same as everybody else."

Leslie later told me what had happened when his friend Kenneth Anger gave advertising agencies a free screening of Scorpio Rising: the filmmaker began to see similar montage and image in TV commercials a year later. Leslie's execution of policies protecting filmmakers always seemed absolute, but the most memorable example of his acting in the interest of a filmmaker came later in the spring. One morning a middle-aged, crew-cut man of average height and enormously wide body—a tight 250 pounds, I estimated, compacted onto his 5´ 9˝ frame—entered the Coop. He asked for Leslie.

"United States Marshall," he said, taking from the inside left breast pocket of his suit coat something I couldn't see, showing it to Leslie, and explaining why he'd come: Harry Smith. Harry—whose likeness I'd first seen in that photographic print on Panna Grady's mantle—was the gnomish, long-impoverished, bespectacled little man with long gray hair and beard who made startling movie animations. An anthropologist and music ethnologist as well, he sometimes billed himself as the alchemist son of Anastasia. Socially, he made a habit of disarming everyone he met with comically offensive insults (He would tell a guru of Ginsberg's, for instance, that he should've been a bellhop.). He was now in arrears at his film lab, and the marshall was empowered to seize his work. Unfortunately, a print of his Heaven and Earth Magic Feature had just returned from a booking and sat there in plain view next to Leslie's desk. Seeing it, the marshall reached for the can (it housed a 1600-foot reel of film, weighed all told at least six pounds, and was a foot and a half across). He lifted it up, turned, and took his first step toward the door.

"Just one minute!" Leslie, firm-lipped as ever, rose from his desk instantaneously, and was suddenly just behind the marshall, who must've outweighed him by at least eighty pounds. The next moment he was embracing our visitor from behind—like Sammy Davis, Jr. hugging Nixon, and no doubt just as startling for the man suddenly hugged. Leslie's body pressed tight against the Marshall's as his hands now joined our visitor's around Harry's print. "You can't do that!" Leslie exclaimed, firm but gasping since he was trying to tilt his head back so as not to shout immediately into the marshall's ear, yet not lose control over the man's enormous— and undoubtedly armed—body mass.

"It's Mr Smith's print!" Leslie gasped again, his glasses working their way down his nose as his face turned a deeper red. "You've got to present him with a warrant for it. And furthermore," he continued after stopping for an instant's breath, "by seizing it you're removing his only real source of income, any ability whatever he'd have to pay it back!" Leslie's face was now fully crimson, his breath halting. "We're empowered to keep it here, and rent it out to customers, and we won't give it up to an illegal seizure!"

The federal marshall, all two hundred and fifty barreled pounds of him, set the print down, gave his body a small shake like a dog exiting water, and trudged out the door.

THE AMERICAN SOCIETY
OF MAGAZINE PHOTOGRAPHERS

"Andy Warhol is here. Shirley Clarke is here. Gordon Ball is here. John Cavanaugh is here."

Under the "starlit" chandeliers of a spacious room in the New York Hilton, the hostess for the evening welcomed her audience—the annual convention of the American Society of Magazine Photographers. Our presentation would include the premiere (outside the Cinematheque Open House) of my *Georgia;* Jerome Hill's *Corrida;* Ed Emshwiller's *Thanatopsis;* and works by each of the others in our hostess's introduction. Jonas had been invited to appear and show movies, to give professional photographers an idea of the latest in avant-garde film—and to bring other filmmakers with him. We were on stage, facing some three hundred mostly male conventioneers. Or rather we were all up there except Andy, who sat in an aisle seat near the front, in his black leather jacket, jeans, and shades, a copy of the new *Newsweek* in hand, one or two companions from the Factory at his side.

Jonas introduced the films in advance: discussion would follow at the very end. Unfortunately the first shown, in its first public presentation in 16 MM blow-up, was *Georgia,* It looked fine, its multiple layers of images rich, its gossamer lines delicate, the startling close-up of Margaret Mullis late in the film haunting: my only disappointment lay in the slightly greenish-golden tint that had replaced the original's fully golden. I heard no audience response whatsoever.

Following *Georgia* came a portion of Andy's *Screen Tests,* three-minute close-ups of various young men and women at the Factory. It included the beautiful one—as I recall it—of Baby Jane Holzer. After over two minutes of her stoical frontal stare, a tear forms, makes its slow way down one cheek toward her chin.

With each screen test the commercial photographers began more and more to resemble Sinclair Lewis creations as they responded with laughter, anger, ridicule: high hand-raised knee slapping, red-faced irritation, sneering and snorting embellished by the elbowing of seatmates. Was this how *The Rite of Spring* was received?

Shirley Clarke's *Bridges Go Round,* which followed, was as short as *Georgia,* and fairly standard fare in terms of subject and treatment. It was a pretty, lyrical paean to bridges, with multiple levels of superimpositions, done in her earlier days before longer works like her film adaptation of Jack Gelber's *The Connection.*

Bridges—like *Georgia*—was received in silence. Then in John Cavanaugh's stationary camera, single-shot silent regular 8 MM, we saw the tall blue-and-red Con Ed smokestacks at the eastern end of Fourteenth Street, the tops of intervening buildings in the foreground, but with an alteration. After shooting his "subject," Cavanaugh—a skinny, six-foot-five twenty year old with moppy dirty blond hair seated next to me—ran his regular 8 roll back through the camera, opening the diaphragm fully to any strong light source at every second, third, or fourth frame. The effect on-screen was stroboscopic. That evening at the Hilton, under now darkened chandeliers, the towers of Consolidated Edison appeared to pulsate.

Lights came on, Jonas called for questions. Several hands shot up. One viewer began, in derision thick as the carpet, "I'd like to ask Mr Warhol just what he thinks he's doing . . ."

I looked at Andy, whose shades still covered his eyes. He'd just opened *Newsweek;* its two covers now shielded the lower half of his face. There was a pause of several seconds before our hostess spoke through her mike, "Andy's reading *Newsweek.*" I remember wishing he weren't.

The remainder of the evening was more or less a free-for-all between John Cavanaugh and members of the audience, in which Cavanaugh, having moved near the front edge of the stage, assumed a long and lanky straight-backed lotus on the bare wood, and lectured them on cinema: "Hollywood knows everything about technique and nothing about content," he instructed, as I sat there thinking how I'd thought it was just the opposite. At one point as I faced the audience I raised my hand to speak, then realized the absurdity of my gesture (Who was going to call on me, the audience?) and lowered it and in fact never did speak—and the evening ended.

Months later, in the slick but pleasant-smelling pages of *Esquire* magazine, I happened to read an account of the occasion by Wilfrid Sheed—his debut writing on film for this monthly. He made the Cavanaugh "lecture" virtually the entire evening, with little or no attention to other films and filmmakers. His tone was superior beyond limit, as he likened the gathering to "A revival, in ultramodern dress, of W.S. Gilbert's *Patience.*" And given to the excess and inaccuracy of yellow journalism:

Messrs. Warhol, Mekas, etc., [sic] had undertaken to roll their
wares at a meeting of the Society, and they arrived, with hair
streaming and eyes rolled upwards and in, to play Bunthorne,
the pure young man, to the photographers' Heavy Dragoons.

I never saw Andy's hair stream, at the Hilton or anywhere else, or
Jonas's eyes, or Andy's shaded ones, roll upward. I'm not sure what it is
about an Oxford education that seems to promote in some men an abid-
ing superciliousness, especially toward the new and the different. Nor
why *Esquire* seems to be so insistently silly or vulgar with some of its inter-
esting topics (see, for instance, the cover of its July 1963 issue featuring
Ginsberg, or Gerald Clarke's "Checking in with Allen Ginsberg," in April
1973). Sheed may at least have deserved consideration in claiming that the
underground (as personified in Jonas) was too all-accepting within itself:
"if some of these filmmakers would turn on each other with a snarl . . . "
But there was far more underground turning and snarling than Sheed
seemed to realize. And far worse was his clear lack of interest in even
understanding what was in front of him, in relating to it from any per-
spective other than a superior one.

Perhaps the judgments of history—decidedly not in Sheed's favor—
have made him more sensitive. In any case, his was not the only written
comment which seemed to have missed something. A week or two after
the program, I received, on the Society's stationery:

January 30, 1967

Mr Gordon Ball
Film Makers Cinematheque
125 W. 41st Street
New York, N.Y. 10036

Dear Mr Ball:
On behalf of the American Society of Magazine Photogra-
phers, may I extend my thanks for your participation in our
meeting, "What's New in Underground Films!"
It was most gratifying to have your interest.
Your cooperation in this effort is most appreciated.

Sincerely,
Regina Benedict
Executive Director
RB/ja

'66 Frames

ANNA MARIE AGAIN

"How'd you get this number?"

"They said you were here, at the Cinematheque."

I was sitting on the hokey, dark, nappy brown Danish modern sofa at Jonas's; the phone next to it had just rung and I'd answered. Anna Marie was coming to New York one of the next weekends. Could she see me?

In the intervening months since I'd responded to her pregnancy claim I'd heard nothing from her, except one letter inviting me to a dance at the country club, with casual dress, "sweaters and slacks." I hadn't answered. Now here she was, by electronic transmission, at the inner sanctum, the Third Avenue redoubt.

"Anna Marie, let me call you back, okay? In twenty-four hours."

Later that evening I checked with Candy. "Here's the deal," I clumsily returned to Anna Marie the next day. "I'm living with a woman here, and you're welcome to visit Candy and me if you like."

She came the next weekend. She stayed at a hotel, but Candy and I otherwise welcomed her into our lives. Though nothing much happened, on Friday night we took her—in a polyester pants suit—with us to Stanley Fisher's.

Saturday night, she came to our apartment—along with Billy Trotter and John Cavanaugh. It was at the end of a long day. We turned the lights low, and Cavanaugh passed around a pipe of nice golden brown hash and at least three of us took some, deep into our lungs. We put on a little music; Cavanaugh leaned against the wall behind him and closed his eyes. Billy and Anna Marie sat there in the semidarkness making occasional awkward conversation. Finally, Candy and I began taking off each other's clothes and making love. Gloop! Glooduh! Dum! went the tabla for Ravi Shankar's probing sitar as Candy and I began moving in rhythm. Then Billy and Anna Marie became entangled, clothes on, on their sheet-covered mattress. A little later still, they left together. Cavanaugh just continued to sit there, large long back up against the wall, legs folded at the knees, a big pleasant grin on his face.

The next time I spoke with Billy, he told me of the rest of his evening: "I got a cab and took her to her hotel room and at the door she said 'I'd invite you in, but my mother's here.'"

Gordon Ball

IN THE *VOICE*, WITH BARBARA AND JOHN

In mid-February—just before Barbara's *Caterpillar Changes* began its run at the Cinematheque—Jonas published in two installments of his weekly *Village Voice* column transcripts of conversations at his loft, recorded a month or so earlier, with Barbara, John Cavanaugh, and (though I spoke very little) myself:

> I have good news. Change is taking place in the under-ground. The youngest generation, a generation that grew up with the Co-op, with Bobby Dylan, with LSD, with Allen Ginsberg, with Brakhage. . . . is entering the field of action . . . Cinema is being reevaluated, redefined. . . .
>
> The people involved in the first conversation are John Cavanaugh, who had his first one-man show at the Cin-ematheque last Saturday; Gordon Ball, whose first film, *Georgia*, was premiered at the national magazine photogra-pher's gathering two weeks ago; Barbara Rubin, whose new film, *Love Supreme for the Free Spirits*, will be shown at the Cinematheque later in February. . . .

John did much of the talking. A sample:

> It seems to me that what the cinematic process is, like where it has value, is in expressing directly certain things that are going on in the body, which I take to be an approximation of certain magnetic energies, magnetic currents. I want to delin-eate this subtle magnetic process, because I think that's like the essence of the mind.

Soon he was speaking of the body as the residence of intelligence, and the importance of LSD and nature for freeing "the swirling energy patterns that make up the actuality of life," using the camera to "trace out . . . the life flux." And he proposed, "We could have movie theaters like rocket ships, we could really take people places. The screens could be like portholes."

Meantime, Barbara was reporting and envisioning:

> I think *Empire* is my favorite . . . the most beautiful movie I've ever seen. . . . He was shooting still camera life. . . . I'm waiting till we project it in the sky. . . .

'66 Frames

That's why all our saints today are the artists. Because it's the whole creating of that, the backwards living we are going to do now. Now we are going to spend all our time watching what we are doing, we are not going to live it. We are going to reflect it, project it, then we are going to rehash it, reedit it, and then we are going to throw it back out, just like the flying saucers. We are going to go through it. Here in America today all those young kids who are turning on and everything, they are all doing the tribal scenes, taking Eastern cultures, you know, doing that whole thing, and there will be little communities in America, "independent states of mind," and they will make the United States. Until, one day, we realize we are not really in America, but we are flying saucers from outer space. Everybody's taking movies. Everyone. Even my uncle had an 8 MM camera, before I had one.

And she continued:

I was thinking, while watching John's movie, listening to the Velvet music. They are like Buddhists, like Zen Buddhists. The kind of person who might, years ago, have gone out and dug that kind of state of mind, living in that, you know, kind of mystery and feeling, that whole generating quality. Now, you understand, he's making movies or playing this music. The Velvets—this tape . . . it's a meditation. They are sending me in that kind of feeling . . . which is just sitting and being very quiet.

In the first of the two transcribed sessions I didn't say a word. I thought Barbara and John talked too much and sometimes sounded ridiculous—but feared exposing myself as stupid if I spoke! Besides, I wanted to shoot, not speak. And I had my Revere—or my new 8 MM Bolex—in hand. When John spoke of "using camera as an energy transforming machine to bind kinetic energy sequences," Barbara allowed, "This is the kind of film Gordon is filming around the room . . . looking at each other . . ."

But by the next week's transcript, I'd warmed up sufficiently to speak a few lines:

QUESTION (TO GORDON BALL): And you haven't said a word. You just kind of sit taking it all in . . .
GORDON BALL: I know very little else.

Gordon Ball

BR: He makes beautiful movies.

JM: There is no city in his work . . . peaceful . . .

QUESTION: What happens to the energy of the city? It gets per-
verted?

GB: Organized humanity always does.

QUESTION: The drift of all modern civilization has been to im-
print your mind, no?

JC: True, very true. But not any more! Me and William Bur-
roughs will rub out all mind imprints.

QUESTION: What happens when you start de-imprinting the
mind, like de-imprinting the astronauts, you know?

BR: Then they set fire to the capsules, right?

QUESTION: How far can you go with de-imprinting the mind?

GB: All the way.

QUESTION: How far is "all the way"?

GB: Whatever you can think of.

I first read some of those words thirty years ago, as Billy Trotter and I
stood with the new *Voice* spread open beneath our tilted faces. Incandes-
cent bulbs lit our dark subway platform, and we could smell ozone and
hear a distant rumble of steel as we waited for a crosstown train.

'66 Frames

CATERPILLAR CHANGES

Barbara and Candy and blonde Susannah Campbell and I had work to do. And we did it all, basically, in a single extended evening at 57 Thompson.

In a matter of weeks Barbara's expanded media Cinematheque program would be upon us, running most nights from Saturday, February 18 through Friday, March 2. Many of those whom Barbara and I had called had responded favorably; among filmmakers lending their work were Harry Smith, Andy Warhol, Jonas, D.A. Pennebaker, Jack Smith, John Cavanaugh, Stan Vanderbeek, Robert Breer, and a close companion of Dylan's, Bobbie Neuwirth; among the musicians scheduled to perform were Gato Barbieri, the Free Spirits, Angus McLise, and the Velvet Underground. Now we had to get some word out.

Now that Candy and I had shared the same apartment for several months, new prints and posters decorated our walls. On our old familiar mattresses we four sat beneath our large, unframed rice paper woodblock print of two lovers in a contemplative moment at the edge of their bed. Near it I'd recently put up my favorite poster: a very large oversize black-and-white photograph, in medium close-up, of three longhaired and barefoot Indians sitting, knees and lower legs erect in front of them, among logs and vines on the floor of a jungle. Most of their bodies were encased in long burlap. The one in right foreground, mustached and bearded, looks intently, almost sternly, into the camera. His counterpart at the left rear, a cheroot clenched between his lips, looks off into the distance—bored, perhaps? The one in the middle, evidently in inner ecstasy, seems to let his eyes fall toward the one hand he holds before his face.

A much smaller image taped to the same wall was an underground press photograph of Allen Ginsberg, in extreme close-up from just below; looking upward, exhaling steamy spirals of smoke. Beneath it I'd written a caption, "Mine eyes have seen the glory."

Now the three women and I sat beneath such artifacts and labored and played and created nearly the entire night, to come up with an artifact of our own that might draw people to the Cinematheque and—perhaps one of us thought of it—that might be looked at again in days to come. It was a poster for *Caterpillar Changes*.

The butterfly was a major icon for both Jonas and Barbara Rubin. Susannah Campbell, who had perhaps the most artistic gifts, helped guide our fingers in conveying its individual parts and lettering. It wasn't easy, and we were sometimes giddy, as the somewhat harebrained fine lettering in the margins—some of which recorded our conversation as we outlined the butterfly—demonstrates:

> come come come come . . . hi hi hi . . . together we'll babysit together hang posters together . . . we'll beg borrow steal together . . . Monica says they're really one hundred and ten . . . together the Cinematheque is broke together . . . How are you Harry Smith . . . Together the cinema is broke together we got busted together . . . what's happening together . . . we lost three thousand dollars of equipment in the last year together . . . Jonas is only answering the phone from two to three-thirty . . . paint the cheese in the Cinematheque ceiling together A. Ginsberg for President Dick Gregory Vice President Secretary of Health Welfare & Education Bob Dylan together Otis Redding Chaplain of the Senate Peter Orlovsky Head of FBI . . .

Once or twice, we argued: Barbara mistakenly insisted that another young woman—later a film critic at the *Village Voice* for many years—named Amy Taubin was Amy Taub . . . "Taub" was how it got written. But considering our nearly ten hours of work, our differences were nearly minimal, our solidarity and fun and indulgence great, and our result? Well, we were pleased with it.

But then there was the program itself, looming. Now that I worked full-time at the Coop, Barbara took on most of the final planning (it had been—and remained—her project) and what there was to be in the way of run-throughs. She had, among other things, a scheme for suspending crepe paper streamers from the ceiling of the Cinematheque auditorium, so that any projected image would be broken up multiple times, in many planes, before reaching the screen.

Unfortunately, the day before the first afternoon in which everything would be set up, I strained my back at work. Just as I finished some typing, I pushed and tilted to the rear in my padded-back office chair. I could feel things beneath me starting to give . . . I'd tilted too far, losing balance. Thinking I might be thrown to the floor, I reacted suddenly; the quick lurch I gave my lower back left me in pain, scarcely able to walk—comic though the event certainly was to anyone watching. In bed for several days, I managed to get some letters written ("I hear you suffered Brakhage of your Markopoulos," Rick Jensen would write back) but missed the preparations the next afternoon and evening at the Cinematheque—as well as some of the programs. But Billy, who'd intended going anyway just to lend a hand putting things up in the auditorium, phoned with his report the moment he got home: "She's crazy! Barbara Rubin doesn't know what she's doing! It was total mayhem! There were streamers every-where! Then she'd want to try something else, try that, try this . . ."

In his *Voice* column three weeks later,Jonas reported:

> More than twenty different filmmakers and two music groups, Gato Barbieri and the Free Spirits, contributed their imaginations to Barbara Rubin's *Caterpillar Changes* program during a two-week run at the Cinematheque. But it was Rubin who was the caterpillar, really, and the show was the product of her imagination. In my judgment, this show, to those few who saw it, and really saw it, provided an insight into the farthest out frontiersland of cinema and of vision. Really, the whole cinema as it is (or was) fell to pieces, and was hanging around the auditorium in shreds, like a leaf eaten out by worms. I said it was the product of Rubin's imagination, but that shouldn't be misunderstood: Her imagination is only part of our imagination. Rubin acted as an architect who was pull-ing out from our dreams the primordial shapes, shred by shred, recreating our own dreams in front of and around us. It was a visionary show and one that marks a very important direction in cinema . . .

And in a single long paragraph shaped like a butterfly, Matt Hoffman would write in *Film Culture:*

> . . . A friend calls her amateurish and mentions setting up for the high school prom. Her work is very simple and direct. No subtle philosophic ambitions—just a direct encounter. Fill the lobby with streamers of color and top it with blue angel hair. The result is as physically involving as it is visually. The lobby becomes a new kind of space—difficult, labyrinthine, chal-lenging, bemusing. One is reminded, quite by his own con-nections, of jungle or carnival. The physicality of her imagination is extended in the auditorium where a spun fiberglass cloth screen hangs in vertical columns at the foot of the stage and then reaches out over the audience to envelop it

one night, to allow its heads to pop through on another, and to form a canopy on a third . . . In *Caterpillar Changes,* differently shaped and sized images intermingle presenting old films in new contexts . . . Tuesday night, February 21, the show opened with a large trapezoidal projection of *The Brig* reel 2 on the left side of the screen, *Jonas In the Brig by* Storm De Hirsch on the right, *Guns Of the Trees* square in the center, and a small square of reel 1 of *The Brig* moving all about the screen. . . . The result of this seemingly abstract and unthinking projection of Mekas's films was to affirm aspects and attributes of his work scarcely noted before. The number of actors on the screen at any time, the constant haunting images of mass suffering; a peace demonstration from *Guns* coincided with one of the shake-ups in *The Brig* while The Mothers of Invention poured out their agonies over the sound system. A weird, fragmented, but pervasive image of multiple horror and perception flooded the auditorium. But the whole thing had evaporated in minutes, to be replaced by a ballet of loving sympathy and tenderness. The projectors were slowed down to silent speed inducing a choreographic element to *The Brig;* it became impossible to sense that shuddering horror of the suffering and instead we were presented with the beauty of all those actors working in harmony . . . Saturday matinee, February 25—The material now was shredded, latticed, laced, and cobwebbed over the audience and throughout the stage. Musicians stood in the midst of a network of spun fiberglass that mostly obscured them from view. The Free Spirits provided very beautiful jazz-rock of a delicate nature. Ed Emshwiller's films were on all the 16 MM projectors. One film of his which is an animated painting threw out a succession of changing patterns over the lines of the screen material so that there was this sense of a continually metamorphosing forest of color. Like lying on the forest floor and looking up at the tree branches and seeing them jump from fall to spring to winter to summer . . . Conversation badly remembered and paraphrased from night before show opened:

John Cavanaugh: The light is diffused, I can't see the images
    clearly.
Barbara Rubin: The light's diffused. That's the beauty of it. The
    lack of clarity is in your head, John . . . Thursday, March 2—

'66 Frames

All the material is gone. A projector hanging on the side near the stage throwing a large trapezoid on the ceiling that is a children's doodle. Rich orgiastic ballet of flesh, Barbara Rubin's *Christmas on Earth,* alternately tinted blue and pink superimposed by the incredible candy concoctions of Harry Smith's hand-painted color abstractions . . .

But bad press, to which Jonas was no stranger, was also on the horizon. Several issues after his review, the *Voice* printed the following from a reader in Brooklyn:

> Dear Sir:
> Jonas Mekas has descended to new depths of pretentiousness trying to breathe life into a corpse. I refer to the *Caterpillar Changes* show at the Cinematheque that he reviewed . . . This cinema environment had about as much imagination as the kind of first prom dance at high school circa 1937. The music by the Free Spirits was bad—a compromise commercial heap of neither good rock and roll or jazz—more like cocktail music —uninspired and making no musical statement whatever. The only creative people involved were the Gato Barbieri jazz group and they didn't need the silly Christmas decorations or rag hangings to enhance them. They deserved much better.
>
> As for the films, they were all reduced to a washed out visual common denominator of endless, hardly visible footage. More amateurish (in the worst sense of the word) shows like this and Mekas will have succeeded in destroying the Cinematheque altogether.
>
> Mekas's column so often illustrates the story of *The Emperor's New Clothes* with such accuracy. Really, Jonas—wake up—the child has nothing on—absolutely nothing on at all.

NEWSWEEK AND *TIME* GO UNDERGROUND

①

And what did I think of Barbara and her work? I thought *Christmas on Earth* was interesting, I wanted to see it again;

I had mixed feelings about *Caterpillar Changes* and some other efforts: the impulse seemed fine, fertile, but there was something unrestrained or haphazard or indulgent in the execution or result—perhaps like some of my own efforts. And though her good humor easily matched her ill temper, I often had the sense that whatever she was doing was, in her view, almost unquestionably right. Personally, even though Barbara was closer to Candy (they were more or less best friends during this period), she was almost always generous and thoughtful toward me, far more than I ever was toward her.

She was always planning, projecting; she even hoped to marry Dylan, the Beatles, Ginsberg. In some ways, she and I complemented each other —she rushed in, I held back. She was stubborn ("Barbara is from Missouri!" Candy once exclaimed in frustration at trying to persuade her of a different viewpoint); I was yielding. And sometimes, she and I were at odds.

I remember a telling moment between us much later in 1967, when after Jonas vacated his Third Avenue loft Candy and I, before leaving for Mexico, joined Barbara and others there. Barbara had taken Julius Orlovsky at a time when his brother Peter ("out of his skull," Allen once said) was unable to look after him. Julius—perhaps Barbara or his psychiatrist or both were the driving force—had reported for work as a soda jerk at Nedick's and brought home an employee identification card with "Orlovsky" handwritten at the top. As several of us sat with him one evening around what had been Jonas's Danish modern nappy sofa, we discovered that he really wasn't keen on having the job, on reporting for work the next day. The medication he was taking encouraged him to talk a little—hardly effusively, but it brought him a step or two out of his catatonia. Barbara quizzed him on his attitude about work: "Well then Julius, what would you do if not this? What is it that you can do, that will make someone else hire you?"

"They could hire me to think!" he answered emphatically, scowl breaking across his face, lower lip asserting itself.

"You can think? Somebody's gonna pay you for that?!" Barbara broke out laughing hysterically, without stop.

I became angry. Perhaps I identified with Julius in his extreme quietude; in any case I'd been sitting there thinking of all our hifalutin cabinet ministers and secretaries and presidential advisors, wondering if they were any more effective—even if they weren't much more destructive than Julius Orlovsky might be. Weren't they paid to think?

"I don't think you're being fair," I interrupted Barbara's laughter.

She stopped midlaugh, eyed me immediately. "Gordon, I think you're missing something in life."

②

"It says you're the Delacroix of the Underground, Gordon." Jeffrey Childress, boot heels dug into the lower rungs of his long-legged stool, was speaking to me at the Coop one morning from behind a small stream of rising smoke. I stood in the doorway to his room for housing and cleaning film prints; his long and broad chambrayed back was to me, but his head turned in my direction. The new *Newsweek*—February 13, 1967—lay cradled in his large hands. Its cover story was "The Divorced Woman," but deep inside, an article entitled "Up from Underground" included three pages of text, movie stills, and filmmakers' portraits.

Of course the article didn't say Gordon Ball was the Delacroix of the Underground; in fact, when I got to see it later in the morning, it didn't mention me—or, for that matter, Jeffrey Childress. Instead, what I read when he handed me the issue was a positive, almost promotional piece, beginning with a 1962 quotation from the late filmmaker Ron Rice:

> "The New American Cinema is just the first crack in the ice. What is going to be made and seen in the next ten years will cause your grandfather to leap from the grave." . . . Rice was right. The American anti-establishment filmmaking movement, with its hock-shop cameras, surplus film stock and hole-in-corner cinematheques, has grown steadily in numbers, self-awareness, audacity and importance. It is now as significant as the more organized, recognized and "official" avant-garde movements in the other arts, which are changing

the face of culture in this country. And, with the unprece-
dented success of Andy Warhol's film *The Chelsea Girls* . . . the
underground has at last surfaced and is moving into public
consciousness with a vengeance.

The Chelsea Girls was screened five months ago at the Radio
City Music Hall of the underground—the Film-Makers'
Cinematheque, a converted downstairs auditorium in a dingy
New York office building, where the screen is far back on the
platform, too many seats are busted, and the ticket-taker is
sometimes too polite to ask for your money . . .

The article by Jack Kroll called Stan Brakhage "the Hart Crane of the
underground film," and Jonas "the symbol of this new cinematic saintli-
ness." It admitted the lure the underground held for many of those
"above," surveyed the works of some of the major artists, such as
Brakhage, Anger, Conner, Markopolous; then closed with that January
night at Jonas's when Candy and I were there:

But the real scene is at Jonas Mekas's apartment in downtown
New York. The place is dark and littered with miles of film,
papers and books. Several very young people are scattered all
over the place editing film in the corner, cooking macrobiotic
spaghetti in the kitchen, sleeping off an all-night shooting ses-
sion on the couch. A not-too-clean movie screen stands near
the wall; Mekas gets up and scrapes off some of the dirt with a
knife and a film is projected. It was made by twenty-one-year-
old Barbara Rubin and it is the sheer galloping metabolism of
her energy turned into an electrifyingly eloquent salvo of
images which her camera has pulled from the street like a jet-
propelled vacuum cleaner.

Barbara Rubin is already beyond cinema—her spiky hair
and dry-cell eyes would scare Marshall McLuhan himself. . . .

Four days later came *Art of Light and Lunacy: The New Underground Films* in
Newsweek's competitive cousin *Time*. It included a medium close-up frontal
shot by David Gahr of Jonas in long hair, startlingly Christ-like. It ended
with: "'You might say,' Mekas murmurs with a sly little grin, 'that the
lunatics are taking over the asylum.'"

There was a brief mention that many filmmakers "wear hair to the
shoulders and beards to the ears; some smoke grass and turn on frequently

with LSD." That last was the closest to any record of my dinner with the two people—Susan Jonas and a male companion—from *Time* who interviewed me at dinner ("Hey Gordon, I hear you were interviewed by *Time* magazine," the neighbor who'd kept Miss Lyn at Christmas greeted me in the corridor of our building when I returned). At a pleasant and tony midtown restaurant where the *Time* couple took the tab, I'd told them some of my psychic energy experiences as well as of the films I liked. But— I was conscious of this at the time, though I didn't know how to evaluate it—my discussion of Kenneth Anger's *Scorpio Rising,* and other movies, focused on some of their more startling images, not on how they worked as a whole.

ON STAGE IN GREAT NECK

"Magic city!" Jonas exclaimed as we approached Manhattan after an evening in Great Neck, Long Island. Before us in myriad gold and amber, Manhattan rose sparkling against a backdrop of black velvet.

Three hours earlier, arriving on Long Island, we were lost, asking for directions—but the first person didn't respond. Jonas called out the window, "Vere is de Kennedy Auditorium?" to a man walking briskly, huddled in coat and hat, on a dark sidewalk. I thought he didn't hear, or perhaps was afraid; Jonas took it as an affront, and shouted as we hummed by him, "Fuck you!"

Luckily the next stranger whom Jonas asked not only heard but responded, and we made it in time to our presentation, sponsored by the Adult Program of the Great Neck Public Schools. The flyer had advertised a "Spring Underground Film Festival" running three evenings from early February to late April, "bringing to Great Neck new filmmakers who are achieving international recognition for their work in the newest form of artistic expression." Our evening in mid-March (Jonas had been here the month before with other works) included "Film portraits by Stan Brakhage and Gordon Ball."

Jonas had in fact brought not a Brakhage but several other films, including Thom Anderson's *Sundae Melting*, a time-lapse portrait of a chocolate sundae undergoing total collapse in fourteen minutes; and *Amphetamine*, by Warren Sonbert, which looked close-up and unabashedly at shooting speed, boys dancing together, kissing.

And then, Jonas introduced me and *Georgia*. I stood right next to him on stage as he referred to me as "one of our best young filmmakers." But right after the film, when someone asked "What is the relation between the images in the film and the soundtrack?" I simply didn't know, and stood there dumbly before two hundred people. I made the film; I never thought how certain parts of it worked—or not, at least, from the standpoint of the questioner. Or I hadn't asked myself such questions. I made the relationship intuitively; I hadn't thought about it abstractly. Jonas, at my side, whispered to me, "De mood, de mood," and finally I bent my head to the shiny round silver microphone and spoke: "The mood. The music sets the mood."

PRUNES: FROM MAIN STREET TO THIRD AVENUE

①

I was more than gratified by Jonas's introduction that night. Though I thought it not deserved, I nonetheless hoped it might be. But I didn't know what to do next in film. When Jonas once remarked "I haven't seen your latest work" at a party where we looked at several recent efforts by others, I didn't know what to respond. Puzzled at what to do, I may have even hoped there was an advantage in appearing mysterious—

And I was surprised at his response when he saw an earlier work of mine. I'd thought of *Georgia* as my first film, and it certainly was, if at age twenty-one I were to have any sort of "canon." But even before *Georgia* I'd made a film at Davidson with that same Revere regular 8 MM camera Jonas had brought me, starting right on the spot with his visit.

The twenty-minute *Prunes* took its term from the word Billy and I and others in our "gang," as Jonas called us, used for representative Davidson faculty—as we saw them from between unwrinkled lids: dessicated, anally clean fellows in their forties, fifties, and sixties with dry minds, dry sex lives, and nonexistent lives of the imagination. For them, it seemed, an original thought, or passion, was akin to a laborious, constipation-breaking, full-tilt bowel movement.

In time, Billy would write a comic novel, *Prunes*—his inspired send-up of the Davidson experience. But what was my little color film of the same name? It aspired to take in the Davidson milieu as I saw it, as I could capture it in the light-burnt emulsion of my final weeks. Having begun during Jonas's visit, I continued filming through nearly the end of the school year in late May. The result, a collage of daily scenes of campus life: one somewhat portly red-headed copain posed beneath a *Playboy* bunny on my wall, stretching himself out on the bed in naked profile, glasses on face and cigarette in mouth; there were portrait sequences of two young women from Charlotte; Jonas at the lake, beer bottle in his mouth as he closed the car door; a trip to the mountains with Billy and friends from Charlotte; my having my hair cut a few days before graduation; and odd, "abstract" rhythmic sequences. I shot one of the last when some of us happened to be walking through the Fine Arts Center parking lot one evening at dusk: I came up to one car idling with its lights on and pressed the lens of my durable Revere close to the illuminated red taillight and shot just one or two single frames; then (to block light) pressed the lens against my thigh and single framed several more times, then returned to the taillight. The result, when the entire sequence of some thirty or so frames—less than two seconds—was projected, was a rapidly pulsating, brilliantly red screen. "Nice rhythm," George Williams (the friend who'd originally suggested I invite Jonas) allowed as he beheld it on a dorm wall three weeks later. I was surprised, gratified. I often worked by "not knowing" what I was doing, not planning, just sensing things, with little idea of how my efforts, or results, might seem to someone else.

There were of course numerous other sequences in *Prunes* besides single framed light experiments—one got me in some trouble at Davidson. Ever since seeing some of the work of Stan Brakhage in the fall of 1965, I'd been greatly interested in the superimposition of two or more images. Once, before Jonas visited in the spring of 1966, I'd forgotten to advance the film in my Kodak brownie after taking the portrait of a dorm-mate. When the shot was printed it merged indoor medium close-up of my friend with swirling patterns of gravel from the roof of our Duke Dormitory. "Isn't this interesting," I said as I showed it to him. "This is crazy, Gordon!" he guffawed, certain he was confronting the ridiculous.

I was determined to continue my investigations and after getting my movie camera shot some sequences of myself reflected in the mirror on the side of the car as I rode shotgun; it reflected as well the at-long-last green trees whizzing by, with occasional bursts of golden North Carolina sun shining through—a natural superimposition.

And here I was making a film about Davidson, about everyday life at Davidson, about the reality of its everyday life as I saw it. And so it must contain some of our hopes and aspirations and disappointments and trivialities, some of the substance of how we actually lived whether we liked it or not or would otherwise point to it or not. And so my shooting included such things. But one that seemed central to life at Davidson— perhaps second only to the frequently expressed, obsessive fear of homosexuality at an all-male school—was masturbation. It was more or less an everyday practice, many seemed to assume, though hardly any admitted to it. Certainly, I masturbated; and the movie *was* about my Davidson activities and my perceptions of what I took as our common experience. But not only was masturbation a daily affair, it offered, even with its obvious limitations, a kind of beauty, a release. Needless to say, I by no means preferred it to sex, but it still could please and relieve, even in May of my senior year, eleven months and some days after the loss of my virginity. And what did it look like? That I'd never seen.

Naked in my small narrow room, I placed my Revere regular 8 MM upright on my desk, angled it toward the midpoint of my bed, and pressed the silver button for continuous. I walked naked the two or three steps back from the desk, lay down on the bed, brushed my long light brown hair from my forehead, stared into the camera and began to masturbate; I continued through the bursts of white liquid that came spurting from the round orange crown of my cock two to three minutes later. The entire sequence, before I removed my magazine of film from the camera several days later, involved a superimposition of another set of images, so that layered intermittently with my body on the bed, fading, holding, then fading, were those traveling shots of green and golden trees immediately overhead, with the sun exploding through.

That semester I was part of a creative writing class which was taught by a man who insisted that the best writing being done in America appeared in *Redbook* and *McCall's*. When during one of our evening sessions a couple of classmates asked me, with some persistence, about my week at Panna Grady's, I mentioned having met Allen Ginsberg and Andy Warhol and Norman Mailer—to which our instructor responded immediately, "Sounds like a queer convention!" But Professor Peter Van Egmond, to his credit, accepted *Prunes* as my major work of the semester, and I—who'd won the college prize in creative writing as a freshman —received a c in creative writing as a senior. And I showed *Prunes* at the last meeting of the semester; not one classmate fainted or was apoplectically seized. And though responses afterward were generally muted, some viewers appeared to have liked it; others looked aghast.

From the former came the suggestion to show it at the college union. The end of the year was around the corner, exams were coming, what harm would be done if one evening the Morrison Room were given to perhaps the first film shot at Davidson by a student? Billy and friend William Walker created a striking elaborate poster, and I approached C. Shaw Smith, Union Director and overseer of my film committee work.

Gordon Ball

Smith was a middle-aged man of medium height and pleasant paunch. At each side of his head dark gray hair, which was beginning to vanish on top, was combed back emphatically in long dovetailing, almost devilish strands. A practicing magician and funnyman, he'd taken his show to American troops in over two dozen countries during World War II. At some engagements nowadays, it was said, he'd stick a lit cigar into his pants pocket while speaking.

Whenever I saw him in the Union he reminded me of Bob Hope—or even Groucho Marx. He'd referred quite deliberately to Carolyn Kizer, in all her large and heeled presence as she loomed over him, as "Miss Kisser." He often could be long-winded, trite, and mealy-mouthed on issues; as Union Director perhaps he felt obliged to always defend standard, non-controversial "good taste." In the midst of questioning me on Kenneth Anger's *Scorpio Rising,* he'd asked if any "male genitalia" were displayed; then, as if in reassurance, he let fly, gratuitously, "I for one know that you're not a pervert, Gordon."

Now, as he discussed my request to show my own film, he offered no reassurance of any sort. Naturally word of *Prunes* had spread overnight on this small Presbyterian campus; though he of course wasn't among the dozen or two who'd seen it, Smith seemed quite familiar with what he took to be its more lurid contents, and I could sense opposition from the start, but only sense it . . . I finally had to ask him to be explicit. "Are you saying that I can show my film if it's censored?" I asked, ingenuously hoping for clarity, resolution.

For C. Shaw Smith, it was an insult, the last straw at the end of a long and exasperating year in which several times at least I pushed him beyond the circumspect limits he felt he must maintain. "Censor" was evidently the trigger word, for he flared, "All right, Gordon, I've had it with you. You are relieved of your duties as Film Committee Chairman!"

I returned weeping to my room. Billy entered almost immediately. When I could still the tears I could laugh at the absurdity of being fired at the very end of two and a half years, with hardly any film programs left, only a couple of exam-period tension-breakers. Promptly, passionately, Billy took himself to C. Shaw Smith's office on behalf of his fired friend, but without significant effect. Years later, revisiting C. Shaw several times when returning to Davidson, I felt affectionate toward him, and when I came once with Ginsberg, he remarked to me on Allen's profound tenderness

'66 Frames

toward all. Years later I sensed that his persuasions were far more generous than he'd ever let on.

There were other responses to *Prunes*—or impressions of it. The very last of the Union's exam-time offerings was a thrilling action-packed narrative, with de rigueur social fluff and rising tension that culminated in violence and conflagration: Marlon Brando starring (as a sheriff!) in Arthur Penn's *The Chase.* It had none of the high quality of his own *One Eyed Jacks,* but it was suspenseful and violent and certainly good for exam-pent college boys. On our way out of the showing, through the now open pneumatic rubber-bottomed doors, a classmate volunteered, "Gordon, if you made a movie like that, I might really like it."

"Oh, okay," I answered and continued out into the lobby.

A different approach was taken one afternoon when I was walking by a dorm and another student stuck his head near his second-story window (behind the dark fine mesh screen, he couldn't be seen) and shouted, "Hey, Gordon, jack off!" And another came when Everett Cooper, a visiting instructor, invited me over to his house one evening, with my film.

Cooper lived in the same place as had my friend Preston Faggart, now happily settled in New York. It was an apartment on the second story of a white frame house on the west side of Davidson's Main Street, in the center of one long block whose clothing store and hardware store, snack bar-bus stop, bank and two barbers, soda shoppe coffered ceiling drug store, comprised the business section of Davidson. From Main Street's facing side stretched the broad green campus, dotted with stately oak and elm and Georgian brick and column.

During my sophomore and junior years, Preston's was a kind of oasis. Here we were all welcome, here I sketched in crayon with Sacha Beck, an intense thirty-five-year-old Russian with brown wavy hair and glasses who taught briefly at Davidson—and here he fought with his girl from the even smaller nearby town of Huntersville, later going home to burn all his original poetry manuscripts in the middle of the night. Here were joyous parties; here the many-talented Preston made an exquisite cream sauce for spaghetti; here we could take our girls; here a roommate played guitar as we drank wine and beer, substances forbidden not only Davidson's students but faculty as well. Here I heard Bob Dylan for the first time. Ambling into Preston's one spring afternoon in 1965, I was greeted by music whose makers, I could hear, were actually having fun, rollicking, nearly falling over themselves doing it, their almost bellows-like instruments oompahing in and out: it was "Bob Dylan's 115th Dream" with its recorded false start, its call for "Take Two!" and its giggles, from *Bringing It All Back Home:*

> I was riding on the Mayflower
> When I thought I spied some land
> I yelled for Captain Arab . . .

But by the fall of my senior year Preston was gone and I must say most unceremoniously since one of the last events of the preceding spring had been a party in which several tipsy guests went out the window onto the roof over the front porch and tossed pebbles at people walking below on Main Street. Someone phoned the police and the several guests landed in jail.

Now the place had been partially remodeled, the downstairs let, and to go upstairs you had to use an outside stairway. Everett was very quiet and didn't bother anybody and I don't know if anyone came over much—I never did get to know him well. But when I came to his place in late May 1966 and showed him my film he became excited and kissed me, saying "You're so beautiful, Gordon"—and I stayed the evening. The next morning, bright and golden, I came out his door, *Prunes* within its circular flat can in my hand, and stepped down the outside stairway in the airshaft between this refuge and the local soda shoppe. Pausing half within and half without, the fine dark mesh of her screen door partially covering her on one side, stood the proprietor, very erect, each sharp elbow at her starched waist gripped in the palm of her opposing hand, sharp blue eyes tracing me.

②

I was made aware of community views of me in other ways too that may or may not have had anything to do with the movie *Prunes;* typically they did have to do with my long hair. A couple of instances:

The Davidson College library was directed by an elderly bachelor of the white aristocracy from Charleston, South Carolina, but the librarian forever behind the circulation desk just after the entrance was Carrie

Britten. It was she—small, single, fiftyish, with glasses and mousy reddish brown fuzzy hair—who monitored all comings and goings. When I'd worked a few weeks in the library the preceding summer and my girl-friend came to visit, she told me not to let her return. And when I entered a week before commencement, she greeted me with "Are you going to get cleaned up for graduation?"

It took me a moment and then I realized she had my hair in mind. "Oh yes," I'd said automatically, not even knowing exactly what she referred to, not showing the hurt I felt. But then I began to think about my parents. In her memoir *Minor Characters,* Joyce Johnson's statement on *her* parents—"Their innocence is the great achievement of their lives"— is one I might've been able to make of my own genteel mother and father, in spite of the war and their years in Asia. After leaving the library, I began to think about my parents—now retired to Winston-Salem to be near my sister, after forty years in China and Japan—coming down to Davidson to watch their last child graduate. Why throw an issue which they wouldn't understand in their face? Not long after they'd returned to the States, I stood next to my mother, observing, as she watched a newscast. It was on how civil rights demonstrators, led by Joan Baez, had confronted the police in a sit-in. My mother let out a worried "No!" as she stood looking down at the screen, shaking her head lightly. It was a disturbance of the social order to which she had adhered, through four decades, from 10,000 miles away, from foreign concessions above and below the Yangtze to a humbled Tokyo in Occupied Japan. And it was all changing.

Some of my friends took my haircut as capitulation. They were right, of course—at least in part. Ironically, even before a mousy librarian's chal-lenge, one of the two town barbers had also offered an opinion on my hair. Mr Johnson, a tall, slender, middle-aged, black gentleman with glasses on his nose, had first cut my hair my freshman year, commenting all the while with barber shop homilies like "Don't see why folks speed, they'll get there anyway," as his silver scissors clicked, telling me how "folks at the bank get kinda persnickety" if customers—especially awkward young freshmen like myself, writing their first—don't fill out their checks cor-rectly. I'd always gone back to him—until I let my hair grow. One pleas-ant afternoon near the end of May Mr Norton, Mr Johnson's competitor for the hair of all the white males, stood at the doorway of his own Main Street shop, hands a-pocket, one or two baby-like tufts of light hair on his

Gordon Ball

starched white shirt front. "Why don't you wear a skirt?!" he offered loudly as I walked by. (Incredible as it may seem, at this time even moderately long hair was often taken as outrageous affront.)

Then, nearly four years after I first went to Mr Johnson, I entered his shop one more time—and brought a friend with me. Handing my Revere to my friend, I stepped up into the empty padded chair: this too would be part of *Prunes*.

③

Of course *Prunes* had its refreshing effects, and some generous friends appeared quite fond of it. There were parts, in fact, that all but the most sober-minded Calvinist might laugh at. As the American onslaught in Vietnam continued to escalate—u.s. troop levels had risen above a quarter of a million, and we'd begun bombing Cambodia—several of us drove to Washington one weekend in May 1966 to join 25,000 others with many a banner urging "Bring the Troops Home Now." Saturday morning before the march as we strolled along the green ellipse, I suddenly asked one of my companions to sit on the grass, legs flat and straight in front of him, the upper half of his body erect, as I lay on my stomach five feet away, Revere in hand. Two hundred yards beyond him, rising erectly in optical illusion from his pants, was the Washington Monument, its faceted top penetrating high into the blue above. My friend seemed to require little instruction in what to do with his right hand, and when this shot appeared on screen in each of the several private showings we did have at Davidson, there was the laughter not only of surprise but of instant recognition.

Another effect I took for the good was an incipient relationship with a younger student. More than once in our careers at Davidson, we—myself, Billy, Eddie, a few others—had welcomed into the fold younger students who'd begun questioning some of the Davidson "givens," just as we had. Now, at the year's very end, Melvin Story, a freshman, seemed to want to learn from me.

I remember early one dusk as the sky's blue dissolved golden behind dark and green spreading trees, standing barefoot on the vivid grass, propounding to Melvin my notion of the absolute, unlimited power of the artist. Appreciating the revival of the green grass, the entire vegetative world, I'd taken to going barefoot late that spring—both in and out of class. (A week later, the bulletin distributed at mandatory morning chapel contained a new ordinance from the dean of students, forbidding his charges to go anywhere on campus without wearing shoes. . . . I ignored it.)

"The imagination knows no bounds," I instructed Melvin. "The world wears a dirty face—but it's only a face." The transcendental effects of full spring—which had sometimes brought me to an idealized woman— now found me in the temple of Art.

In the excitement after Jonas's visit, Melvin, who had his own movie camera, was quick to make a film himself. At one of those several show-ings of *Prunes* we projected it onto the wall of our dorm hallway, and even, for a few moments, onto a friend's bare chest; at another, we showed the three-and-a-half minute silent regular 8 roll Melvin had just completed, with himself in hooded drag at a piano.

(4)

Half a year later at Jonas's invitation, I projected *Prunes* on the folding portable screen at Jonas's loft—the very screen *Newsweek* depicted him cleaning with a knife.

One among many sequences was devoted to that weekend peace march in May. Here in a sign-bearing procession were students from Ivy League schools; midwest centers of enlightenment like Oberlin; and here, for several dozen frames, a sign proclaimed, was Davidson College: it too was taking its stand against an illegal and immoral war. Since several or more rows of marchers appeared fore and aft of this placard, perhaps a good part of this redoubtable institution was in attendance! You couldn't quite tell—it was a movie, after all—but there were in fact no more than five of us. Also included in the march sequence were shots of the demon-stration's program of speakers; of some unexplained disturbance which brought mounted police in a flurry; and a quick succession of single frame shots, no more than a few per man, of every policeman stationed at the end and middle of every block for over a dozen blocks as we made our way to the gathering: the effect was startling, and turned its subjects comic.

Jonas was interested in such things as documentations of campus life at the time. "I am putting together a program," he said, "and this could be part of it." But I couldn't believe it, I didn't think he really wanted to show *Prunes* with all its homemade embarrassments—after all, wasn't it very personal and arbitrary, not the objective picture of campus life it ought to be? I actually thought that. I never gave it him.

IN SHEEP MEADOW

Near the end of March 1967, a very large get-together would coincide with Easter Sunday. Two and a half months earlier, what was called the "First Human Be-In and Gathering of the Tribes," had taken place in Golden Gate Park, San Francisco, with Allen Ginsberg and Timothy Leary among those presiding. Now a similar event—without programs or presidings— was scheduled in a large meadow at Central Park. I'd just strained my back again, and wasn't sure I'd be able to go—but Billy announced, maybe not wholly in jest, that he and his visiting friend from Charlotte, Alex McIntire—a mountain of a man at six-foot-three and two hundred and eighty pounds—would carry me there on a litter.

As it turned out, I was well enough to walk carefully by myself. Candy painted our faces in rich paisley bands of white, red, yellow, black, and green grease paint, and with my Revere in hand we four took off. It had rained recently. Across brown-and-yellow meadow, spring hinted its existence in tiny spots of green, as hundreds and thousands of humans, infants to old people, gathered in groups. They danced in circles; idled; played flutes, drums, guitars; stood and talked or spread out on blankets; shared food and sacraments. More than a few hugged each other. Occasionally we'd see others with their faces painted like us; many were in jeans, with shirts or jackets in bright natural color. Some wore headbands; some wore skin jewels, diffraction disks; some stood in the ample warmth of serapes. Occasionally you'd see feathers, flowers, buckskin. The great majority were white, but now and then blacks mixed in. Occasionally, I smelled marijuana.

And we saw friends. Billy and Alex had gone off in another direction, and Candy and I had just finished a sort of ancient round dance; as Candy talked with one of her partners, a blonde woman of twenty-six or so, in brown jacket and jeans, came up to me.

"Louise!"

"Hi Gordon! How are you?"

"Good—you?"

"Beautiful today, isn't it?"

"Yes—you look well. And David too!"

Turning to a bearded man with curly red hair, who held in his arms a now larger David, she introduced us.

Gordon Ball

The six months that had intervened made my stay in her Perry Street apartment seem decades from Sheep Meadow. Now, as afternoon hours passed, swelling circles of new acquaintances seemed friends. Not all was joyful, however: an antiwar flyer circulated, featuring two large black-and-white close-ups side-by-side: one, the Mod-ish face of a model, every inch of skin stroked, brushed, layered to doe-like commercial perfection; the other, a young Vietnamese victim of American napalm, her—his?—face hideously transformed into a gaping, gasping grotesque . . . I thought of the *Voice* piece I'd read of two Vietnamese children recently flown to England by a Swiss group for treatment of their napalm-inflicted wounds: paper bags over their heads spared fellow passengers the sight of what remained of their faces.

Moments later we ran into Stanley and Carri and hugged them in delight: they both wore big grins. It was pleasant, surprising to see Stanley so disarmingly sociable, as if he were on a level with everyone else! But he was also distributing small white flyers packed with miniessays, testaments, and psychological commentary. One was headed "Above All—Be Truthful to Others":

> We are a commune dedicated to the ideal of being absolutely truthful with one another. Absolute truthfulness has never been tried before upon this planet and is the sole solution to the problem of man's misery.
>
> Absolute truthfulness is the only means by which need can be communicated to others. We must learn to show our need so other people can respond to it and express their own needfulness. . . . Until now the expression of needfulness was conditionally sanctioned by laws designed to insure survival but not sanity. The ending of these regulations will lead to sanity although the transition will appear to be a threat to survival. The closer we are to being absolutely truthful, the greater our awareness is of the world as a magical amalgam of the mundane and the mystical, synchronistically leavened for the spiritual edification of man.
>
> The immediate hurt or discomfort caused by telling the truth is far less devastating than the long-range confusion, despair and alienation left in the wake of deception. We must unswervingly adhere to the conviction that, regardless of how

the truth may be received, the more truth, the better. Being totally truthful also frees one from the crippling anxiety of having to guess how much truth is acceptable from one moment to the next, and thus frees the mind to discover its passionate role in the creation of cosmic perfectibility!

Total truthfulness to one another constitutes the only true love of one another. Telling the truth always leads to doing the right thing. One is spiritual to the degree that one has no secrets.

Total truthfulness leads to the understanding of the universe.

Under "Remember . . . Remember . . . Remember . . . Remember . . ." another entry instructed:

1 Ask for love directly and simply when the need is felt.
2 Endure the pain of sexual jealousy without retaliation against anyone in any way, and encourage and help those around you to find happiness in love.
3 Share all of your experiences with your mate, including the loving of others.
   Never keep secrets.

Remember
THOU SHALT BE TRUTHFUL ABOVE ALL ELSE.

And beneath a rubric of "TRUTHFUL IS GODLINESS" came an exposition of lying as social norm:

Lying is the sanctioned way to deny your need for others while plagiarizing and peddling the stuff of others. Lying creates the classless society by creating a single class of liars. Lying is what the topman does as well as his bootlicker. . . . Lying has created a vast mental institution in which the ruled and the rulers change hands without rhyme or reason, a case of the clever insane leading the less clever insane. Lying creates the inner emptiness of TV titillation and the desire to possess and value the worthless. Lying is not them, or the fellow down the block, or the other guy, or the enemy. Lying is you. Lying is me. Lying is all of us. Lying is the swaggering of your secret dreams and the desire to be lied to so that you may have them answered.

Gordon Ball

At bottom, hand-written block lettering directed the reader to write the author at a 42nd Street office address. I was surprised by this, but much more by the name given for the author: "Stan Sher." Was Stanley covering his Jewishness? What was he doing? Worried about his part-time employers? (His substitute teaching give him quite a decent day's pay, when he was called.) I felt vaguely disillusioned.

"Did you get the saint?" Billy asked; we'd met up with him and Alex once more. At the center of a circle of some thirty or forty people, two or three deep, seated on somewhat muddy turf, pushing and pulling the bellows of his small dark red harmonium as he chanted, was Allen Ginsberg. Peering into the circle from its outer ring, I'd raised my Revere over my head, tilted it downward, and shot him.

A month or so later, Candy and I sat in the quiet living room of my parents' rather modest red brick house rising from Carolina clay. It was their new home, after returning to the U.S. from their four decades in China and Japan; at Christmas I'd shown *Georgia* here. Now, on a newer, regular 8 MM projector, we showed them the twelve-minute movie I'd assembled from the Sheep Meadow footage. "It's just a bunch of people who like to get together and do whatever they want and have fun. Some of them might even take off their clothes!" Candy had offered in an introductory chirp—though no nakedness was in the film. We then sat there, in that well-insulated room with thick gray wall-to-wall carpeting and storm windows to keep out the cold, with the ebony sideboard from Shanghai in the thirties, the teak bust figurines from Java in the 1950s, and the ebony, ivory, and jade screen of Buddhas from Tientsin 1933. And there we watched my silent film of the 1967 Central Park Human Be-In. Silently.

WALDEN IN MANHATTAN—AND JONAS'S NEW REGIMEN

①

"Den you vill vant to edit vid your eyes as you vatch, to eliminate de faster parts."

In a scissors-like motion, Jonas pointed his big long fingers just to one side of his narrow eyes. He faced an audience of some 200, after a spring-time showing of his own in a spacious midtown theater. Had the recent *Time* and *Newsweek* coverage contributed to such "overground" attention? Perhaps—and perhaps it had also contributed to improved relations with the city, for around this time Jonas asked for my help in getting an 8 MM movie camera to give Barbara Lee Diamondstein of the Parks Department.

On this spring evening, he'd just premiered a portion of *Walden,* his diaristic film record of his own life, New York, and its avant-garde. This seventy-five minutes or so was only a small part of autobiographical work that would run many hours and represent many decades, much of it shot handheld with his 16MM Bolex, much of it single-framed. Action was often quick and truncated. This night's section consisted of footage from roughly a year earlier: slow, loving shots, some in close-up, of actress friend Amy Taubin, heavily coated in Central Park, with its poor pitiful signs—so late to come—of a New York spring: greening grass, birds in trees still otherwise denuded, tiny yellow suggestions of buds hobbling along a few bare branches; men with jackhammers in city streets girded by sawhorse barriers; critic P. Adams Sitney and other friends at a brightly lit diner, smiling into the camera; the Chinese New Year; mailing *Film Culture;* the Velvet Underground's first appearance, at a psychiatrists' convention; Leslie Trumbull's view out the Coop window onto Park Avenue South; Sitney, then Director of the Cinematheque, being fingerprinted by the police; Adolfas's and Pola's wedding; Ginsberg and Mailer trading Uncle Sam hats; sparrows grasping bare winter branches, ministering (as Jonas narrated it) to an ill Flo Jacobs indoors; a visit to Timothy Leary at idyllic Millbrook the year before the raid led by Gordon Liddy and other agents of government; Mel Lyman ("God") making coffee; a flashback to a 1959 antinuclear demonstration of women at Times Square led by Judith

Gordon Ball

Malina. Commenting on it all was Jonas's unadorned, lyrical, lamenting, ironic, wistful voice, with occasional interludes of Chopin and other Old World resonances. Intertitles flowered by his magic-markered hand divided some of the scenes: "IN NEW YORK WAS STILL WINTER BUT THE WIND WAS FULL OF SPRING" was the most wistful—and abiding.

(2)

"We're going to be shooting this weekend. Why don't you come to this address Saturday evening—"

Andy was on the other end of the phone, giving me the apartment and street. But I chose not to come, because Jonas was going to a party at the apartment of a "rich lady," who evidently could be interested in helping avant-garde film. Candy agreed with my decision and together we went to the "rich lady's" only to find—aside from Jonas—several rooms full of people, nearly all strangers, in slick suits and dark evening dresses. Drink held at waist, they'd greet one or the other of us and ask, "Oh, and you're one of them too?"

But if my own life had its miscalculations, so evidently did Jonas's. In the vein of Rilke's "You must change your life," a proclamation and schedule had been posted on the Coop wall two months earlier. An eight and a half by eleven sheet, it was typewritten single spaced, but embell-ished with a cheery handwritten heading in semiscript; the left margin was illuminated with magic markered flowers; at bottom, resting next to a large butterfly, lay Jonas's signed first name. The telephone schedule and the note following it were bracketed at the right margin with "READ THIS TWICE" written alongside:

> To friends & everybody,
> During last five years I have, practically, lost my private and my
> creative life. I have been completely pulled away from my own
> work as an artist. My life has been consumed by the Under-
> ground Empire. At this point, in my life, I face two choices:
> either I pick up my own creative work or you'll have to pick me
> up and put me away. Since I have my own apprehensions about
> being locked up, I have worked out for myself, for these com-
> ing months, a very strict schedule which will allow me to regain

my own lost life—unless this is already a sign of total insanity. Anyway, I have to ask you to put up with me, at this stage of my insanity, and forgive me that I will be quite difficult to reach, these coming months. Of course, you are perfectly welcome to make bets how long I'll be able to keep this schedule:

8:00	get up
8:30 — 9:30	correspondence
9:30 — 10:30	meetings, appointments (preferably, in MY neighborhood)
10:30 — 12:00	my film work
12:00 — 1:00	"church" "meal" a short stop at the Coop; buy a Flower
1:00 — 3:00	film work
3:00 — 4:00	*Film Culture* work
4:00 — 6:00	my writing work
6:00 — 8:30	meetings, appointments, anything for "Others," "meal," C'teque
8:30 — 9:30	"church" (by which I mean: doing nothing, walks thru the city, even, reading)
9:30 — 12:00	my film work
12:00	closing the day

SUNDAYS no rules will be followed

TELEPHONES will be answered ONLY DURING the following hours:
9:00 — 9:30 A.M.
3:30 — 4:00 P.M.
9:00 — 9:30 P.M.

SPECIAL note to the COOP, CINEMATHEQUE, CENTER:
appointments for me, or meetings in which I have to participate can be made only for the following hours:
9:30 — 10:30 A.M.
6:00 — 8:30 P.M.

The above Iron Rules become effective as of NOW, February 3rd, 1967

Regardless of the many exasperations and disorders in his day, Jonas's singlemindedness, his one grand vision, his bedrock commitment and devotion, never wavered. Once when he entered the Coop, I reported having read in the paper of the will of a man recently deceased: he'd left a million dollars to anyone who could prove there was a soul. "Art is de proof of de soul," Jonas responded immediately, quick as a whip.

SEX AGAIN

(1)

"I don't see how he can do that without coming." So Billy confided to me one winter evening at the Cinematheque as we beheld a multimedia performance by Jud Yalkut: a moving image projected onto oversize balloon suspended from the ceiling. On the balloon, a few feet from our eyes, a young longhaired couple engaged in yabyum, a Kundalini yoga or Tibetan Budd-hist method of intercourse in which the two partners face each other seated upright, legs around each other, the male member inside the female. One of its effects is to delay orgasm for the male and enhance the possibility of orgasm for the female; its overall goal, to add almost infinitely, meditatively, to appreciation of sex and partner, to yin-yang recognition of interconnectedness. (I'd first encountered such—though I hadn't fully understood concept or even logistics—in a papberback *The Dharma Bums* on the bedside table of my parents' room, Tokyo 1960; it was there, age fifteen, that I first read of this strange sex: I asked my father about it; he told me not to read it; and I no longer saw the book on their table—or anywhere else.)

In the spring of 1967, Candy and I continued as before in sexual explorations—but with some differences. The frequent sex we had together continued to be complemented by love with friends and strangers. Candy—as I could see and as she told me—was possessed of an almost incredible energy, and was fully satisfied by men only infrequently; even when satisfied she could welcome more. As she was the first to point out, the modeling studio—"Model and Photo Equipment Rental Center"— at which she now worked was often merely a sleazy cover for various forms of titillation, foreplay, and, on occasion, sexual intercourse. Though Candy said she never had intercourse with customers, she told me of an older Chinese man in suit and tie and hat who visited every once in a while, and liked to perform cunnilingus.

The clientele were, of course, almost exclusively male, generally straight, and older. Some paid simply to see a pretty young woman partly or totally naked and to sketch and photograph her, with their own equipment or with rentals from the studio. A tip on the side would cover more revealing in-bed shots.

Gordon Ball

The studio, up a narrow flight of stairs from a relatively quiet side street in the low thirties, was run by a short, brawny, slightly pudgy fellow named Ron. He had pale skin and short dark wavy hair, and kept a black .38 in his desk at the entrance. He and his wife—Irene had short light brown hair, fair skin, an engaging smile—were ten or so years older than us and perhaps not "hip" in some of our ways, but they did experiment with sex and were much more streetwise than we. There were perhaps a dozen or so girls attached to the studio, three or four there at any one time. Everyone seemed more or less friendly, Ron and Irene especially so.

With Ron and Irene, and some of the studio girls, Candy and I went to several orgies. One was at a rather swank and spacious midtown apartment, carpeted wall-to-wall in deep dark red, where we all stood around naked, under dim light, talking when we weren't screwing. Among us was one entirely straight couple (so they appeared) who seemed to be first timers. Both were quite attractive, he with medium length brown hair combed and parted, she with a gentle, full head of well-brushed blonde like in Breck commercials. But she didn't seem to want to come even near any of the other men, and so they stayed to themselves.

Then late in the evening, on a double bed in one corner, in full view of others, her tightened long soft thighs raised over the broad bones of his thrusting shoulders, he loudly slammed and smacked against her again and again. It seemed strange to come to an orgy to end up by yourselves, making love only to each other—but Candy and I too had done the same at least once.

And what was I doing that evening? There was a woman there from the studio whom I'd admired from afar: Angie was tall, with permed flaming red hair, long legs, a pretty face with high cheekbones, teeth that were vaguely bucked—and very large breasts that asserted themselves authoritatively high above her midriff. This was the first time I'd seen her undressed; and now, after only beholding her (she partly clothed, me tongue-tied) from across a small studio waiting room, I had my chance! As I made love to her on the carpet, I realized her breasts were hard, they didn't have the right give and softness. Instead of changing their shape when she lay on her back, they poked up. As I kissed and sucked and held them, I realized there was some unnatural substance there.

That was early in the evening. Much of the rest of it I tended to draw back, even as I talked with others. Perhaps the disillusioning effect of my

'66 Frames

moments with Angie had something to do with it; perhaps I felt sad for her and, for the time, unenthusiastic about more sex.

(2)

My everyday life now—from early 1967 on—held one new constraint. Given my ten-to-six work at the Coop, I was meeting fewer new people. One was Carol, a black seventeen year old high school student. She came to our apartment one gray afternoon and fucked me when Candy wasn't there. We listened to music and she allowed, almost scornfully, that she was "the only black in my school who likes the Beatles; everyone else likes Soul!"

Candy and I continued to visit Stanley's and Carri's every so often; sometime in the early spring I met a new young woman there whom I'd come to see again and again. Yvonne Adams was talkative, slender, with a narrow face, thick lips, blue eyes, short brown hair. She was very, very sexy in body, face, speech, manner, gesture: her overall effect was of some all-encompassing liquid sexuality that filled every dimension and pore with regenerative vitality.

Mentally she was fast, focused, ambitious; she was thinking of law school. "You've got a first-class mind," said Stanley, naked, to Yvonne, naked, as he held forth one evening on the floor in a small circle of naked couples. Two years later, she asked me to marry her.

(3)

Often Stanley Fisher could put me uptight with the pinpointed psychological scrutiny and bluntness he accorded everyone: "I think you want to make it with Jane, Gordon, and you're afraid to say it." Once, after several minutes listening quietly, blue eyes unflinching, to a new fellow talk not about the heart or sex of his life but the logistics of his workplace, he interrupted, "This bores me."

But one evening in the spring of 1967 I loosened up with him and asked questions that I'd been tossing around in my own mind; though at the time I didn't know the term, I was perhaps considering him as a possible role model. I was trying to figure him out. He'd just agreed with my proposal that "Most fundamental truths are simple." Then as discussion took a somewhat different direction, I asked "What really interests you?"

"Communication."

I followed, almost pleadingly, with "What do you live for?"

The two-syllabled response came instantly, powerfully, without hesitation:

"Pleasure."

I wish that pleasure had abided in all my meetings with Stanley. Though I could appreciate the workings of his mind, his focus was so intense there was little room for let-up. Yes, he *was* given to spontaneity and humor, but one couldn't casually visit with him (that's what made our Be-In encounter so exceptional). Sooner, rather than later, the familiar psychological scrutiny, with or without sex, would come to dominate. Obviously, being young and somewhat sexually inexperienced (within that milieu), I found Stanley intriguing: he had a purchase on the body and mind of life which I thought I sought. The pain could be ignored— or learned from. So I felt then: though I admired his directness, I finally, over time, found him restricting.

Through Stanley, I may have learned more of my limitations than I did of the needs of Candy and Carri and others. Thirty years later, I think Candy was possibly right, that his power over others came to preoccupy him. Coming to terms with Stanley Fisher hasn't been easy.

AGENT FRALEIGH OF THE FBI

①

One week later I answered the phone at my desk early one afternoon at the Coop:

"May I speak to Gordon Ball?"

"This is he."

"This is Agent Fraleigh of the FBI. I'd like to speak with you about a matter concerning Jake Floran."

"Oh . . . "

Agent Fraleigh made an appointment to come to the Coop the next morning. I don't know how pale I turned. I'd helped Jake Floran, two years behind me at Davidson, get some acid when he visited New York in the fall. Without my saying a word to him, Leslie could tell how I felt: "Are you all right? Is there anything you want me to know?" he asked.

I filled him in; he gave me permission to go back home and "clean house." (Naturally, we both assumed it could be drug-related—though the courtesy of a call in advance was quite puzzling.) Jeffrey Childress came in from his film cleaning and took in our conversation.

I left quickly—as soon as I filled Candy in (in safely veiled terms) on the phone. But as I reached for the door, Leslie called out from his desk: "One other thing. Remember your own dignity."

"Okay," I answered. What, I thought to myself as I rushed down the steps, through the twin glass doors framed in black iron and onto the vigorous street: I have dignity? I have self-respect? I have such things? I do? What are they?

Returning to our quiet, entirely civil apartment, no bodies bared and reclining together, no music, no candles, no incense, all silent and still, I hated to even consider throwing things out: the small brass pipe with its rich dark center, its residue of not only hashish but DMT, that amazing "instant" psychedelic which gave me great red and green and yellow inner visions of luminescent paisleys, ancient Mayans, and helmeted Roman soldiers in profile, in almost neon-like patterns. . . . The grass and the roaches, the withered, wrinkled, brownish gray-and-black butt-ends of M.J. cigarettes that were thought to possess added potency; the Zig-Zag

rolling papers, the bust of a North African fellah on their cover; what-
ever we might've had at the time in the way of diet pills. And was there
acid? Any of Dave's methedrine crystal? How dispose of it all? Or keep
some? Would the family who tended the small bodega next door, and
who lived in the apartment immediately above us, see that instead of
being away at work I was depositing something in the garbage at the
curb? I should walk farther down the street? Someone else might see me
and wonder?

In virtual shock, I robbed a grave, desecrated a temple. Some grass
went to a neighbor, some things went into the garbage, some into a secret
place. And this was not terribly long after, in paranoia, I'd asked for my
key back from Robert.

②

The next morning, a somewhat slender man an inch or two above aver-
age height, combed gray hair, late forties or early fifties, appeared in the
doorway. He wore a gray suit, held his hat in his hand; his raincoat—it
was wet that day—lay draped over a forearm.

He came over to my desk.

He introduced himself.

Leslie quietly lay down his papers and watched. He lit a Pall Mall and
breathed in. He breathed out.

Jeffrey Childress came in from the next room, unfiltered white ciga-
rette hanging by a prayer from the corner of his mouth. He slouched his
big long body against the white wall, knees bent, still taller and decidedly
larger than our visitor. He wore a long sleeved denim shirt, a wide black
belt at his small waist, and dark blue jeans over dusty black stub-toed
boots on which little splatters of rain had dried in circles. He folded his
large arms above his waist and eyed Agent Fraleigh intently.

Fraleigh started to speak to me, then stopped himself, turned to
Jeffrey. "Would you mind leaving?"

"Yes," Jeffrey replied phlegmatically.

The enormous admiration and gratitude that welled up in me then
for Jeffrey was tempered just slightly by a fear that things could turn con-
frontational. But they didn't; and though I worried that Fraleigh was

'66 Frames

becoming suspicious of the entire Filmmakers' Cooperative, he began with me once more.

"Jake has applied for conscientious objector status, and he listed you as a character reference. We like to ask for a few minutes to interview each reference."

A little relaxed, still largely nervous (there was no time or reason to revel in my nearly unbelievable relief) I told Agent Fraleigh of Jake's good character; of how he earnestly tried to reconcile his strong religious and moral convictions with the duty, if necessary, to kill; I improvised; I embellished (how to make a strong, emphatic statement on the spot, without overdoing?). As I spoke, my heart pounded within, as if trying to push its way up into my mealy mouth. For twenty-one hours I'd primed myself to expect the worst, and now couldn't fully believe it wouldn't come about.

Within ten minutes, Agent Fraleigh was on his way out the white doorway of the Filmmakers' Cooperative, returning to the rain—had I wanted, I could've turned and watched him head down the slick gray sidewalk right outside my window. Jeffrey went back to his film prints and rewinds and Carbona as Leslie continued with his Pall Malls and his papers.

My feelings for Leslie (I hadn't forgotten his remark as I left the day before) and Jeffrey had changed—as had my feelings for myself. For it was also Jake Floran who'd visited me that night at the Syracuse warehouse, when I'd shown him around and we both took several items; it was Jake Floran whose name and address I gave when interrogated several days later by my superiors. I could've made up a name or not even mentioned a second person, but, cowardly, I didn't. Now I was more than conster-nated; I was extremely upset with Jake Floran for not having ever asked me if I were willing to be a character reference for him, for not even at least informing me after the fact that he'd listed me as one, never even mentioning that he was even considering C.O. status. With just that addi-tional morsel of information, "a matter concerning Jake Floran" might not have triggered the severe anxiety that rushed over me. And a morn-ing at the Coop might've been far less tense—and less dramatic, too—for two coworker friends. But what did happen was—I knew all too well—poetic justice.

Gordon Ball

WORDS

By April 1967 Candy and I had been together half a year, and seemed to be getting along. Her gregariousness and initiative complemented my introspection and self-consciousness, and we both still seemed vastly curious about new worlds emerging within and without. Her dark eyes flashed bright, she was quick, talkative, demonstrative, down-to-earth—and so full of spunk and initiative that every now and then I thought of her as almost a kind of Tugboat Annie—but with insight, creativity, accomplishment. Evidently she liked me—or her comparative freedom from her husband—well enough now to go ahead, in the spring of 1967, and plan for a divorce in one of its easiest, least expensive forms. She'd lived with Bill O'Brien two years in Quajimalpa, an Indian village off the Carreterra Mexico-Toluca, spoke fluent Spanish, and would have no trouble locating an appropriate justice or lawyer in Juárez.

The cost would basically be that of a quick flight to Mexico—$300— and another hundred or so for the lawyer. We could make some of the expense, but not the three hundred. "My father will give it to me," Candy announced one evening after some deliberation. Less than a week later, I found myself sitting at a large polished oak table in a high-ceilinged living room in a spacious house set back from the street in Somerville, New Jersey where Candy Mills had once been a senior in high school. Not long after Fats Domino's "Blueberry Hill" came out, all the boys had gone around singing of their big-busted classmate with the long auburn hair, "I found my thrills/On Ca-a-a-ndy Mills."

Across from me sat a tall, neatly bearded, dark-complected man. Balding, he had a narrowish face, and wore glasses; coils of big black hair tumbled forth from the open neck of his knit shirt. He was big, long-limbed, masculine.

A St. John's graduate in engineering, David M. Mills was now an assistant manager at Allis-Chalmers.

"I want to thank you for—" I volunteered.

"I'm not giving it to you," he blocked and parried. "It's for Candy."

The major discussion of our afternoon in this Catholic home of many kids (of which Candy was one of the eldest) soon proved not financial but generational—and argumentative. Candy and I remained at one side of the table, her father at the other. Tied to chores for dinner and the

'66 Frames

evening party at which Julian, Candy's oldest younger brother, would perform with his band, her mother appeared only intermittently. The question that heated up our table, meanwhile, was what we—Candy and I—stood for: how we lived, what we valued. All that the darker, older eyes of Mr Mills seemed to see across the table from him appeared suspect. Perhaps it was only natural; our striking differences in posture, body language, hair, and clothing only advertised the deeper differences we labored vainly, with words, to reduce.

"Give me some philosophy!" his low and rather gruff voice demanded, after we'd tried at length to explain our values, beliefs, theories. Perhaps he wanted Kant, or Plato, or Schopenhauer, the celebrated rational Prunes, if you will, of the western world. Perspectives on life drawn in part from some of the world's oldest religious scriptures seemed not to count. Had we had our Ali Akbar Khan record with us to play, to offer what I thought of as the sounds of eternity, discovered long ago in India, I doubt we'd have fared any better. And utterly veiled though we kept it, he disapproved wholly of our sex life, even though we made only the most reserved and indirect references, based on the inescapable fact that we did live together. He disapproved too of our opposition to an illegal and immoral war, and mention of drugs of any sort was out of the question.

Argument ended but unresolved, we decided to stay long enough to take in some of the party and Candy's brother's band. Numerous young people in their midteens—and half a dozen or more grown-ups—began piling into the house. For the elders, a large punch bowl now rested at the center of the oak table where we'd fought with words. Julian, a large, hunkering, chubby sixteen year old with short blond hair, came out of the dining room and announced to assembled old and young alike as he joined his band, "Try the punch. It's really alcoholic and not only that, it's super psychedelic!"

Many years ago, in high school in Tokyo, I was in love with words, their etymologies, their nuances.

I began to write short stories, both for my own pleasure and for class assignments, and though they tended to be limited in diction, occasionally a new word might work its way in.

Gordon Ball

And, excited by advertising, I made numerous class dance posters whose dramatic effects came from a few telling words I'd place beneath one or two provocative images—sometimes my own photos, sometimes those of magazine ads. When I ran for Vice President of the student body, I made a large poster with a photo of the main school hallway, lined on both sides with lockers, thronged by students at the noon hour as classes let out, and the same hallway, empty of humans, framed only by the same skeletal lockers, after the end of all classes in the afternoon. The caption, in large block letters, read, "All for Ball or None at All."

But over time, as I read and heard more, I began to pick up on what life in the advertising profession nine thousand miles away in the United States was like. I saw the way *Time* magazine used words: not only for empty and flashy effect but for snide, arbitrary put-downs. I saw that even the new instructor at A.S.I.J. who assigned us the writing of short stories was impressed by the glitz in *Time* magazine. I later came to live in the United States and began to hear and see, in loud and startling verbal promises of radio and television advertisements, how black was turned into white, and how that seemed taken for granted as everyday reality. Within a few years after my return from Asia, I began to hear and read daily how, according to our government, our armed aggression in a small Asian country was for "freedom"; I saw how in commercials our culture evidently valued what was "incredibly delicious" and "the real thing," yet banned chemical substances that not only offered immense pleasure but profound, spiritual perspectives on "the real." I saw in my own life how pleasurable and healthy and athletic and aesthetic and varied sex could be, and how it was suggestively championed commercially in word and image—and also how any deviance from heterosexual, marital monogamy, and its few "approved" positions and manners, was put down with severity. When I saw all this taking place in my mercantile homeland, I became disabused of any illusions regarding the efficacy of words.

One night after a program at the Cinematheque I sat amidst the wooden seats of the auditorium with Elenore Lester of the *New York Times*. The long article that would appear nine months later was devoted to how more and more college students (I appeared somewhat prominently early on, but numerous others were also cited and quoted) were turning to film. The first page of *Shaking the World With an 8 MM Camera* included the following:

. . . this new age has produced a new crop of creative young people who see an almost magical potential in making films themselves. These embryonic artists speak of their film mission in tones of revelatory rapture. They see the camera as uniquely the instrument of their generation, still rich with unexplored possibilities. "Do you realize how you can rock the world with an 8 mm camera?" asks Gordon Ball, a recent graduate of Davidson College in North Carolina, who gave up writing for filmmaking. "Words are so limited and film is still so unexplored as an art form."

Certainly (though it hadn't been my intention) I'd rocked Davidson College's enclosed world; and though much more time would pass before I eventually turned again to writing, I also eventually made more substantial films than *Georgia*—and used words on the soundtrack.

To return to the Mills household: it was of course possible that Candy's brother may have wanted us to know we shared a common interest, but our argument with his father made a discussion of psychedelics with Julian more than I was willing to take on. And so, later that same evening in the spring of 1967, Candy and I, done with our verbal fight with her supportive father, done with the fancy of alcohol being combined with psychedelics, walked out of the large frame house under the trees, into the now dark front yard, and pulled open the big heavy doors of my deep green, horizontal-finned v-8 Chevrolet Biscayne. We drove out of Somerville, New Jersey for home, for the illuminated island to the East.

RETURNING MY CAR TO THE GREEN WORLD

①

We'd use my car in a few more instances and then, within a few weeks, I'd drive out of the city and never bring it back.

One evening Andy Warhol and a couple of Factory people—one was Edie Sedgwick—rode in the back seat; Edie was in a fit, in tears; on one side of her sat a friend, trying to comfort her; on her other side, Andy. The cause of her upset? Andy had been asked to show *The Chelsea Girls* at the Cannes Film Festival in May, and was bringing several people from the Factory, but not Edie. Another night, Candy drove Andy (riding shot-gun) from Max's Kansas City to his uptown Lexington Avenue home as I sat between them, holding hands with Andy on his blue-jeaned thigh.

Then one unusually cold spring morning a week or so later, I walked to the far West Side, where I was parking the car: it was the only place I knew where I wouldn't have to move it daily from one side of the street to the other. And there it was, as before, safely parked and locked at the curb—but all four tires were gone. I phoned Candy and we discussed what to do. As with the FBI visit, I was close to being in shock. "I love you," I said as we hung up.

Not long after Christmas my father had received an overdue notice, addressed to me, on payments for the car I'd gotten (with my parents' $100 down payment as college graduation gift) from my uncle's Riverside Motors in Madison, West Virginia. "YOU TOLD ME THAT YOU WERE KEEPING UP THE PAYMENTS," Gordon Senior had typewritten immediately in a letter of some length, "SUGGEST YOU DISCUSS THIS WITH YOUR EMPLOYER." Now with the vandalism I could see no point at all in even keeping the car: I would give it to my sister and her husband, who'd pick up the remaining pay-ments.

One Thursday night in April, rolling on four new tires purchased at the equivalent of one of the several monthly payments in which I was behind, we were en route to Winston-Salem, North Carolina. Billy—he'd stay a while with his family in Charlotte—was riding down with us. Hours and hours into the trip, off to our left behind shivers of white-and-gray mist over green grass, between dark pines and a rude stand of

Trees of Heaven, the red sun began to grow. We pulled over and got out.
I stood in the silent green grassy dew, camera in hand, shooting, facing
the slowly rising red and mist, as Billy at my side softly urged "Get it, Gor-
don," as if to say "Show what the South is like." We were back, brief as a
dewdrop, in the Green World again.

②

During our visit in their modest red-brick home, Candy and I showed my
parents the silent, twelve minutes of the Easter Be-In in Central Park.
Afterward, my mother took me to the rooms—wall-to-wall carpeted,
like the rest of the house—where Candy and I would sleep. "Couldn't
we share the same one?" I asked my mother with a smile on my face;
I'd thought I'd try being candid, and give it a playful tone. "No!" she re-
sponded sharply, affronted, frightened.

A little later that evening, neither of us able to sleep, Candy and I tip-
toed into the living room. My parents had recently acquired two new
items of furniture: one was a salmon-colored love seat which sat at the
foot of the screen of the Buddhas; the other was a large RCA color TV.
Quietly, we turned on the television and played with form, color, and
motion on screen, watching closely, changing the dial gently. Though we
were being quiet, my parents woke and came in, standing there behind us
in pajama and night gown—and disbelief. The pain on my father's squint-
ing face seemed to say "What a waste of time!" "Wha—? What?" they each
asked us—and our chipper explanations were of no avail. Disheartened
and baffled, undoubtedly, they left the site of news and drama and sports
and soap opera and returned to their room—and we went once more to
our separate ones.

During our time with my parents, Candy, ever garrulous, had spoken
rather volubly about herself, including her marriage. She talked so much
I began to wonder if she'd taken speed. On the way home she volun-
teered, "I think they think of me as a Fallen Woman."

In a year and a half we'd learn of my mother's Alzheimer's.

③

During that weekend Candy and I drove around town and shot azaleas, lilacs, dogwoods, and redbuds in bloom; at one moment, as we stood hugging and kissing in a parking lot by the side of the road, an older man drove by and shouted angrily, "Why don't you go to a motel!"

Later that night, having trouble sleeping alone, I went into the living room and began shooting the ebony, ivory, and jade Chinese screen of infinite Buddhas. Suddenly, my father was in the room, inquiring. "What are you doing?"

"I was trying to shoot all these Buddhas."

"For whom to see? Where will you show it?"

I stood there looking at him, exasperated, inarticulate. Eventually, he explained his worry: "I don't want the IRS to find out."

'66 Frames

ENTER BRAKHAGES

When I was running the film program at Davidson College and began to learn of Jonas Mekas and films carried by Filmmakers' Cooperative, one of the first filmmakers I read about was Stan Brakhage. For his *Dog Star Man,* an extraordinary blurb by Guy Davenport claimed that:

> Not since D.W. Griffith educated all American eyes to see cin-
> ematographically has a different pattern of eyesight been
> offered us, and Brakhage, praise be, is the offerer.
>   . . . American art has had four great masterpieces: *Moby Dick,*
> *Leaves of Grass, The Cantos of Ezra Pound,* and Brakhage's *Dog Star*
> *Man.*

I tracked down the article from which this was excerpted, and discovered it was in the *National Review*—a fortuitous source since its rock-hard conservativeness might appeal to many Davidsonians. I was, of course, already thinking of trying to bring the film to campus: its sixty-minute version, not its completely permutated four-and-a-half hour long *The Art of Vision.*

Dog Star Man was a silent, seventy-five minute amalgam of superimposition and scratching and painting on color film, all shots made with a handheld 16 MM Bolex. Since Brakhage's camera extended the human body, the "errors" in using it off-tripod could be as intrinsic to the work as the heartbeat is to the body: not extrinsic, as in Hollywood and academic presumption. His subject matter was largely, subjectively "home movie" material—and in fact one of his several great, revolutionary contributions to the art of cinema was his demonstration—through his work—that "art" and "home movie" can meet.

But such recognitions came to me some time later. We showed *Dog Star Man* at Davidson in March 1966, three weeks after Teshigahara's *The Woman in the Dunes,* one week before Jonas's *The Brig* was originally scheduled. That we were between or within two worlds—dutiful Presbyterian obligation and unrestrained aesthetic discovery—is suggested by the short film we chose to accompany the Brakhage: *World in Remembrance,* the funeral procession of Winston Churchill.

An audience of perhaps thirty or forty attended. In the ensuing discussion (films were often introduced by faculty or students who then led earnest, semiformal and semipainful discussion afterward) even C. Shaw Smith was laudatory of *Dog Star Man*. Only a week earlier Smith had given me a brief, Babbitt-like in-office lecture on cinema and its depiction of the negative in life: "Oh, we all know life has bad things, the negative and the dreary and the sad," he began, then spread his white-shirted arms, his swivel chair emitting a soft squeak, as he challenged, "Show us some of the good things about life." But this silent work of five parts—a Prelude and four Latin-numeraled sections organized, according to P. Adams Sitney, along the lines of seasonal myth—had been celebrated by poet Michael McClure as a "colossal lyrical adventure-dance of image in every variation of color," and was now proclaimed by Smith as "positive."Positive in what regard, other than basic outlook on life, wasn't clear to me. *Dog Star Man* is not narrative or dramatic in anything like the usual senses (though Davenport saw it as "extraordinarily dramatic"). And its themes, he claimed, "are immemorial: love, death, the family, the man of action." Though there's a repeating sequence in which a man (Brakhage, filmed by wife Jane) struggles—axe on shoulder, dog at snow-encrusted boots—to climb a winter mountainside, there's no clear resolution of his effort. Nonetheless, perhaps it was his effort that pleased Smith.

Brakhage had begun filmmaking over a dozen years earlier, at nineteen, and among his many relatively early works was an exquisitely beautiful piece I saw at the Cinematheque in the fall, *Window Water Baby Moving*. It was a great example of home movies "raised" to art (or art "raised" to home movie), a twelve-minute exposition of Jane's last stage of pregnancy and childbirth, edited with extraordinary power.

By the mid-1960s, Brakhage had become a prime mover in "underground" or "avant-garde" or "independent" or "personal" cinema. After the first weeks of spring 1967, the small New York community of filmmakers eagerly awaited the appearance of Stan and Jane in our subterranean vault just off Times Square, two thousand miles east and nine thousand feet below their snowy Rocky Mountain cabin home. As it happened, the visit followed a week of "FILMS OF JOY/In Honour of the Angry Arts Against the War in Vietnam" that included Richard Aldcroft's *Infinity Machine*, Brakhage's own *23rd Psalm Branch* (part one), my *Georgia*, and Jonas's *Hare Krishna*.

The major event of their visit was the premiere of the second part of Stan's *23rd Psalm Branch*. This was his twenty-third in a series of silent regular

'66 Frames

8 MM *Songs*. A "study of war" that included footage of the Holocaust, it was prompted by the Brakhages' having brought a new TV into their small mountain cabin home: it brought with it America's War in Vietnam. He wrote that this was:

> . . . something in the house that I simply could not photo-
> graph, simply could not deal with visually. It was pouring
> forth war guilt, primarily, into the household in a way that I
> wanted to relate to, if I was guilty, but I had feelings . . . of the
> qualities of guilt and I wanted to have it real for me and I
> wanted to deal with it. And, I mean, it was happening on all
> the programs—on the ads as well as drama and even the
> comedies, and of course the news programs. And I had to deal
> with that. It finally became such a crisis that I knew I couldn't
> deal directly with TV but perhaps I could make or find out why
> war was all that unreal to me . . .

The Cinematheque's ad in the *Voice* billed the April premiere as "THE ONLY PUBLIC APPEARANCE STAN BRAKHAGE IS MAKING IN NEW YORK ON HIS COMING TRIP TO THE EAST COAST," and used a blurb from Allen Ginsberg, who with Peter and Julius Orlovsky had spent several days with the Brakhages in January and seen the new work. Ginsberg celebrated this "collage of visual memories," claiming that "All modern phenomena are crazy and transient as proved by this movie."

Add to the anticipation Jonas's recent inclusion in *Film Culture* of Brakhage's *A Moving Talking and Picture Book,* that home-scale how-to manual of experimental play with the substance of film; Jonas's publishing the critical monograph *Brakhage* by Dan Clark; and my laying hands, around the same time, on Brakhage's own extravagant, extraordinary *Metaphors on Vision,* a multifaceted compendium beginning with a remarkable romantic manifesto:

> Imagine an eye unruled by man-made laws of perspective, an
> eye unprejudiced by compositional logic, an eye which does
> not respond to the name of everything but which must know
> each object encountered in life through an adventure of per-
> ception. How many colors are there in a field of grass to the
> crawling baby unaware of "Green"?

Its range of material, including interviews, poems, letters, and diaries, and excerpts from film scenarios, was no less astonishing—or challenging.

"I don't see how an artist can live in New York," Jane began in answer to a question following Stan's movies as she and her husband stood before two hundred people packed into the Cinematheque. Stan had just spoken of his work, of inspiration from the music of Messiaen. Now much of the audience broke into applause at Jane's words, as if underscoring an argument already developing between Barbara and Candy. Though Barbara had been with us one cold Sunday in the fall when we and filmmaker Piero Heliczer and one or two others drove up into the "wilds" of Westchester County, and though she'd speculate about Jonas, "He's just a fahmah—eventually he'll settle down in the country," she thought living in the country would be boring. Candy, like Jane, was much quicker to condemn city living—for its dangers and unhealthiness—and to propose that we all live someday somewhere in the country.

After the program I talked with Jane near the doorway to the auditorium as others shuttled in and out, milled about. She was tall, slender, bright-eyed, smart, and generous. As we stood talking close to each other, face-to-face (she was two or more inches taller than I), she volunteered her worries about young people taking drugs. I listened quietly, recalling the Black Beauty I'd taken in the morning, while she looked earnestly into my eyes as she spoke.

Stan had visited the Coop earlier in the day. "I've heard of you," he offered kindly when Jonas introduced us, as he shook my hand, wrinkling his brow, staring close into my face. Given his upper body size, his hands were surprisingly small, delicate, with tapering fingers, fresh-skinned, almost the texture of a child's. He was tallish, serious, slightly heavyset, with straight black hair and a black moustache and black eyes wherein I couldn't see the pupils. Though I recall once hearing this man of highly individualistic vision claim to be almost legally blind, his works contain some of the richest images and visual relationships I've seen on film.

BILLY AND ME

the war

Let's begin with a scene from late May 1966 at land-grant, all-male Davidson, where two years of ROTC were required of all students, four for those intending to become military officers: One Tuesday afternoon at 1:30 —the time of the weekly drill—a handful of those of us who weren't pursuing a commission appeared on the low graveled rooftop of our old redbrick Duke Dormitory. Billy Trotter had rigged up an amp-lification system so that when we—in mock military attire, helmets and overseas caps at rakish angles—played excerpts from his LP "phase 4 stereo spec-tacular" *Battle Stereo,* they easily reached the athletic field-parade ground below and beyond. The album, one of those early stereo demonstrations, contained simulations (and live recordings) of battle, marching songs, and speeches from the American Revolution through the Second World War. On one band the voice of an actor playing Jeffer-son Davis declared, amidst rising cheers, that the Confederate states would "make all those who oppose us smell Southern powder and feel Southern steel," and was followed by strains of "Dixie." But the one we played the most and the loudest included gists of a nearly apoplectic Adolf Hitler proclaiming the glories of the Third Reich, followed by thundering cheers of "Sieg Heil! Sieg Heil!" from the German people—and air raid sirens rising over London as the Lüftwaffe bombed.

The Davidson parade ground—a bare hundred yards distant—was filled with young, erect, close-lipped, rifle-bearing men in uniformed for-mation: it was the final and most auspicious ROTC ceremony of the year. A little over a year earlier our first Marines had been sent to a small Southeast Asian nation; only weeks earlier the United States had begun bombing Cambodia as well as the North. Only weeks earlier, "our man" President Nguyen Cao Ky had ordered 1,500 of his troops to crush students, Budd-hists, and military personnel—his fellow countrymen all—who protested his expulsion of a Buddhist general. And there were now over 250,000 lethally armed young Americans in the Republic of Vietnam.

Our prankish demonstration—Billy's brainchild—lasted for some minutes, until an ROTC instructor came running from the parade ground and halted suddenly two stories directly beneath us. Thrusting his clenched, white-knuckled fists in our direction as we peered down over the edge of the flat gravelly roof, young Lieutenant Lawrence threatened us with bodily harm. We (my hair was long enough for North Carolina, May 1966, for someone to report afterward, "They had a girl up there!") tilted our heads, cupped our ears toward our interlocutor. His face now apoplectic, he continued to shout and spit his worst invectives up into our faces. Then, as Hitler's furious volume began to subside, some of my colleagues in grim silence extended raised flattened hands in his direction, in fascist salute.

In New York City throughout the spring of 1967, I continued seeing my friend Billy on and off; different as we were in some ways, we were never really out of touch. In his Twenty-Seventh Street apartment he slept with a prized .30 caliber rifle near his bed, even as his disaffection with the Vietnam War was beginning to match mine. Back at Davidson his active interest in military history, his valorization of military glory, and his basic support of the war (even while parodying militaristic pomp and vainglory from our rooftop) had inspired at least one teasing caricature of him as a militarist. We each had scatological nicknames; he was "Scrotum" as I was "Ballox." Upon seeing my cartoon captioned "General Scrotum Arrives at Tan Son Nhut to Review the Troops," he'd become solemnly offended.

One spring evening in 1967 as I sat in an overstuffed chair in the dark living room of his Twenty-Seventh Street apartment, I spoke what was for me the unspeakable. It came, not without some hesitation, in a moment of rare—if not foolish—candor: "Your love of violence worries me."

And though my suddenly glum companion received my statement essentially in silence there in his small dank living room, Billy was changing some. His responses to two events in the larger world, several months apart, show as much. One evening early in 1967, he'd come to the Cinematheque to tell me that journalist Bernard Fall had just been killed in Vietnam. He wore a scowl of depression on his face as he sat close-mouthed on the imitation marble steps leading into the lobby. As well as regretting his evident unhappiness, I wondered if he were overdoing this: where was his concern for the hundreds of Vietnamese we killed each day? Of course, believing in Fall and his mission, perhaps he would've said Fall was their best hope. I resolved to try to say something; I wanted to extend some fellow-feeling or understanding. But the question I asked,

'66 Frames

awkwardly, was somewhat vulgar, and Billy's answer was sharp and immediate:

"Which side was he on?"

"Both sides."

Billy obviously identified with Fall, whom he saw as a single man carrying out exploits of extreme commitment and risk, facing large terrors, to bring accurate word of them to humanity: a solitary, lonely role for one just and dedicated man.

Fall died in February. I don't remember if Billy was with us on a large peace march to Central Park a little later. On that occasion, a fellow marcher just ahead of us scuffled with one or more bystanders watching from behind the gray wooden NYPD sawhorse barricades. Before companions pulled him back, a few blows toward the face were exchanged. A tallish, slender young man in jeans, with broad shoulders and long blond hair, he explained, emphatically, "He called me a girl!"

But at some point Billy did attend a springtime peace march that also culminated in Central Park. I missed it; he filled me in; he was almost ebullient, euphoric. "Allen Ginsberg spoke," he said. "He got up and declared an end to the war. He read a poem in which he said the war was over." I thought and thought. He did that? Now what does that mean, exactly? How wonderful! There was a vague, puzzling quality to hearing about it secondhand, yet it seemed a brilliant, enlightened, and enlightening thing to do: a breakthrough. It seemed that Billy, too, was exulting some in it, and that added to my joy. What the poet had read was of course, as I'd learn later, the portion of "Wichita Vortex Sutra" where after studying the government's use and mis-use of language to justify the war, after considering war as language-habit, he declares:

> I lift my voice aloud,
> make mantra of American language now,
> I here declare the end of the War!
> Ancient days' Illusion!—

his genius, my curiosity, our history

The same spring evening in which I came out to Billy in halting syllables on what I saw as his love of violence, I also told him that, in a literary sense, he was "possessed." More stumblingly, less directly, I was trying to say that in his dedication, imagination, and accomplishment I saw genius, demonic possession. Inspired by the 1956 Hungarian uprising, he'd written his first novel in his early teens; before turning twenty, he'd completed an extremely long, lyrical, and autobiographical one, as well as much other work of substance.

While he was a small child his father had left for good and his mother remarried, upward, to a quiet, congenial, well-situated contractor. Billy had grown up comfortably with them and a stepbrother, stepsister, and dog in a large upper-middle-class home in Charlotte. He was good looking, with sharp, dramatic features, and dark, luxurious waves of hair; he always seemed to be coming out of a crouch, out of some great knot of absorption and imagination. When he moved, he moved quickly. He wrote nearly constantly, and listened daily to classical music. He was supremely taken with many Romantic works, Sibelius foremost. Davidson had no junior year abroad program, so he'd engineered his own, sending himself to Finland to study Sibelius and the Russo-Finnish War. When I told him I'd be taking Music Appreciation my senior year he offered, "I'll teach you music."

He tended to emphasize the age difference (nineteen months) between us. I've no doubt he saw immediately the even larger difference in psychological maturity and commitment to writing—as he perhaps felt some threat in a younger companion with some aspiration and a little accomplishment. Once in a Charlotte cafe before we knew each other well, he introduced me to some of his friends. He kept saying "This kid," as in "This kid has won more attention for his writing than I have." Then his head would tilt slightly toward the table.

That was shortly after my having won the writing prize my freshman year, which after two years (and volumes of writing) had eluded him. In the middle of my first year I'd gone to look him up in his single upper room in the large four-storied redbrick Belk Dormitory for upper classmen. My knock-on-the-door visit came, ostensibly, in response to an ad he'd posted on a bulletin board to sell a complete set of an Abraham Lincoln correspondence. I wasn't actually interested in the book, but rather in meeting this strange, hermetic upperclassman about whom I'd heard only very little. About whom, it was exclaimed, "He's already written novels!"

I stood there on the greenish-gray linoleum parquet floor of his room as he sat, manual typewriter before him on his formica-topped desk, in a metal chair whose padded plastic seat and back, he complained, wouldn't absorb sweat. I tried desperately to make conversation, and ended up to a much greater degree just smiling a lot, more or less repeating what he was saying, or saying "Oh," or "Yes," and then left. He remembered me later, probably correctly, as "simpering."

We may have run into each other once or twice again that semester. In early June I wrote asking if he'd like to hitchhike to New York with me: this was my New York initiation trip, funded by the $75 prize money. He answered that he couldn't due to previous plans.

So he didn't come, but gradually we became friends. Though he'd read much more and listened to much more, he saw fit to include me in his socializing. He'd come by my room and if I wasn't there leave a note saying "Let's do some serious drinking tonight," and we'd set off together up the road to a gas station tavern a mile north where unlike on campus we were allowed to drink. There behind a counter at an old zinc grill a small, nearly balding blue-eyed gnomish man with tiny points of white on his round head, would tend to our hunger and thirst. In white shirt and apron, he'd cup and shape fresh oily red meat with his hands, then spatula up for us great little vinegar-and-mustard hamburgers as we reveled.

In the sober day-to-day, Billy could sometimes be close-lipped, authoritarian, arbitrary. When once I mentioned I'd been reading poems by Rupert Brooke, he informed me that Brooke wasn't a good poet. To my "Why?" he offered only "I won't tell you." Much more often, he was a generous friend. Already before he left for Finland I'd visited overnight at his Charlotte home. Then after his return—he'd extended his travels and also gone to the Soviet Union, Moscow and Red Square (where he posed for a shot of himself underneath a massive metallic Lenin)—I went there frequently and we enjoyed going out together on many a foray. Once when his parents were away he hosted a large weekend bacchanal, and my girl at the time stayed there with me, overnight. Carla and I were greeted in the morning by a cheery note from our host, found later by his parents, wishing us a good morning, telling us where the orange juice and bacon was.

Looking back thirty years, I wonder that he tolerated me, considering my extraordinary conversational limits alone. "Lo, set we forth, Hrothgar, the world lies before us all beauty and bounty!" I can hear him say one weekend's eve, raising his cup as we supped on mighty bachelor's fare before rolling out for women and song; and I can hear myself answer, quite agreeably, "Yeah."

So we'd ramped and romped together, and he was welcoming, and I learned from him. And always he kept writing, that hacking smoker's cough bracketing his rapid and mighty punches of typewriter keys— "Akh! Akh! Tap!Tap!Tap! Akh! Akh!"—as he hunched over his small, undefended portable typewriter with its thin curled slice of paper. A friend mocked these characteristic sounds of his labors that emanated nightly from his Duke Dormitory room; we could always hear them easily whether we were walking down the hall or outside his open window: his wages of a daily pack or more of Kools, his constant keyboarding.

Billy smoked (like the rest of us), and he drank. He seemed far older, more Southern, than I. He did well with bourbon—which I could scarcely tolerate. He wouldn't really turn on to pot until mid-1968, but he'd taken LSD once in Charlotte, just over a year before I first took it in New York, and had written of it beautifully, intensely, with lush descriptions of even such "simple" pleasures as biting into a ripe red tomato.

He loved the work (and perhaps also the mystique) of that other Carolina étranger in New York, Thomas Wolfe. He once addressed—that is, he lectured informally, like the resident in-house expert that he was— a small seminar class at Davidson on Ernest Hemingway, castigating critics like Leslie Fiedler for their "crocodile tears" at the isolated author's recent suicide.

Most recently—spring 1967—he'd read with admiration John Barth's voluminous *The Sot Weed Factor;* a little earlier, he'd spoken highly of Henry Roth's *Call It Sleep.* The latter could serve as a register of difference between us: Billy relished its raw, vivid depictions of Lower-East-Side immigrants just after the turn of the century, and knew their larger history as well. But he scarcely ventured out among the descendants of the novel's characters two generations later. I, as was typical, didn't read the book, yet I found myself from time to time within the area of Tompkins Square Park, noting from my first visits there in the fall the strange gray quiet people with canes and old pants or floral print dresses, idling eternities on park benches. I never paused to wonder at the fading of their history in the New World, the sad sharp glow of their passing isolation. And never made the connection to my own life, to the white Russians I'd known and even loved at the American School, in Tokyo, many years before.

'66 Frames

Of all contemporary writers Billy most admired Mailer (for both literary gifts and bravura, it seemed), and it was Mailer whom he emulated. And though not without some qualification sometimes, he liked Jack Kerouac as well. In his sophomore year he'd begun reviewing books in the *Charlotte Observer;* in thanks for his "wonderful review" of *Desolation Angels* he received a handwritten page-long letter from Kerouac:

May 13, 1965

Mr William Trotter

Dear Mr Trotter:

Just a note to thank you for the wonderful review of May 5th—I've never written to any of the thousand reviewers who covered the dozen books of mine published here & elsewhere since 1950, but in your case I feel I'm writing to more than a reviewer, to a kindred spirit really—I'm glad you noticed Doctor Sax and the symbol in it, other reviewers & critics merely glanced at it & pronounced it "a childhood reminiscence" & all the time there's that Snake a hundred miles long—I hope to live up to your expectations of a goodly great next "novel"—I'll pin your second-to-last paragraph above my sheets—Yea, "essential goodness to life" and thank God for you.

—Yrs, Jack Kerouac

new york

In New York Billy wrote daily, and went two or three mornings a week to rehearsals of the American Symphony directed by Leopold Stokowski, on whom he was gathering material for a biography. But his efforts at breaking into print weren't succeeding, and he attributed at least part of the problem to the severely arbitrary world of publishing he found within a decidedly "crazy" city of eight million vivid people torn from the green earth to push together upon some few squares of concrete. Take his long novel—autobiographical, Romantic, prolix, and Wolfean—of a young man growing up infatuated with a young woman. Who'd risk marketing that, he might've reasoned, in a mod world of Barnaby Street and psychedelics and Eastern religion and war protest? And at that frenetic

moment how many people read novels, when there were so many excit-
ing things to do?

Of course plenty more or less traditional fiction writers were being
published—his admired Mailer was one example—but they'd broken
through years before. Nonetheless, Billy wasn't utterly without publish-
ing contacts in New York: though follow-up efforts like getting an agent
seemed not to work out, his editor and advisor was the respected Bob
Ballou from Viking Press. And very occasionally a connection with a well-
placed friend might be renewed, as happened one night early in spring.
Carolyn Kizer, our poet friend who'd visited Davidson our senior year,
was reading with Stanley Moss at the YM-YWHA, Lexington Avenue and
92nd Street.

Billy and Candy and I took the subway uptown together. Candy, with
her full, long splay and splash of luxuriant auburn hair, was dolled up in
a black evening dress that came just short of her knees, and surely rav-
ished if not provoked most any male possessed of a pecker.

Carolyn, imposing, big-boned, blond, in a deep blue ankle-length silk
gown, stood easily over six feet high in heels. Her sometimes histrionic
manner of speaking, of dropping names; her occasionally hifalutin dic-
tion and elocution ("autobiography" became "auto-bee-ography"), and
her sheer physical, broad-shouldered blue eye-batting almost John
Wayne-like presence had intimidated some of our fellow students the
previous year at Davidson. They'd found her pretentious: for them, a later
visit by James Dickey with his old Southern drawl, his "That's ver' fahn"
response to every classroom comment on poetry, his smile that broke
across his face like white ocean spray over granite, his strummy guitar
and his ease among males, offered welcome relief.

But for Billy and me, Carolyn was ballsy, generous, and loved to talk,
drink, and arrange things for others. We looked forward to seeing her
again. At the Y we were part of an audience of one or two hundred, the
great majority of them two decades older than the three of us, in a spa-
cious comfortable auditorium with all seats slanting gently down to the
stage. Carolyn read well, except when she twice told the same joke about
an editor—exposition, narrative, punch line. Billy and I exchanged smiles
as the auditorium filled with uncomfortable silence.

Afterward, stageside, she exclaimed, "Oh, Gordon, I know just the
part for you in a movie! I had lunch with Mike Nichols last week, and he's

'66 Frames

planning one with a role you'd be just perfect for!" (It was to be *The Graduate,* with Dustin Hoffman taking the role. But the logistics of how to apply for the role never came up, and I didn't press—until I did call her about it several months later.)

Later at the private reception—Carolyn invited us—our mutual efforts focused on moving Billy in the direction of another guest who'd attended the reading: Norman Mailer. I'd "met" Mailer back at Panna's in April 1966, when Andy Warhol and I were talking, and he had intervened with his self-amused challenge.

Now Candy and I stood in a crowd of formally suited older folk, drinks in their hands; we watched Carolyn (easily half a foot taller, and broader shouldered, than either Billy or Mailer) swoop one long arm, brilliant before it tapered to its pointed end, down around Billy's shoulder as she thrust their way into Mailer's inner circle. Even though we gradually moved quite close, Candy and I couldn't hear a word, but we could see that Billy—whose back was to us—was getting in a good ten minutes with the writer who amounted, more or less, to his idol. Only later could we learn through Billy the gist of what the god had spoken: he'd read a prose sample Billy had sent, praised it generously, then chided: "You write with such emotion that the pencil point breaks. You have to learn to do it without breaking the pencil point."

As Candy and I stood watching, we saw how the two men resembled each other: both were somewhat short, and though the elder was gray-haired and the younger better-looking, the ears of both stuck out widely at their tops, outspanning a head of active hair, tapering into the rest of the flesh at their lobes: in that respect, it was as if one man were speaking to himself.

His discussion concluding, Mailer turned away from Billy and directed himself, bright-eyed and eager, toward Candy in her sophisticated dark dress. "And are you having a pleasant evening, Mrs Trotter?"

Gordon Ball

CANDY ADVISES

Candy was equally appealing one night a little later when Preston Faggart —my art assistant instructor friend whose Main Street apartment had been a Davidson oasis—held an opening for an exhibition of paintings by himself and others in his group. It was a warm evening; daffodils had at last raised their delicate yellow heads somewhere around glass-and-stone Manhattan. Candy attended in tight jeans, tight white T-shirt; a layering of yellow blooms pushed between folds of her rich auburn hair. Preston, a tallish, lanky lover of Duchamp with a way of tilting his head back as he smiled, seemed entirely taken with her on this their first encounter.

Though she was mesmerizingly so at times, Candy wasn't "only" sexually attractive. Older than I and possessed of a far stronger sense of self, she was more the head of our two-person family, more level-headed, more worldly wise, more observant in many ways than I. When later in the year we decided to leave New York for Mexico and held an apartment "yard sale" to get rid of unneeded belongings, it was she who spotted a teenaged kid making off with some of our things when we were distracted by another customer. She ran right out the door after him, shouting, nabbed him on the street, and pulled the goods right back out of his hands. It was she whose voice was calming on the phone after I'd found my car suddenly tireless, it was she who cooked and, at least fifty percent of the time, managed our finances and planned ahead.

And it was she to whom I turned for advice for how to deal with others. For perhaps two weeks I'd been stewing about a notice Jonas had posted at the Coop regarding a European tour he was planning. Together with film critic P. Adams Sitney (the young scholar of long beard and small spectacles, whom I'd heard at Lincoln Center) he'd be taking a package of recent American avant-garde work for showings in England, France, Italy, and the Netherlands over the summer. *Georgia* was not among them; I simply rolled it back and forth in my own mind, taking it as another sign of my inferiority, some sort of "just" rejection or neglect. Finally, as Candy and I lay side by side in the comfort of our mattresses on the floor a fortnight later, I broke loose and mentioned it to her. Immediately I heard her reply: "Why don't you ask Jonas if he'd take it? You don't know but that he might've meant to."

'66 Frames

The next time I saw Jonas, we stood face-to-face in the Coop; I asked, and he answered "Yes," without hesitation. I felt gratified, but a little vexed, too: feeling I'd manipulated him, knowing that it would be going not on his but my initiative. Likely I'd become too attached to one good thing. Candy would tell me later, "I thought you just wanted to keep showing *Georgia* and getting praise."

MILLBROOK

①

Come May the air turned mild, windows could stay open by day, and heat pipes were cured of their coughs. In the late winter and early spring we'd thought several times of going off to the country, even if just briefly, but the city kept us within its canyons. Now, as the warming world seemed to call irresistibly to venture forth, the running city-versus-country argument between Barbara and Candy moved to a back burner: Barbara Rubin had a boyfriend.

David Hoff was a photographer who had a loft in the lower midtown area, on West Twenty-Eighth Street. He was, in manner and appearance, as Barbara rightly said, "an angel." No older than she, he was slightly built and slender, very pale skin with a flat, beautiful white complexion, large broad forehead, mass of curly black hair. He was utterly striking; the only resemblance I've found was in Johnny Depp as Edward Scissorshands.

This new relationship tended to preoccupy Barbara; at gatherings the two of them could be seen quietly and closely together: it seemed strange to see her physically close with someone. In the meantime, Candy was giving increasing consideration to the idea of our visiting Millbrook, the large ten-mile square (2,500 acre) estate which Mellon heir Billy Hitchcock had loaned to Timothy Leary as a haven to continue his psychedelic inquiries. Why not spend a weekend there, Candy had wondered.

She'd already checked with Leary. One late February afternoon had found us seated with two dozen or so other young people on the floor of the small storefront headquarters of Leary's League for Spiritual Discovery, at the corner of Hudson Avenue and West Tenth Street. As late afternoon slants of light illuminated floor and carpet, Leary, on the floor along with everyone else, responded to question upon question:

"I've been asked to address what we should do about those who are starving in India. . . . Don't get too involved in the antiwar movement; it will tie you up fruitlessly when you want to be exploring inner space . . . 'Give to Caesar what is Caesar's.'"

As discussion came to an end, Candy approached Leary, smiling easily above his long jutting chin, and asked if we might spend a weekend at

Millbrook. "Yes, sure," he answered. "The main house isn't really open, but there's an ashram there with Art Kleps, and you can sleep on the grass or in the woods. There are also just a few people scattered around, camping—living—among the woods."

Leslie let me go an hour early from work on Friday, May 4, and in late golden light we boarded the train at Grand Central for the small upstate town of Millbrook. From this community a year earlier, zealous District Attorney G. Gordon Liddy and twenty-one fellow government agents-in-arms—Duchess county Sheriff's officers—had launched a middle-of-the-night raid into the main house on the Hitchcock estate, arresting Leary and three others. Doing so, they'd found, to their alleged shock and horror, some of the thirty people there totally naked in bed as they slept. Only three persons, all guests, were found with drugs—a miniscule amount of marijuana. Liddy and other agents of the state had planned the raid in part because, as the Duchess County Sheriff explained on the soundtrack of Jonas's *Report from Millbrook,* they'd seen "strange" goings-on: signs of interest in Eastern religions. Their suspicions proved justified, the Sheriff suggested, beyond the slight amount of marijuana that was found. Evidently an orgy was going on, because "There was one fellow playing a guitar and another playing a banjo. Someone was blowing a flute. There were colored candles giving off a strange light and I think I smelled incense."

By the time Candy and I—walking on foot, small packs on our backs —got to the estate, the last of the day's tiny mayflies danced in dying amber light. We visited only briefly in the ashram—Sri Rama Ashrama— then went down to the extremely large flat green lawn beneath an extremely large white frame main house—"The Big House." Painted on its front was an enormous, Hindu-styled smile in reddish purple. We laid out our ground cloth and blankets, and slept soundly.

The next morning we visited at the ashram again with large blond Art Kleps and several others in the kitchen that was locked nightly so strangers wouldn't help themselves. They offered us breakfast. Things seemed to be proceeding nicely until one of them saw Candy with my Revere in one hand, and said immediately, "You'll have to leave." Meaning, the ashram.

Once suspicions have been aroused, even within people whom you feel sure are of like mind, how do you explain you're not police or their

Gordon Ball

accomplices? A year later in Mexico I'd wonder how to explain I wasn't guilty, as strangers and acquaintances alike eyed me while I walked along the Puerto Vallarta beach in the commanding khaki presence of the Chief of Police—and again, two days later, as suited federal agents in the capital escorted me onto a Delta plane for deportation. How to speak?

Candy and I headed into the woods, up a trail littered with the fall's once brilliant leaves, past a stone gate—the ten miles square were ours to roam. We walked farther into the woods and came to a clearing. Joyously —after the manner of Jerry Joffen, as I'd seen in Jonas's *Film Magazine of the Arts*—I started my Revere on continuous and threw it up in the air, that it might move, in great big washes, sky and cloud and sun and tree and leaf and ground and air.

We continued into the woods, past large naked scraggly trees with scarcely a hint of tender green; we stepped across gullies and looped along hillocks. We came to another sort of leaf-floored clearing only smaller and hillier than before; we were in deep now. We decided to set up camp.

We were on somewhat of a ridge, bare deciduous trees stretching up forty feet or more all around us, and to one side, distant, there seemed another ridge, perhaps with a road on it, for I once thought I saw or heard a car. The views in other directions were filled with trees near and far, and hardly any had started to bud or leaf. Though it was now in the sixties and seventies, warm enough for mayflies, it was still early May at 42° latitude. The thick layering of last year's fall shuffled and crinkled with our every step.

Setting up camp was simple: clearing a small area of myriad layers of orangish brown brittle leaves, laying down groundcloth and blankets, food and utensils for tonight's dinner over a fire. Then we had a snack and at one o'clock in the afternoon we each took a half tablet of ritalin, a "psychic energizer" (as it was called) which a friend had given us—and one small white Owsley "White Lightning," the LSD said to have been manufactured at the underground lab of Stanley Augustus Owsley.

Against a log we lay back side by side, on—in—within the sea of leaves, looking up at sky, waiting for the acid to take effect. As it did so, my eyes began tracing Buddha faces in the gentle cumulus clouds hanging in the blue. After some minutes—twenty, a half hour or so—Candy, at my left, turned to me. "Gordon, are you all right?"

"Yes, I think so."

"I think we're dying."

'66 Frames

Immediately I sensed myself melting into the earth, into the old brown mottled leaves. I looked at my hand and saw no longer the mayflies that had danced about us; now maggots crawled in my flesh, which was drawn tight and thin: brown, scaly, wrinkled. We helped each other to our feet and I looked Candy in the face and watched her age a millennium in a moment—as when a child I'd beheld a lovely woman on a Hollywood screen become an instant's thousand-year-old mummy: Candy's face, like my hand, became drawn and tight and brown and richly scored, scaled, even, with leathery wrinkles. We looked to the trees, and found them full of silver webs of energy: each looked the same as the other. There was an overriding sound of a generator—it seemed to be the generator of the universe and it kept winding up and winding down. When it began to wind back down we'd sink back into the earth, into the leaves, become buried with all the other decaying organic matter as we became part of it—and when it would again accelerate we'd rise back up—but only to continue back down. We couldn't resist it; our bodies simply melted back into earth and leaves.

We would again summon ourselves to our feet, and then the generator of the universe—an audible force that sustained us and all other things—would again begin to close down on us, come to a halt, bring us back to the earth and its decay. Then slowly we'd rise once more. Over and over again: the sky would grow darker, the trees would begin to bend, a drone that seemed to be life-sustaining would bend downward on the scale into a diminuendo, and we would sink back into the earth again. We tried to break loose and went running in one direction and then another but each gave the same prospect: a forest of denuded trees with silver bands of energy lining the branches.

We kept rising and falling, melting back into the leaves, rising again, only to melt back into the earth. "Don't you see, Gordon," Candy said at one point, "We're just going through cycles—it's life, death, and rebirth"—but I couldn't grasp that. And it wouldn't stop.

"We're gettin' out of this!" she fairly shouted, erect, defiant. But wherever we turned we saw the same trees with the same silver webs of energy. We could no longer find campsite, groundcloth, camera.

And we kept going through it, rising and falling, as the sky would darken and the droning generator of the universe continued to plunge again and then start up again, with a rhythm of its own that yet was in tune with our individual organisms, earth, and universe. I thought that through the bare trees on that other ridge in the distance I saw a car move along a road—and then it seemed as if we might be hearing a helicopter and might be in Vietnam. I thought of Allen Ginsberg and called out loud for him, realizing I didn't know how to communicate. The sky seemed to be growing darker even on the ascending cycles and I could sense that hours had passed. I imagined a filler in the *New York Times,* "Bodies of Couple Found at Millbrook."

Now the sky turned even darker. We continued to look and run in one direction, then another; every side was the same, each tree was identical with silver webs of energy lining its boughs, and the degeneration, our sinking back down then rising up, sinking down and rising up, continued. Finally we went running, screaming through the darkening woods, yelling "Help! We're dying! Help!"

We stripped naked and tried fucking but we couldn't. It was as if we were already no longer alive. I put a rock into my mouth and tried biting it as hard as I could to force life, sensation, into our midst. We tried biting each other to bring ourselves back to life. But we were still dying.

Then we found ourselves on a path under a much darker sky, near a large tree. By now it was dusk; we went over to sit at the base of the tree. "Gordon, think of your mother," Candy said, and I saw her face.

Way far away up the path a hazy yellow light appeared. I couldn't tell the nature of its source, only that it seemed to be coming gradually closer. We could make out a figure, some kind of upright humanlike figure moving within the yellow light. But I couldn't tell the nature of the light, the nature of the figure, nor the time or space plane to which it belonged.

The figure came closer through the darkness. We'd risen to our feet and now stood in the path, watching.

"Do you people need help?" the figure's voice called as it drew closer.

"Yes, we're dying," I explained, running several steps toward him. I could see he wore something like a gray jumper over a plaid shirt and I reached out and pressed his upper arm between my fingers. It was alive, whole, rubbery, and responded to the touch. I pressed my own and it was no longer brown and scaly but white and rubbery. Candy and I pressed each other.

'66 Frames

"You have to understand," the figure said. He was tallish, young, dark-haired, square-jawed. "I live in a world where there's supermarkets, high-ways, and cars. I'm Jackie Leary," he said. "How did you get here?"

We explained, and as the darkness above turned to a clear night sky, a rich deep blue with stars, he led us on the path six or seven minutes to a campsite. There up on a hillside around a fire was another couple five or six years older than ourselves; the man had left his career in radio and advertising. They had two small children. They welcomed us, Jackie left, and they gave us food to eat around the fire, and blankets; then they retired to their tent.

Candy and I huddled together, bright flesh upon bright flesh, hair and lips and ears and cock and breasts all alive, heart beating, heart beating, under the blankets, next to the breathing and dying red fire in the darkness, under the old dark blue sky and high silver unblinking stars, and slept.

②

"Bardo Follies."

"What?" I answered.

George Landow was another young filmmaker, seemingly older than I. He had reddish brown hair, a handlebar sort of moustache, spectacles; one evening early in the year he sat in the front seat next to me as I drove the small cross streets of the East Village.

I thought George was referring to Brigitte Bardot, but he explained that this title of his new film referred to the Bardo planes found in the *Tibetan Book of the Dead,* the handbook for priests and family to guide the dying one through levels of consciousness, ego surrender, death, and reincarnation.

Months later, not long after that early May weekend in Millbrook, an analogy had become clear to me: I began reading the *Tibetan Book of the Dead,* translated by Evans-Wentz. Leary of course had seen the connection early on, and with Ralph Metzner and Richard Alpert had published their own adaptation. Though some readers complained that *The Psychedelic Experience* too easily appropriated Eastern archetypal imagery for Western assimilation, that didn't bother me. Leary, in any case, had been quite sensible in his laying out in print elementary ground rules for the taking of LSD, centering on the importance of set and setting: his advice was to take

acid when you were in a good state of mind (calm, relaxed, not undergo-
ing a crisis); to take it with a trusted friend (perhaps who was not himself
tripping, but who was experienced in psychedelic voyaging); to take it in
a place that was familiar, comfortable. In leaving for Millbrook as we did
we were of course running a risk. But we'd taken LSD nearly forty times,
and seemed to do well, and to trust each other—and of course had asked
Leary himself about going there, assuming he realized we might well trip
there. And we chose to take, perhaps wrongly, the ritalin with the LSD,
introducing a new chemical agent along with a new setting. "Don't bite
off more than you can chew' would seem to be the moral," said Stanley
one evening when I told him of it. I thought too of a line Leary had writ-
ten somewhere, that he who begins in laughter ends in tears.

The experience had affected us profoundly and though I wanted to think
I hadn't become an obsessive Ancient Mariner, I did tell others besides
Stanley of it, I did speak with something like new authority. An instance
is etched strongly in memory: a young Argentinian perhaps a few years
older than I—I forget what he did or why he was visiting—came by the
Coop one day later in May, and wanted to see some of my work. A devo-
tee of surrealism, he was a short fellow with long black hair, glasses.
    We used the projector down the hall at the Filmmakers' Distribution
Center, after working hours, and Billy came over too, from his apartment
just a few blocks away. After the showing our guest seemed pleased; then,
somehow, I got into a discussion of LSD with him. As the several of us
walked through the Center's narrow doorway and into the not much
larger corridor that led past the Coop to the street, I continued our dis-
cussion. "LSD prepares you for death, you see, that's a basic purpose in tak-
ing it, to deal with, to bring about the loss of ego," I allowed.
    Billy was just behind us, and I thought I could sense his shudder.

Viewed from a distance of thiry years, were the drugs I took a good thing?
How about those available now, such as crack? Is it time for me to renege?
    I—and I assume many others like me—took psychedelics and mari-
juana not for oblivion, not for escape from pain. As the Millbrook episode
suggests, sometimes the experience afforded could be quite painful—and
also life-enriching. Of course, one might counter that "Millbrook" as

'66 Frames

experienced by others, or by ourselves in somewhat different circumstances, might have resulted in personal injury or even death. But as Allen Ginsberg once reported, the death rate associated with LSD use at its height was lower than that of suicide among people who worked in television. Naturally there was an element of risk. I recall being in the company of an American minister and a fellow hippie once in Mexico. My companion asked the minister, "What do you think of LSD?" As I heard him begin, "I think it can be dangerous . . ." I sat there quietly thinking to myself, "Can't believing in God also be?"

I was, as I said much earlier in this volume, searching for Absolute Reality: I believed there was such a thing, and thought or hoped I could find it by psychedelic voyaging. Robert Du Peintre proposed that I might see my soul, which would manifest as a white light. I never did, and today have a very different sense of "soul" and "reality"—but remain indebted to psychedelic experiences in my early days.

Of course, not all drugs open doorways to truth. Amphetamines, for example, as I learned years ago, are destructive. But today I am shocked to see all or many drugs frequently lumped together, indiscriminately (see, for example, the "public service" message, "Your Brain on Drugs"). LSD is (or can be) educational; heroin closes down awareness; crack invites mayhem and destruction of the sort falsely attributed to marijuana by Narcotics Commissioner Harry Anslinger two generations ago when he convinced our politicians to criminalize it in the first place. (A statistic commonly cited today associates over 400,000 deaths a year with tobacco, none with marijuana.) And I take exception to the way our government has handled our "wars" on drugs so as to make the problem worse. This includes Nancy Reagan's simple-minded "Just Say No." Thirty years ago we were just saying, with curiosity, "Oh?"

In 1969, I visited my parents from the upstate New York farm that Allen Ginsberg had purchased as a retreat for fellow poets. While visiting I tried, for an extended moment, to build a bridge of understanding. "I'm a truth freak," I began by saying, not without some anxiety as to its reception by my mother and father. I proceeded to express my feelings about life and—well, not drugs (that seemed beyond the pale)—but a matter only slightly less controversial: the war. But certainly I had drugs in mind as well.

My father proposed, "You should write and publish your views." Before responding, I thought not only of the illegal use of government power against war protestors, but also of the attempted set-up of Gins-berg himself (because of his outspoken candor on drugs) by New York Narcotics Bureau agents. "No," I answered my father, "I'm afraid I'll be arrested." Now, thirty years later, I rise to my father's challenge.

3

DEPARTURE

THE COOP IN SUMMER

Meanwhile back at the Coop, visitors would stop by from time to time.
One early summer afternoon Andy called to me, just to talk, from imme-
diately outside the unscreened open window where I typed. I hadn't
sought any further movie work with him; perhaps I was constrained a lit-
tle ever since, late in the winter, I asked Leslie what he thought of Andy,
and Leslie pronounced him, in a negative sense, a "magician." But I always
liked seeing him.

I had, actually, been shy about another opportunity as well: Michel-
angelo Antonioni had come to town—in fact, I'd later learn, his visit
included a look at some of Andy's films at the Factory. He was casting the
male and female lead in his next movie—at the end of his search, he'd
select two unknowns to star in *Zabriskie Point*. I expressed interest in it to
Leslie, who said I could take part of a day off to go downtown for it—but
I hesitated, held back.

Later in the summer a fiery, earnest, "conscience-bound" letter came
from two thousand miles away, nine thousand feet up. Stan Brakhage asked
that all of his films at the Coop be returned to him. He explained, in part:

> I cannot, in good conscience, continue to accept the help of
> institutions (for that is what they have become) which, thru
> the imbalances of the works of unaesthetic and thoughtless
> self(ish) expression they do mostly distribute and show-forth,
> have come to propagate advertisements for forces which I rec-
> ognize as among the most destructive in our world today:
> "dope," self-centered Love, unqualified Hatred, Nihilism, vio-
> lence to self AND society. . . .

Though he never identified Andy Warhol or any other filmmaker by
name, some of us wondered if it weren't in some measure, at least, a reac-
tion to Warhol. A story which I heard later was that in 1965 Jonas had given
the visiting Brakhage a viewing of *Eat* and *Sleep* so that he could see, as
Jonas remembered the words of his guest, "'what's the noise all about.'"
After looking at *Sleep* Brakhage complained angrily; Jonas proposed that
he look at the films at sixteen frames per second instead of twenty-four.
Brakhage then gave Warhol a more favorable viewing—at slower speed.

But in the summer of 1967, Brakhage's prolix, fulminating letter shocked me, and I worried about the Coop without him. Of course, regarding the two filmmakers (assuming, as we surmised, that Warhol was the biggest bee in Brakhage's bonnet), their fundamental differences were striking. For Stan Brakhage, the manner and matter of Andy Warhol might well have represented much that was "wrong" with cinema: a demythifying stationary camera with its mostly single takes of a single, sometimes static activity—eating, sleeping, a blow job depicted unblinkingly from the recipient's neck up; all of Andy's silvery, voyeuristic, reductive detachment. Such approaches may have flown in the face of Brakhage's romantic, lyrical sturm und drang impulse for myth-making, autobiography, multilayering of images, rapid camera movement, rapid cutting, and rich almost fauve-like color and composition, his wholly expressionistic involvement with subject and medium. And he may well have disapproved of what he took to be Warhol's values. But in the end, he kept his films at the Coop—and Andy moved toward larger scale production and distribution.

"Bonne chance!" The large, somewhat puffy-faced olive-skinned man in an impressive gray suit waved jauntily at Leslie and me as he left the Coop one day. He'd been in only a moment, chatting briefly with Leslie, on his way out from a longer interview at the Distribution Center.

"Ooh, yuck!" Leslie exclaimed, laying his Phillip Morris in its ashtray next to his lighter and pinching his nose, barely an instant after the other gentleman was out the door. "That cologne'll be with us all month!"

The man's world was "film," but it was virtually as different a world as there could be from Jonas's world, our world: as different as his fine suit and cologne from Jonas's corduroy and large peasant hands; as different as Brakhage from Warhol. Andrew Sarris, whom I'd seen on stage in Lincoln Center, had advanced the auteur theory in America, championing not only Bergman and Antonioni in their early and relatively unknown days, but American directors such as Howard Hawks. And though he and Jonas had been colleagues at the *Village Voice* (and even worked together on Jonas's *Film Culture*), his interest was the narrative feature: he once wrote that *The Life of Maria Montez* was the best movie he'd ever seen. He was distinctly uninterested in, even unsympathetic toward, the nonnarrative, experimental, lyrical, minimalist, or personal: in a story headlining the front page of the *Village Voice* some years later he'd proclaim, after seeing the religious experience brought to film—*Wavelength* by the Canadian artist Michael Snow—and other recent works, that AVANT-GARDE FILMS ARE MORE BORING THAN EVER.

office guests and workers

Another afternoon brought a friend from Davidson: tall, slender, serious, narrow face, dark hair, rosebud lips and glasses. Under the aegis of English and drama professor Goodykoontz, Robert Chumbley had, with Billy Trotter, "gotten into trouble" at Davidson my freshman year. How? As a result of their efforts to get a typewriter and other humble forms of support for the drama program. Feeling hornswaggled by the administration, they made their cause public in the student paper, and a frustrated Goodykoontz ended up erecting a bulletin board display attacking the college president—and resigning. For their efforts, Chumbley and Trotter were chastised by one of the Davidson community's most venerated pillars, the cadaverous Dean of the Faculty, Frontis (we called him "Frontispiece") Johnson, who in his own letter to the *Davidsonian* fulminated over their "puerile fulminations." A year later, Bob Chumbley was the only Davidson student of the nearly one thousand in chapel one morning whom I saw remain seated when we were asked to stand in honor of the excellent performances of our recently returned basketball team. I admired him.

Now in his second year at Yale graduate school, Chumbley was in the city on a brief visit. I showed him around the office, showed him my large desk, typewriter, telephone, oversized black loose-leaf notebook filled with filmmakers' account sheets, and the film room. He smiled politely, nodded, said "Oh, I see," once or twice. Then he extended his hand and shook mine as we said good-bye. What was I doing, I asked myself.

Over the summer, a recent NYU graduate helped part-time in the Coop. Jon Sholle was quiet, modest, sensitive, with a big craggy friendly face, broad shoulders. He'd majored in filmmaking, but—since he hid it under a bushel basket—it was months before I learned that he was an extraordinary guitar player. At age twelve, he'd left his Great Neck home for the Union Grove Fiddlers' Convention in North Carolina, where he won the major guitar competition, defeating many southern bluegrass musicians four and five times his age.

Now the days were long and my side of the office would sometimes light with stretching shafts of gold. Traffic outside my open window could grow heated; a little carbon monoxide would push its way in— along with shouts and yells and softer clusters of sidewalk syllables. The small grocer at the southwest corner of Thirty-First raised his green awning and arrayed the near end of the sidewalk outside with shiny fruits. The deli across from him had its usual coffee and sandwiches ready-made and made to order, and the welcome, in both Barney's sharp cheery Bostonian and Raul's voluble Puerto Rican, grabbed you like instant rec-ollection each time you pushed through the aluminum frame glass door.

But at the Coop we had work to do, even though rentals—many of our customers were universities—tended to lighten in the summer. Still, we were young—Jon and I were only twenty-two—and sometimes when Leslie stepped out a moment we'd toss wads of paper at each other and loosen up; I even drew a cartoon of the office at play in moments when Felix the Cat was away. The whole phenomenon of Zip Code, introduced two years earlier, was now taking hold; the Post office had launched a large promotional campaign to encourage its use, featuring a rather silly big-eyed, smiling but responsible citizen cartoon stick figure in postal uniform named Mr Zip. I applied the name to Jon, called him "Mr Z.," and we carried on, like the boys we still were, as the days were long.

CATALOGING THE COOP

By midsummer, new material arrived daily for listing in the Coop's fourth catalog, which would be two and a half times as large as the 1964 edition. When it appeared in the fall, it would list four hundred works by over sixty filmmakers. In dignified white block lettering near the bottom, its optimistic red cover would proclaim:

TWO SERVICES

nontheatrical orders to: commercial/theatrical orders to:
Filmmakers' Cooperative   Filmmakers' Distribution Center

ONE ADDRESS
175 Lexington Avenue, New York, N.Y. 10016

Among the entries were new ones such as Thom Anderson's *Melting;* classic works such as Kenneth Anger's *Fireworks* and *Scorpio Rising;* Bruce Baillie's *All My Life,* his three-minute pan across a fence full of climbing red roses while Ella Fitzgerald sings "All My Life"; many silent "songs" from Brakhage; *Breathing, Fist Fight,* and *66* by animator Robert Breer; and a number of antiwar films, such as Peter Gessner's *Time of the Locust,* made with "American newsfilm, combat footage shot by the National Liberation Front of South Vietnam, and suppressed film taken by Japanese cameramen."

There was Jeff Begun's *Please Cancel My Conscription to Your Army, Or How I Learned to Stop Worrying and Drop the Bomb,* made "with a cast of dozens." There was *Antifilm #2* by George Binkey, a career diplomat-bureaucrat-lion hunter who in actuality was Adolfas Mekas. Pola Chapelle was represented by a funny film: *A Matter of Baob* scoured the 1967 Montreal Film Festival's purple paean to cinema as the most ennobling art of all. For the fifty seconds in which a voice-over reads the festival flyer's bombast, we see Adolfas and Pola, Storm de Hirsch, and others, in formal attire under chandeliers at a white-linened dinner table, glasses and elbows swinging high in mock riotous drunkenness.

Stan Brakhage listed some sixty films: thirty-seven in 16 MM, including *Window Water Baby Moving* and many other classic works; and all twenty-three of his 8 MM *Songs,* including the recently premiered *23rd Psalm Branch.* Shirley Clarke's ranged from *Dance in the Sun* through *The Cool World* and a documentary on Robert Frost. And there was the most memorable work I'd seen at Lincoln Center in the fall of 1966, Tony Conrad's *The Flicker* ("The first fully atmospheric development of stroboscopic light as an expressive medium," explained Conrad).

Wheeler Dixon, a young, energetic and good-looking blond fellow from New Jersey, listed four short works. He came by the Coop one afternoon, went back to Thompson Street with me, and visiting till it grew late, stayed over. He slept with us on our mattresses, and though I knew he knew of our rather extraordinary sexual hospitality, I made a point of doing nothing to encourage any interest he might have in Candy. As we three began drifting off to close-quartered sleep, I imagined his desire while I thought, uncomfortably, of my closing the door on it. I knew nothing of what Candy felt.

There were three delicate color films by Nathaniel Dorsky, who in later years would edit *What Happened to Kerouac?* and other works. There was Robert Downey's *Babo 73,* with the girlish, campy, delightful Taylor Mead playing the President of the United States. The group of artists known as Fluxus, headed by George Maciunas, Jonas's friend and fellow Lithuanian, were represented in a "Fluxfilm Program—Summer, 1966 Version" that included John Cavanaugh's three-minute "Blink" and Yoko Ono's five-minute "No. 1."

There also was Robert Frank's (and Alfred Leslie's) *Pull My Daisy* with Corso, Ginsberg, Orlovsky, Larry Rivers, Delphine Seyrig, David Amram, and others, and Kerouac's improvised voice; Jean Genet's "un-adorned anecdote of prison life," *Un Chant d'Amour;* the "discovery" of the 1965 Pesaro Film Festival, Peter Emanuel Goldman's scriptless dramatic feature, *Echoes of Silence;* and John Hawkins's LSD *Wall,* an accurate representation of psychedelic experience.

Ken Jacobs's first *Little Stabs at Happiness,* a home movie recollection of friends or friendships mostly gone, was followed by all of Peter Kubelka's magnificent work, from *Mosaik im Vertrauen* through *Unsere Afrikareise.* Gregory Markopolous claimed five pages, from his adaptation of *A Christmas Carol,* made at age twelve, through recent releases such as *Galaxie.* In making each of *Galaxie*'s thirty three-minute color portraits (of Jonas, W.H. Auden, Ginsberg and Orlovsky, Panna Grady, and others) he ran the film through the camera as many as ten times, so "all fades, dissolves, single frames were literally conceived and executed during the moment of the 'sitting.'"

Jonas's first release, his 1963 "bitter but lyric" *Guns of the Trees,* with poetry voiced by Ginsberg, was followed by a handful of others, including *Film Magazine of the Arts.* He began this 1963 work (which depicted, among other scenes, the Joffrey Ballet in rehearsal, Warhol in the Factory, Shakespeare in the Park), only after asking the producers from *Show* magazine "why did they want me to make it—didn't they know I was a bit unusual. . . ?" "We want something unusual," they said, before destroying the rough cut he brought them.

Accompanying over a dozen works by Marie Menken was a blurb from Stan Brakhage: "She, Gertrude Stein, and my wife are the three women who have most influenced my life."

And there was Ron Rice's *The Flower Thief,* and several works by José Rodriguez-Soltero. In the spring of 1966, as the U.S. commitment to war and destruction continued to mount—B-52s raided North Vietnam for the first time—Rodriguez-Soltero had shocked even most of a small Village audience by burning an American flag as he performed his *LBJ* at the Bridge Theatre. Early in the fall of 1967, when he heard I was about to leave for Mexico, he asked me to interview Luis Buñuel for the new film magazine he was putting out. I loved *Exterminating Angel*—I laughed out loud when I saw it—but beyond *Un Chien andalou* and *Simon of the Desert,* I'd seen nothing else by him. Quietly, I backed out.

And here at last was Barbara Rubin's thirty-minute *Christmas on Earth* with its call for two projections (one, smaller, superimposed within the other) for its two reels of engaged human flesh, faces in white grease paint. The film, Barbara told us in a note, "has neither head nor tail—it can be projected either way." Jonas commented extensively:

> *Christmas on Earth:* A woman; a man; the black of the pubic hair; the cunt's moon mountains and canyons . . . image after image, the most private territories of the body are laid open for us . . . the first shock changes into silence, then is transposed into amazement. We have seldom seen such down-to-earth beauty, so real as only a terrible beauty can be; terrible beauty that man, that woman is, are, that Love is.
>
> Do they have no shame? This eighteen-year-old girl, she must have no shame, to look at and show the body so nakedly. Only angels have no shame. . . .

And Barbara returned with a postscript:

> A week out of nine months of mental hospital indoctrination
> and I meet Jonas and he gives me a camera and film love and
> trust and I shoot up down around back over under and shoot
> over and over speedily slow back and front end, the subject
> chosen by the creeping souls of the moment cocks and cunts,
> love supreme can believe to fantasy I then spent 3 months
> chopping the hours and hours of film up into a basket and
> then toss and toss flip and toss and one by one absently
> enchanted destined to put it together and separate onto two
> different reels and then project one reel half the size inside the
> other reel and then show it and someone tells me what a good
> editing job I did . . .

Harry Smith's "cinematic excreta" (his own words) followed *Christmas on Earth,* with a blurb from Jonas that "Harry Smith is the only serious film animator working today." And here was Jack Smith's *Scotch Tape* and *Flaming Creatures,* with the Fifth Independent Film Award from Jonas's *Film Culture,* proclaiming that he:

> . . . has graced the anarchic liberation of new American cin-
> ema with graphic and rhythmic power worthy of the best of
> formal cinema. He has attained for the first time in motion
> pictures a high level of art which is absolutely lacking in deco-
> rum. . . .

Billy Trotter listed his Eisenstein parody, *The Battle of Goat Island:* it was "the world's first 8 MM epic," shot "on-the-run" with "over 100 bellicose" Davidsonians; at times "this chamber epic" "even transcends the limit-ations of 8 MM." And finally there was Andy Warhol, with forty-three films described over seven pages, the last three or four given to fine-print blurbs on *The Chelsea Girls* alone. It began with an excerpt from *Film Culture*'s Sixth Independent Film Award:

> Andy Warhol is taking cinema back to its origins, to the days
> of Lumiere, for a rejuvenation and a cleansing. . . . he has
> abandoned all the "cinematic" form and subject adornments
> that cinema had gathered around itself until now. . . . he
> records, almost obsessively, man's daily activities, the things
> he sees around him. . . .

A descriptive listing of films completed between 1963 and 1966 included *Kiss; Sleep; Eat; Blow Job; Couch* (with Ginsberg, Orlovsky, Ker-ouac, and others); *Henry Geldzahler* (a hundred-minute "two-reel portrait of Henry Geldzahler smoking a cigar"); *Camp* ("Warhol's first film to utilize bad camera work, zooming, panning, acting"); and *My Hustler.*

As I review these promotional notes from yesteryear, I'm preparing to leave for a major American film festival, where I have been invited to speak on a film by Robert Frank, and to show a portion of my own work. Ken Jacobs is to be one of the festival's featured filmmakers, and Shirley Clarke's *The Connection,* as well as Warhol's *Chelsea Girls,* are among the films.

Meanwhile, Jonas Mekas no longer has to move locations from season to season: his showcase and repertory Anthology Film Archives is not a subterranean outpost but a center of film exhibition, study, and preservation in Manhattan. That circumstance, and the health of Filmmakers' Cooperative (and San Francisco's Canyon Cinema), as well as the existence of numerous other distributors for independent films and videos today (Women Make Movies is a prominent example), testify to the soundness of Jonas's pioneering concept and models.

The term "independent film" is used much more broadly today than in the 1960s. I find myself still sentimentally and aesthetically attached to the earlier sense of it as a highly individualistic work, concerned more with personal vision than PBS or larger audiences. At the same time, I appreciate the wide range of approaches I see today. Broadly speaking, "Hollywood" films remain far more visible, but Hollywood has been profoundly influenced by "underground" films (even as, astoundingly, it continues to pump out much of the same vacuous fare). Martin Scorsese, for example, thanked Jonas Mekas "for teaching me patience and teaching me how to see"; Woody Allen is on the Board of Directors of Anthology Film Archives. While in many theatrical films the Steadicam is de rigeur, expressive use of handheld camera is far more prevalent than a generation ago. Much of the cutting in commercial cinema (as well as music video) is reminiscent of that in some works from the 1960s; and today's expanded content (in subject and language) can be seen in light of groundbreaking "transgressions" from that earlier era: the everyday jazz musician talk in *The Connection* which caused the film to be banned a year in New York; the "lurid" content of works by Jack Smith and Andy Warhol.

With all its hyperbole, Ron Rice's 1962 prediction that the films to come would make Grandfather "leap from the grave" was a fair one. As to whether the entire blossoming of the arts in the midsixties was, as Jonas claimed at Davidson, "more important" than the Renaissance: I don't know. But I continue to cherish many of the films I first saw then, including, for example, works by Peter Kubelka and Stan Brakhage. Over three decades ago Jonas claimed that Kubelka's twelve-minute *Unsere Afrikareise* was "about the richest, most articulate, and most compressed film I have ever seen." Today, having seen the film at least fifteen times myself, having taught it in class and presented it publicly, I agree.

I'm grateful to have been associated with Jonas and others a generation ago at a crucial moment in the development of American art in general and film in particular. Today, I'm a Prune—to use the term we so eagerly applied to elders at Davidson. Yet I continue to work on films and books and photographs. For the Gordon V. Ball, Jr., of thirty years ago, Jonas Mekas and the "culture" he brought to Davidson promised that imagination can live and grow in spite of circumstance. That promise continues to be fulfilled—for myself and countless others.

Gordon Ball

ANDREI

"I lawst my teetth on tthe wway ddown. I lawst my cellophane bag of poetry."

Gummily and goofily, the small figure onstage three dozen rows in front of me explained why he spoke funny and had no poems in hand as he stood before a crowd of fifteen or sixteen hundred in the Village Theater. He was short and his dark hair seemed rumpled. He wore a light gray suit, coat unbuttoned, white shirt collar open at the neck. He was Gregory Corso.

Gregory was part of a group of American poets including Clayton Eshleman, Paul Blackburn, and Robert Creeley—Ginsberg was reading on the West Coast—who gathered partly in celebration of the American visit of Andrei Vosnesenski. Vosnesenski, in long-sleeved sweater and necktie, also read—in his powerful Russian declamatory manner. Manuscriptless, he stood flat-footed at the edge of the stage, fists clasped together behind back or raised and moving in sudden fury of emphasis. His repertory, bound in his heart, burst from his lungs: "Goya," "The Call of the Lake," "Striptease on Strike," "Moscow Bells." This "3-Penny Reading for Life Against Death in Vietnam"—admission three cents—had been sponsored by the Angry Arts for Life Against the War in Vietnam; according to the *Village Voice*, it was Vosnesenski's inspiration— "only he had wanted to call it *Fuck War.*"

Candy had gone to Juárez for her divorce, and over the next several days I saw a little of Vosnesenski, as he visited Shirley Clarke in the Chelsea Hotel (where he too was staying, in Arthur Miller's room). Barbara would invite me over and we'd smoke marijuana together. Vosnesenski tended to be quiet and I don't think his English was as fluent as it's become: my Russian—our Russian—was nonexistent. I scarcely spoke to Andrei, but I still can recall an anecdote he told, fingers curved to lips in thoughtful pause and explanation.

It had to do with an Italian woman with whom he was once involved. He thought of her as "Orange" because she looked so great in that color. One day before her plane was due back in New York, Andrei asked for several crates of oranges in a nearby store—would they deliver them to his room at the Chelsea? They did. He carefully prepared the anteroom by covering its floor with them, then set out orange candles, lighting them:

"I've never seen anything so beautiful," he said. Then suddenly she was knocking on the door before he was done. He let her in; she marveled at the beauty of the scene; they blew out the candles, and made love on the oranges.

During these days Barbara (David Hoff seemed to vanish for the time being) would always display a largish pin-on plasticine disk just above her bosom. Upon a white background, it exclaimed in vibrant dark blue, "Vosnesenski Glows in the Dark!" "Andra," she'd call him, delight and mischief on her young face, across the space of Shirley's penthouse.

REX LONGCHAMP MEETS STANLEY

"My name is Rex Longchamp. I sculpt in light." This was reportedly one man's self-introduction, realized or anticipated—I never learned—upon meeting Bob Dylan. Longchamp was an old friend of Candy and her ex-husband, and had been part of an extended "colony" in Mexico. From 1963 to 1965, Candy had lived, fluent and happy, outside Mexico City in Quajimalpa. While there she met Longchamp and other expatriates around the university several miles down the road, on the city's northern edge. It was with Longchamp and her husband that she made one of her most incredible journeys, beholding Acapulco Bay when it was still relatively idyllic, still in some ways like the quiet mountain-and breaker-girt fishing village it had been for centuries.

Candy had referred to Longchamp frequently enough in conversation with me for him to have become a figure of mythic proportions. Tall, dark, broad-shouldered, and handsome, he at last appeared at our door one summer day, cigarette in hand. Striking but quiet, his wife Lisa stood at his side. They were in the city for just two days; our time together included an early restaurant dinner with Stanley and Carri, during which we learned it was Stanley's forty-second birthday. Once we parted, Longchamp determined to do something for the occasion; left to his own secret sculpting, engineering, and culinary skills back at our apartment, he had a major presentation ready within two hours.

That evening found the four of us bearing an enormous white cake as we knocked upon the familiar red door at Hudson Street. Stanley seemed startled to see us, but let us in. In short order, Longchamp set the cake down on a table in the center of the room, led everyone in singing Stanley happy birthday, then pulled a string attached to the cake, whereupon a large artificial cock arose from within, shooting and spraying forth a sticky white liquid substance at everyone. On face, shirt, and forearm, Candy and I, as well as Carri and Stanley, caught dabs and splatters. Stanley wasn't appreciative. I was embarrassed. "I wish I'd known you were thinking of coming by," he announced with dry dejection in his crisp voice. "Carri was tired," he added, not looking at anyone.

In the meantime, Rex Longchamp smoked furiously at the edge of the kitchen. "Goddamn it," he complained to his wife, "he could've appreciated it. After all, the guy's whole life is sex—what's he so down about?"

No one answered him. We didn't stay.

'66 Frames

RICHARD ALDCROFT—
ENGINEERS—CRACKPOTS—COMMUNITY

Something appearing at the Coop around this time so disturbed me that after I first saw it and sensed what was going on, I scarcely wanted to continue reading. It was the "Expanded Arts" issue of *Film Culture* (subtitled *Happenings, Neo-Baroque Theatre, Expanded Cinema, Kinesthetic Theatre, Acoustic Theatre, Neo-Haiku Theatre, Events, Readymades, Puzzles, Games, Gags, Jokes, etc.)*, on which I'd worked in the fall. Now in the summer it came to life, in huge (seventeen by twenty-two inches) illustrated newspaper format, eleven columns across a page, with photographs, collages, diagrams: its genius of graphic design was George Maciunas, Jonas's bespectacled, dark-haired Fluxus artist and Lithuanian friend. Its wide-ranging wealth of materials included even a 150-word blurb with photo for Mel Lyman, as musical performer, that cited a forthcoming album on Vanguard as well as his *Autobiography.*

None of that bothered me. Nor the transcription of the "Expanded Cinema" symposium at Lincoln Center in the fall, with Henry Geldzahler, Stan Vanderbeek, Robert Whitman, and others.

Nor entries for Yoko Ono, Anthony Cox, and Jeff Perkins; nor the small notice for Andy's mixed media event with the Velvet Underground and Nico, the Exploding Plastic Inevitable; nor Jonas's minianthology of his columns on expanded cinema from early 1964 through mid-1966.

What dug beneath my skin had to do with the transcript I'd made of my interview with Richard Aldcroft, that quiet, thoughtful man in his early thirties, at whose seemingly always-open loft I'd first met Robert Du Peintre, first lain next to Candy on mats and beheld the wonders of Aldcroft's Proleidoscope machine. What disturbed me now wasn't the presentation of our interview itself, but an addition to it.

Alluding to our having smoked DMT just before we spoke, I'd entitled (jejunely, perhaps) the interview "Triptape: An Interview with Richard Aldcroft."

After talking the first few minutes about his machine, Aldcroft had focused on LSD and some of his other ideas. Some appeared transparently crackpot, but his basic thesis was sound. In any case, I was not about to edit out ideas that might seem foolish; my purpose was to accurately represent the artist. And his basic thesis was sound, defensible, I felt:

Gordon Ball

> You know, Tim [Leary] is saying LSD is good for everyone . . .
> But I don't think he places enough importance on what can
> really be done with LSD. I mean he says LSD is good, society is
> wrong, and the best thing to do is to move out of society, to
> drop out of it. But I think that society needs to be changed by
> the people who took LSD. Technologists need to take LSD and
> direct their consciousness into a program of reorganization.

But in elaborating some ideas, Aldcroft began to seem cuckoo.
Though he proposed, for example, "using the materials of construction
as design," and related it to an "ancient Japanese structure, the boha," he
also predicted that clothing will no longer be needed in the future:
"Effective air conditioning will make it unnecessary." He distinguished
between his building design idea and that of George Maciunas.

Aldcroft envisioned completely air-conditioned spherical housing
with a transparent trap for sunlight and a transparent bottom for ocean
viewing, cushioned on water, with food conveyed from land when not
coming from the ocean itself. Crops could be grown indoors, in fact,
using rainwater and desalinated salt water. In the larger dwelling units,
nuclear power could generate electricity: "even in the small ones you
could have a stat 3 nuclear generator. They're small enough now—they
could fit into a station wagon."

At this point I pressed him: "And you think this can all come about
from heightened consciousness through LSD?" And he reaffirmed his
claims. What would make technologists want to turn on in the first place?
Through such things as listening to the tape he and I were making,
through effective communication through the underground press,
through appreciating what technology can do for design. "The Amer-
icas," he asserted, "this new continent, should be made an international
monument right away, and housing should begin on the ocean."

To my surprise, the transcript of our interview was followed by an
"Editors note" nearly one-third the length of the interview itself, aimed at
utterly ripping apart what the interviewee had said. Arguing that our hous-
ing shortage was caused by a lack of funds rather than space, it asserted:

> This floating sphere scheme goes an incredible distance away
> from solving this important problem. It is neither economical
> nor efficient. Therefore much fewer of such housing could be
> built than today.

It cited four areas of difficulties: problems resulting from the tenfold greater force of sea waves than wind; the shortening of the housing's connection to public utilities by continuous movement; the corrosive effects of sea water; the inefficiency of spherical surfacing. It concluded, "This scheme, if inspired by LSD, should be the best argument why engineers should not take LSD."

I was miffed: at least I could've been told that such a lengthy (and problematic) put-down was being attached to the interview I'd been asked to do. Thirty years later, I might be tempted to conjecture that if engineers were to choose to take a moderate dose of lysergic acid, under safe and sound conditions as prescribed by Dr Leary, it's possible that they, their mindset, and ultimately their work and our world, might benefit.

In the meantime, I'd heard from Leslie at work that Richard Aldcroft had been arrested. Sitting on a stool at a diner counter, cup of coffee at his wrist, a uniformed policeman perched next to him, Aldcroft was said to have turned to his neighbor and offered, "Hey, Cop, want some acid?"

Leslie read my face. "I don't know if I'd worry too much, you know. He seems to be one of God's fools who go through life in the midst of all its disasters, emerging all right in the end—" He paused just a second to add, "—blessed by Providence."

I remembered a moment a month earlier toward the end of a much smaller Be-In that followed the one at Easter. (It took place, in fact, around the time of a violent Memorial Day confrontation in Tompkins Square Park—which I didn't witness—when police with clubs attacked a group of hippies sitting and singing on the grass after they'd failed to quiet and disperse when ordered.) Candy and I, having spent the afternoon at a small public gathering uptown, were starting to leave when my attention was drawn to a girl whom I'd seen before: now she was one of several women and men wading around in a fountain on a warm afternoon. She seemed nutty: I'd noted her not only on Easter but maybe also once at the League for Spiritual Discovery? I wasn't sure; somewhere, perhaps, sometime, I'd seen her before. She had long brown hair and was vaguely pudgy and wore a sleeveless white blouse and jeans, now rolled half up her calves. And now she was yelling—she tended to be voluble—I couldn't quite hear, but it was something about police. And she said something that suggested she was on acid. My first impulse, of course, was to shut her up: Don't blow the whole scene for everybody! But I noticed that others—I assumed (but didn't know) that they weren't themselves police, bent on information-gathering and arrest—were milling with her, both in and out of the fountain, shoed and barefoot. And that they tolerated her, allowed her rant.

It was something about a community, about absorbing a risk through the entire body so as to let one person be as she was, rather than triggering aggression, violence, hysteria, the intervention of armed suppressive force and its greater hysteria and destruction. As I've not forgotten the longhairs cleaning up after opening night at the soon-to-be-closed Boston Cinematheque, I've not forgotten the image of Richard Aldcroft on his counter stool next to a cop, and this young woman calling, calling—to whom, to what?—from the fountain.

'66 Frames

STP

Thirty years earlier, following a legislative campaign led by Narcotics Commissioner Harry Anslinger—without a word of testimony from any-one who appreciated its use—marijuana had been declared illegal. "The marijuana user," Anslinger had assured the compliant House Ways and Means Committee, "is a violent criminal, with an insatiable appetite for rape, homicide, and mayhem." Now, a generation later, the *Boston Avatar* reported:

> President Johnson has signed the Single Convention, a multi-lateral treaty which provides for strict international control on marijuana. Former commissioner of the Federal Narcotics Bureau, Harry Anslinger, was the U.S. representative to the U.N. Commission on Narcotic Drugs. The only nations who have not ratified the treaty are China, North Vietnam, East Germany, North Korea, and Outer Mongolia. . . .

Around the same time, no effective attention was given a report to a Senate Subcommittee by Dr James Goddard, head of the Food and Drug Administration, on legalizing marijuana. And Dana Beal, "Provo" and promoter of a series of marijuana "Smoke-Ins" at Tompkins Square Park in the summer of 1967, was reported beaten as he was arrested in his office by federal narcotics police.

Meanwhile, the psychedelic compounds—far stronger than mari-juana—had not only been criminalized federally but were increasingly falling victim to state statutes. This came in spite of Allen Ginsberg's remarkable heroic testimony in June 1966 before the Senate's Judiciary Subcommittee on Juvenile Delinquency. He was worried, he said, "that without sufficient understanding and sympathy for personal experience laws will be passed that are so rigid that they will cause more harm than the new LSD that they try to regulate." He concluded optimistically:

> . . . maybe these hearings are a manifestation of that slightly changed awareness. . . . That we are more open to each other is the new consciousness itself: to reveal one's visions to a con-gressional committee.

But LSD was criminalized in California in October 1966; by March 1967, merely possessing it had become a felony in Illinois, Colorado, and Texas

(where ten years' imprisonment was a possible punishment). This outlaw-
ing of psychedelics went hand-in-hand with a virtual prohibition of
human-subject research on the most basic questions: How can the good
points of psychedelics be made better? How can potential risks be reduced?
What more can we learn from them of human beings, of the nature of
consciousness? How can we apply what we learn to improve society? How
can we try to ensure a permanent, safe set of conditions for their beneficial
use, rather than respond with ignorance, hysteria, armed aggression and
imprisonment, wasting lives, public funds, and institutions? Given increas-
ing illegalization and escalating punishments, problems concerning their
uses and effects only increased—naturally!

For LSD, really bad trips could be treated chemically with the tranquil-
izer Librium. However, in the summer of 1967 a new psychedelic appeared
in the underground pharmacopoeia, its chemical makeup such that a dose
of Librium administered during the high could be fatal. I'd read of five or
six people appearing at emergency rooms following ingestion of Librium
within hours after taking this new compound; some of them died. Since
psychedelics and effective research had been prohibited, it was no wonder
such problems arose. Luckily Candy and I had never relied on tranquiliz-
ers to deal with bad moments on LSD, and got through our one really bad
trip out of forty by ourselves—with help from Jackie Leary.

I first learned of STP through the underground grapevine. There
seemed an element of irony in its name, an implied psychedelic critique of
a capitalistic, competition-driven, roar-ahead society. As an alternative to
the values of that society, its contents offered a reaffirming primal, spiri-
tual energy: an entire "engine-cleaning" like the fossil-fuel product bear-
ing its name. In actuality, as Martin A. Lee and Bruce Shlain later reported
in their *Acid Dreams,* the name was an acronym for "Serenity, Tranquility,
Peace," and the substance was developed at Dow Chemical (makers of
naplam), who sent samples to the U.S. Army.

I first read of STP in *Inner Space,* a short-lived periodical effort to discuss,
without substantial commercial sponsorship or police harassment, differ-
ing states of consciousness and their media. There, the author of an article
on the new psychedelic characterized his experience with it as "pure
energy." Our experience was triggered by two modest orange tablets that
Candy and I slipped down our throats one warm Saturday in early July;
it was subhallucinatory but felt like a psychedelic, full of extraordinary

energy. We walked from our apartment all the way to Manhattan's west end. As a high sun stared down at us we looked across the deep green wrinkled liquid at the gray teeth-like buildings of the Jersey shore. Then we hiked block upon block uptown and crosstown, amidst trucks and vans and thousands of other folks a-strolling or hurrying or sunning on a Saturday afternoon, hot and dusty, with occasional blasts of busly carbon monoxide, glimpses of quiet midtown side streets, only an infrequent doorman or a poodle under a sheltering plane tree waiting for the dark-glassed lady with large lightweight boxes hurrying nervously to the yellow cab at the curb's edge. . . .

We returned home in twilight, Italian kids on the streets, a few grandmas in windows beneath crusty painted raised frames, others on dark stoops beveled by footsteps' decades. Our neighbor man and wife were talking together, just barely audible upstairs over our heads as we lay down on cool white pillows and sheets to rest and reflect.

JOHNNY CARSON—AND LOUIE

(1)

Now a young kid from the Long Island suburbs came to 57 Thompson, just "ended up" there. We met him on one of the charmed narrow streets of the West Village, discovered he had nothing, not even a place to sleep that night, and invited him home a while. He was one of a growing American multitude in the summer of 1967 abandoning inherited values and a materially comfortable existence, pursuing curiosity and life itself.

Johnny Carson: barely sixteen, slight, slender, wavy dirty blond hair a good four or five inches longer than mine. He stayed maybe a week or more, fit right in: we didn't need to explain anything to him. Perhaps from his example I coined a definition of friends: people you don't have to explain to. By contrast, I thought, too, of my interview with the Norwegian journalist, his query about "needing" LSD.

Johnny was quiet and gentle, and went with us wherever we went. We took him to Stanley's and Carri's one evening, where he sat shyly, only partly unclothed, as others made love. A few feet away, Stanley, his face at a loved one's breast, interrupted himself long enough to raise his head and say, "Make love to Susan, Johnny."

"Gee, why do you want me to do that, Stanley?" Johnny returned, candidly. It was the only time I saw him ask for an explanation.

Now Stanley didn't even raise his head; he stopped barely long enough, blue eyes twinkling, to utter two syllables in reply:

"Pervert."

Our neighborhood just below the heart of Little Italy was still largely Italian, with rumors of Mafia "insurance" and other benefits for humble store owners and residents. Though it seemed equally as much—if not more—a rather quiet old folks neighborhood, the young people there reminded me by and large of those in the Bronx. All that I sensed of it seemed to be whole cultures, worlds, decades removed from our experiments with sex and psychedelics. By mid- or late-teens the boys (the girls were much less conspicuous) seemed to prize cars, beer, tight tapering pants, and loud voices. The only time—I was passing by on the sidewalk—that I heard a drug mentioned, it was "phenobahbital," in husky New York tones.

Of course I didn't sense that these young fellows were friendly to Candy or me, and I tended to give them space and not look them in the eye whenever I came near. Johnny was not so lucky: he came home early one evening—it was still a golden twilight outside—with a black eye, puffy cheeks, swollen lip, bloody nose: the wages of his long hair. Candy applied compresses to his wounds as he lay without complaint on the white mattress and we sat and talked and were quiet together.

②

Our building was six stories high and in the one next to it lived Italian kids younger than those who beat up Johnny: twelve-year-olds, thirteen-year-olds. The leader of a small group of them was Louie, a dark-haired, good looking twelve-year-old given to performing daredevil acts, egging his followers on: not merely smoking cigarettes or tossing firecrackers, but performing acrobatic high jinks out on various parts of the upper stories.

One weekend afternoon Candy and I were indoors, our large single living room window open into the air shaft, and we suddenly heard a loud clanging, colliding sound, then a second lesser sound, a sort of a thump. We looked out our opened window, but couldn't see a thing. We went into the hallway, heard one or two others already out in the corridor, running up and down the stairs, saying something about "Louie." We went up to the landing, looked out the window on the side opposite ours; there on the shaftway concrete, fifteen or twenty feet below, supine, T-shirted and jeaned, his face utterly neutral, his unmoving glazed eyes staring up toward all of us and the sixth story and the sky above, his chest rising and falling barely, lay Louie, immobile, soundless.

Others too stared out windows as what I took to be family members and friends gathered around him. No one said much. An ambulance had been called, we were told. A priest was coming.

Then two policemen appeared. Louie's little sidekick Robbie lunged at them, thrusting the two uniformed, armed men up against the brick wall an instant before being subdued. When the priest arrived, Robbie broke down, blubbering, "You never gave us a thing! You never gave us a thing!" I looked back to Louie, who continued to stare upward, unblinking.

That evening, several hours after he was taken away, we learned he'd died. The story we got was that he and his friends had been sniffing glue and had gone to the rooftop, where Louie performed a daredevil catwalk on the ledge for his pals to follow. Only he missed his footing, fell over into the air shaft, and clanged into the drainpipe on the way down.

Still later that evening—it must've been eleven or after—our phone rang. It was Billy, in one of his all-systems alert modes. The father of a young woman we both knew in Charlotte had died. I'd filmed Liz Booker in one short sequence of *Prunes,* but had scarcely seen her outside my visit, Revere in hand, to her Queens College redoubt. Now according to Billy she'd recently appeared in the East Village, and no one at home knew how to reach her. Would I comb the Village with him in search of her, he asked.

No, I answered. Not that night.

MARIJUANA, MUSIC, AND TELEVISION

①

Life went on. The Beatles had a new album out and Amy Taubin, who first announced Dannon Yogurt's new individual-sized cup to us at the Coop, was now the first to acclaim *Sergeant Pepper's Lonely Hearts Club Band*. It was nice, but strangely brittle in its campy "one and only Billy Shears" self-consciousness. All the references to drug culture ("I get high with a little help from my friends," "Lucy in the Sky with Diamonds," and even the trippy jacket covers) of course only confirmed what we thought we knew the Beatles had smoked or ingested.

We listened to *Sergeant Pepper* now as we continued to hear "old" favorites from fall, winter, and spring: Ali Akbar Khan and Ravi Shankar, even an LP I'd recently gotten by Swami Bakhtivedanta, of Krishna Consciousness. Stirred by the primeval sound of his strong ancient voice as he chanted the "Mahamantra" ("Great Mantra") "Hare Krishna," I'd gotten a pair of finger cymbals to strike along ("You're missing the beat," Billy once critiqued). And we continued to place on the plastic turntable of Candy's portable the Stones' *Between the Buttons* with its "Let's Spend the Night Together," and Dylan's *Blonde on Blonde* . . . And his earlier *Bringing It All Back Home*, the album which had so impressed me when I walked into Preston Faggart's Davidson apartment. At least until *Sergeant Pepper*'s multicolored brassy collage, its cover had been the most talked about: well over a year after my first encounter with it, speculation as to its contents persisted. In Preston's narrow fourth-floor walk-up on First Avenue between Ninety-First and Ninety-Second on one of my first New York nights in September 1966, one of his roommates, a large heavyset Georgia boy, wondered almost endlessly about who was who and what exactly was going on. In a Daniel Kramer color photograph we met the direct stare of a French-cuffed, hunched-over Bob Dylan clutching a Persian cat; a Lyndon Johnson *Time* magazine cover and LP albums (including Delta bluesman Robert Johnson, Lotte Lenya, and even the previous Dylan), lay strewn about the sofa-settee; and a mysterious svelte dark-haired woman in a clingy red sheath sat upright at the rear. She was Sally Grossman, I learned later, but it was Henry's fancy that she just might be Bob Dylan in drag. On the back, a beardless Allen Ginsberg appeared in tie and top hat next to the shot of Barbara Rubin with Dylan.

Candy and I fucked and smoked a lot to some of these records.

(2)

Early in the winter Jonas had broken down and gotten his first television, a small portable black-and-white which he plunked onto a bare, flat wooden chair in his small loft. "He's a fascist!" he exclaimed, flipping channels one after another in mounting dissatisfaction, only to end up with William F. Buckley, Jr. It had shocked one or two of my friends, but I'd admired Buckley when in his 1965 mayoral campaign he said he'd rid New York of cars and encourage everyone to use bicycles: it was far worthier than, for instance, Norman Mailer's pronouncement, during his own 1969 campaign, that "Drugs numb the mind."

Within a month or so after Jonas had gotten his, Candy and I found a secondhand black-and-white for twenty dollars. A good part of the time we looked at it on acid—not at the midpoint or height of the trip, but later, after the main part was over, after we'd peaked. Or smoking grass: we watched its patterns of dots and light and dark in between channels, or of ghost images near the channel to which we were tuned, altering the dial setting at almost stroboscopic speed, listening to the hum or fuzz or soundtrack, fading it in or out: it was all in appreciation of what Maxine Hong Kingston would call the "snow show." Though the color TV of my parents (which we'd used briefly in our April visit) had capacities of its own, color—as I'd learned on seeing Tony Conrad's *Flicker* in the fall of 1966— could be generated by rapid alternations of black and white. At the other end of the spectrum, I'd seen high-tech performances by videomeister Nam June Paik, but for me these late-night amusements were enough: I never felt inspired to pursue video formally as "art."

Nor did we watch programs as such, though a few times we sought one deliberately. The subject of flying saucers never interested me greatly, but Stanley Fisher, who was interested, was a local channel talk show guest one summer evening. "What would you do—how would you feel—if a flying saucer landed near you?" his host asked. "First, I'd be afraid," Stanley began.

I'd become curious about the Joe Pyne show after reading of Paul Krasssner's appearance on it—or rather, of a question Krassner had asked which was edited out of most broadcasts. Pyne, a veteran who'd lost one leg in battle, hosted a show that was a little like the later *Donahue* but without, of course, walking down the aisle among his audience. He was quite right wing, like today's Rush Limbaugh, with perhaps a similar potential for willful misunderstanding and ugliness. Of Krassner's visit I'd read that Pyne had repeated insulting remarks about Krassner's facial scars, and that finally Krassner had asked "Do you take off your wooden leg before you make love to your wife?"

When Candy and I did watch the show, we found a discussion of drugs ensuing, with firsthand testimony from a young woman guest who claimed to have lived in a commune and smoked marijuana there; since then she'd "seen the light," "reconverted" to the straight world. Pyne at one point in the discussion gave her new position his blessing, as if hers were the one and only gospel: "You've absolutely come to your senses. I can only hope that all the other pitiable people in your generation will do the same." Immediately we heard a woman from the audience yell out, to Pyne's great chagrin, "Aw, come on, man!"

In what was formally the audience response part of the show the mike was given to a large fat kid with dark hair and glasses, in mid- or late-teens. "I don't want to escape reality," he began, "so I don't smoke pot."

That evening Candy and I made love, the next day we went over household finances to see if we could afford a two-week trip to California before summer reached its end. I could have that much time off, Leslie had said, if we could somehow make the trip. And we cleaned the kitchen and spruced up the living room-bedroom. Monday morning I went off to work as usual.

AT DR G'S

Sometime early in the summer I'd given Billy my "joke" movie: that single-reel "In Case of Nuclear Attack" I shot with Candy and me fucking. Perhaps if he looked at it once he was amused; I don't know, I didn't see him a lot in July and August. Some of the time he was at a Long Island beach house with friends old and new—a respite from frustrating New York. But one evening he and Candy and I got together at the Jane Street apartment of Dr William F. Goodykoontz. Goodykoontz—"Dr G," as many of us called him—was Billy's mentor; and though he'd taught at Davidson only my freshman year and I never studied with him, he'd influenced me as well.

While I was in Tokyo preparing to leave for college in the States, Billy (a year ahead of me, but his junior year in Finland would put him in my class) was spending the entire summer of 1962 typing a lengthy novel on G's back porch. Once I entered Davidson, an older student, Bill Ferris, read some of my writing, and told me "Go to Dr Goodykoontz and show it to him." Goodykoontz taught with extraordinary inspiration and devotion, took the basically ad hoc student drama program under his wing, and seemed generally to extend himself beyond measure for the sake of student literary interest.

Reading several samples of my writing, Dr G was remarkably encouraging, particularly with the long story I'd written my senior year in Tokyo. "He's doing something that I've seen only André Gide in The Counterfeiters do," he told my parents when they met. When Eudora Welty visited campus in the spring of 1963, he gave her a copy of it; she read it and offered me her agent's name and address. Around the same time, an older student told me that one day in his Shakespeare class Goodykoontz had volunteered, "Sometimes I think Bill Trotter and Gordon Ball are the only writers we have."

Among his favorite readings was Billy Budd, though the word "favorite" is light in the extreme: for Dr G, books and their encoded teachings were a matter of life and death, models of inspiration that profoundly altered the lives of individuals and whole societies. He seemed ever the champion of the voiceless, the unrepresented, all the way through the end of my freshman year and his protracted attack on the President for neglecting student drama.

'66 Frames

Goodykoontz not only championed underdog causes in public, in classroom, and in play rehearsal, but in his home, where he welcomed students in a manner unlike all other Davidson professors. Typically, faculty home visitations that I participated in were held underneath ticking imitation Vienna clocks on solid imitation marble mantelpieces, with proper coffee and cake teetering on awkward kneecaps as everyone sat upright on Victorian furniture which sank properly into wall-to-wall carpeting—after an hour in straight-backed, straight-bottomed pews at compulsory Sunday evening vespers!

At G's—a place I discovered for company and talk only late in my freshman year, after he'd seen my writing—you were made to feel as if you could drop in most any time: fill an overstuffed chair, sink into an ancient sofa. You'd never have to dress up; evenings, you could enjoy the host's generous supply of beer and nuts and unprescribed conversation— even though alcohol was never to touch the lips of faculty or students anywhere on campus or in town.

As we snacked and drank, G would sometimes tell, wistfully and poignantly in his soft Blue Ridge tones, of young Davidson men from the past; of their various confrontations with authority, with Presbyterianism, with status quo or reaction. Mug in one hand (the other reaching for nuts or pipe), tilting his head back, eyes to the ceiling, his black blind poodle Lancelot at his feet, he'd tell of loves and battles in larger worlds: of Shakespeare, Shakespeare, Shakespeare; of the political figure he virtually idolized, Franklin Delano Roosevelt; of socialism, of communism, of man helping man. With a rueful sigh he once evaluated the community of elders on our campus: "I'd rather be tried by a court of Chinese Communists than be judged by some of these Calvinists around here!"

Late in the fall of 1966 in New York, Billy and I had gotten together with G and a couple of visiting Davidson pals—Bill Ferris, a Vicksburg, Mississippi cattle rancher's son who left the South for Yale and would return years in the future to set up a center for the study of Southern culture; and Jay Federman, a Philadelphia Jew who'd come to Davidson most deliberately, to experience a Southern WASP education. (With Ferris and others, he started civil rights efforts within the Davidson community.) The night of our fall 1966 get-together we'd looked at *Prunes,* and the laughter in a few instances, especially at the Washington Monument shot, approached hysteria.

Gordon Ball

Now, late one summer night in 1967 in his apartment on Jane Street, several years removed from Davidson College, in his third year as editor at *Scholastic* magazine in New York, Goodykoontz remained somewhat quiet, hanging back, as we—Billy, Candy, and I, and Chuck, his athletic, younger, live-in friend and former editor of the *Daily Tar Heel* at Chapel Hill, looked at some footage Candy and I had brought with us. This evening's more recent work, however, was more tenuous, more tentative than *Prunes.* We showed, for example, the footage Candy and I had projected at my parents', from the Be-In: twelve quiet minutes of various people, various modes of being coming together for the first time. I'd done little in the way of forming or shaping as I shot, and nothing at all afterward, except for splicing reels together.

Following the showing, something of the old rift between Billy and me surfaced as he made it clear he didn't like what he saw. I couldn't tell what I felt . . . perhaps his resistance was at least in part justified. In making what I'd shown, I hadn't known quite what to do (other than basic documenting), and felt that maybe there was something lacking in my approach. Yet weren't there moments in filmmaking, of which I'd seen some inspired examples (without even considering Warhol), in which one needed do "little more" than be there and shoot? (And though *Georgia,* with a magic of its own, involved more than that, it was entirely impromptu.) Were I articulate, I might've asked the point in judging what was essentially a document as if it were a work of art for art's sake. Part of the time I feared Billy would call my shot, put his finger on my own uncertainty. But I remained silent, as did Goodykoontz, easy-chaired in a corner, the ghostly remains of Cherry Blend tobacco slowly escaping the dark wooden bowl trapped between thumb and index finger. Chuck, a man of considerable competence and grace, joined right in, however: "I like Gordon's movies. I think it's interesting to see people as they are, without makeup or pretense. I want to see more."

We embraced other topics—Billy's stay at the beach; the war (as we spoke, B-52s were preparing a week's bombing of the North). We talked of Billy's continuing efforts to get published; even, strangely, of why my hair was long (I was silent; Goodykoontz offered, "a rebellion against false values"). The night wore on and beer followed beer—though Candy and I, in our usual commitment to psychedelics, had little or nothing to drink.

Then Billy broke down and wept. He was an immensely proud man, and though in the future he'd meet with great success in writing, nothing seemed more unlikely to him at this moment. Sitting in a low chair with his knees not far from his face, he lowered his curly head, hunched his broad shoulders forward, and in tears expressed his frustration, his grief at a whole long year's effort at breaking into print in New York. For an instant I watched; then I went to him, got on my knees at his feet, put my arm around him, hugged him, held him.

When it was time to go, Goodykoontz saw me a moment in the corridor by myself: "Gordon, what I saw you do tonight was one of the finest things I've ever seen anyone do."

"Oh—I learned it from you, G." I answered. I might've also said I'd learned it from Billy, too.

MY SISTER AT 57 THOMPSON

Traveling separately, but arriving around the same time in the summer of
1967, my sister and Emmett Grogan came to town. Maylee, ten years older
than I, had been a history major in college; marrying just after her fresh-
man year, she'd recently managed to complete her undergraduate degree
over the course of a decade while raising a family. Taking a short leave
from husband (like her, a registered Republican) and three children in
Winston-Salem, she joined Candy and me for several days. "I told Cliff
there is social history being made, right now, today!—And I wanted to see
it for myself. And that I was coming whether he said yes or no," she
looked me in the eyes, smiling eagerly, as we hugged.

She slept with Candy and me in our small floor area among the same
sheeted mattresses. I wondered if that living and sleeping arrangement
surprised or shocked her, if I should've prepared her for it—and if I
hadn't done so in part, at least, for the sake of that shock. In any case she
saw us day in and day out, dirty linen and all. "What's wrong?" she asked
early one evening as we crossed the street amidst a line of pedestrians. I
was in a huff, walking righteously, not speaking to Candy, for some rea-
son long gone.

One night we took her to Shirley Clarke's rooftop party at the Chel-
sea. It was a fund-raiser for the Diggers, the group associated with Emmett
Grogan (it wasn't, of course, appropriate to suggest that such a group was
"led" by an individual). The San Francisco-based free-food-and-shelter
group was modeled after a revolutionary seventeenth century English
organization of the same name; believing in the commonality of human-
ity and resources, it was committed to altering the foundations of society
through enlightened acts carried out with methods developed from San
Francisco Mime Troupe and LSD experiences. I don't think I realized that
many of the other guests were being asked to pay (or make donations),
and I was miffed when we—Candy, Barbara, and I—were invited to come
early and help with preparations: slicing fruits, carving watermelons into
big boats, laying out spreads. "I'm an artist!" Candy recalls me protesting.

Once there, we all helped out—and met a number of new people. Sev-
eral guests came from the city's Parks Department. I introduced Maylee to
Andy Warhol, and to Jonas, who exclaimed, his eyes nearly closing asiati-
cally as he smiled, "Oh, you are de sister of de dropout!" Emmett Grogan,

Hugh Romney from "the Hog Farm" on the West Coast, and Paul Krassner were also about, as well as various prospective donors. It was a large, paper-lanterned affair ("Who's that?" someone asked as a short man with curly blond hair passed by. "Simon? or Garfunkel?"); a new psychedelic band from California performed: the Grateful Dead.

When the sky darkened as it must even over Manhattan, several short films, including a Shirley Clarke; a Kuchar; my own *Georgia*; and one of my favorites, Bruce Conner's *Cosmic Ray,* were shown. Afterward, to my surprise, my sister volunteered, "I thought yours was best." I was pleased, but defensive for the others. Then the band picked up once more and Candy and I danced, using a kind of high-in-the-air hand-jabbing we'd derived from psychic energy experiments with LSD. It reassured me in a way, as a sign of our having our own private language—in a world whose tongues still seemed arcane, forbidding.

Later in the evening, as yellow moon arched above pink clouds, we passed by a white metal-grilled love seat of Victorian fretwork: seated there, with a formally dressed gentlemen from the Parks Department whom we'd all met earlier, was my sister, talking avidly: her companion was a friend from her early days in Tokyo long ago.

EMMETT & OTHERS

"'We longhairs are just bedbugs.'"

Candy was reporting how at a recent clinic visit a nurse had asked, "Will all who are here for venereal disease testing please rise?" One of the many young people on their feet was known publicly as Gallahad. In bright headband, jeans, vest—colorful, and socially committed—he was at that moment in the city news as a representative of his culture. He ran a communal crash-pad which had received more than one unwarranted police visit in the last two weeks.

After the January Be-In in San Francisco and the Easter gathering in Central Park, with the almost daily discernible increase in young people choosing alternative modes of living, the media was beginning to identify "spokesmen" for what Candy had likened to a new race of people. I recall seeing a young Californian explain on a TV talk show how he was a "people person": it seemed at the time an extraordinary challenge to a "people" who allowed their authority to be located not in heart and mind—the sense of humanity within each of us—but in armament, aggression, muzaked media image.

More prominent than Gallahad and others was Emmett Grogan, who with his cohorts seemed committed to radical transcendence of the dreary politics of the New Left through a socially activated love ethic, an applied metaphysics of acid. I watched a Digger talk show guest say, when asked how one became a Digger—"You're a Digger." On another show, a young woman guest identified herself as "Emmett Grogan."

Now, one warm late summer evening, shortly after Shirley's benefit party, Candy and I approached a tall building at 829 Park Avenue, a doorman waiting just inside the glass of its deeply recessed front. Moments later, we moved softly down the carpeted hallway of Peggy Hitchcock's darkened, quiet well-appointed twelfth-story apartment. There in the innermost room was a slender, handsome, strongly framed, high-cheekboned and freckled young Irishman with light brown hair. Emmett Grogan, glass of pink champagne on the coffee table at his feet, sat in a couch at a right angle to the one we would take. Several pretty young women were in the room, one or two sitting near him on the dark red deeply carpeted floor.

Emmett, street-smart and assertive, spoke of introducing psychedelic ideas into the business community. "They won't want that, will they?" I asked. "Don't businessmen think they have to be conservative, keep things as they are?" Inwardly I'd almost shuddered at his words, since Business seemed basic to War.

"No. Businessmen *want* change," Grogan answered. "They can make money on it."

I was surprised. And I was much more pleasantly surprised just a few weeks later when Abbie Hoffman, Jim Fouratt, and others squeezed their way into the New York Stock Exchange visitors' gallery. "You're hippies and you've come to burn money," the initially resistant guard asserted. "That's not true, I'm Jewish," answered Hoffman. Reaching the balcony, Hoffman and Fouratt began throwing dollar bills down onto the floor of the exchange; as some brokers cheered, many began scuttling after them.

Several years later I had dinner with Emmett Grogan—who didn't approve of Abbie Hoffman—and Allen Ginsberg at the Chelsea. That evening, Grogan did the talking while Allen (one of the great talkers of the world) and I listened. He told of having recently gone with Dylan to the Ali-Frazer fight; of the busts and shooting of Fred Hampton and other Black Panthers in Chicago, after their efforts to help the poor with winter fuel bills; of "Big Mouth" Jesse Jackson; of how Janis Joplin's mysterious recent death from an overdose of heroin (no fresh needle mark was found) could be explained ("She skin-popped it"). And of how he'd been with a couple of friends earlier in the year, carrying on, depressed, ornery, and riled, when finally his exasperated companions asked, "What do you want?!" Whereupon Emmett had replied, "Tuesday Weld." He and the actress, he continued, then spent three days together at the beach.

Over the next few years, after our night at the Chelsea, Grogan published two books, *Ringolevio: A Life Played for Keeps,* and *Final Score.* Several years after that, his body was found on a subway car; he'd apparently had a heart attack. Now, as I consider some of today's more dynamic social activism—Greenpeace, for example—I can imagine the inspiration of the brash Emmett Grogan.

Gordon Ball

ON THE BEACH

①

Candy and I still had hopes for California. That is, Candy especially wanted to see firsthand the extraordinary flowering of San Francisco in the summer of 1967; now summer approached its end.

We could hitchhike there, but we couldn't count on making a real trip of it inside of two weeks, the most I could be gone from the Coop. We couldn't afford a bus, not to mention a plane. Through someone at Ron and Irene's studio—the "Model and Photo Equipment Rental Center"— Candy located a driveaway car with a man at an agency in New Jersey. Late one Friday afternoon after I got off work, we headed, full of expectation, for an obscure location across the Hudson. We'd leave for California the next morning.

Candy's contact, a dark curly-haired man in an open-neck white short-sleeve shirt named Mr Lentriccia, met us inside his weakly-lit garage under a large ancient wooden ceiling fan that turned slowly with a tic. He smiled—I could see spots of saliva around his gums beneath his lower teeth—and showed us a big black Cadillac which he said was ready to roll. But it had no license plate. That didn't matter, he quickly reassured: just in case a policeman some time or some place should express interest, he was having a letter drawn up for us. It would explain everything; the license would be arriving in just a few days.

We returned to 57 Thompson as we'd come—by bus and subway—except now glumness replaced expectation. Yet we remained determined to break from the city, even if just for the rest of the weekend. Candy called her parents, who were vacationing in the completely white resort town of Asbury Park on the Jersey coast. Excusing the sudden notice, might we join them?

Saturday morning each of us rolled up a sleeping bag, slung it over our shoulders, headed for Port Authority. We arrived in the mid-afternoon. Candy had been looking forward to thanking her father face-to-face for his help with the Mexican divorce; then we'd have dinner, visit some more, and the two of us would sleep on the floor or out on the porch. We knew they already had friends staying with them. In case we ended up with extended free time, we brought two hits of acid.

'66 Frames

Such was how we imagined it, at least. We didn't get to the Asbury Park bus station until late afternoon. Sleeping bags on backs, we asked for directions as we left the station. But having trouble finding the right house, we asked further as we walked along, first one way and then the next. Tired to begin with from little sleep after Friday night's fiasco, we finally found the right single-story frame house, raised high on stilts like so many of its nearly identical neighbors.

The Mills' house guests were out when we arrived and Candy and her mother and father, both in dressy sports attire, hugged each other warmly as I shook hands. With zest Candy got in her expression of gratitude to her father. Then we made chitchat for some moments, then for a few more. Then I began to wonder what was going on: both her parents seemed to be withholding something—yet they looked straight at us, as if studying.

Finally her father came out with it, eyeing us up and down as he spoke: "We're not sure it would be a good idea for you to stay the night. We don't like the way you look, the way you dress; we don't like your values and that—and that" (in all his looming seriousness he stuttered an instant) "you persist in making a show of it! We don't know if we want you under the same roof."

His blonde, curly-haired wife, who'd stood next to him endorsing his words with silent emphatic nods—not without a tremble at her lower lip—then took the floor. "And what do you think our neighbors here will think, seeing what you look like?!"

We were dressed much as in our spring visit to Somerville, perhaps more openly so in the warmer weather: jeans, tight bell-bottoms, paisleys; perhaps one or both of us wore beads. Candy's splaying auburn hair was as always Candy's splaying auburn hair. Her thin sleeveless blouse naturally revealed the dramatic outlines of her breasts. Perhaps my hair was slightly longer than in the spring; I hadn't shaved in a day or two—but my beard was always very light—and, it was summer anyway!—and the beach! And likely I wore my shirttail out, as I often did in warm weather. . . . We were dumfounded, hurt, angry. Had her father thought his $300 would straighten us out? I wasn't going to find out—

—And Mrs Mills hadn't finished. She turned to her daughter:

"You look like a failure! A loose woman! And you come here on foot, with bundles on your backs! What do you think it looks like?!"

Gordon Ball

I got furious and shouted back. "We care more about reality than appearances!" I turned to Candy; she was weeping profusely. We reached for our sleeping bags, rushed across porch and down stairs, and were back on the street again.

I kissed Candy and holding each other tight we retraced our steps (except with none of the false turns; now it was as if we'd been coming there since childhood) to the Asbury Park bus station. As we started to enter I heard a large metallic hum just behind us. I turned. There was Mr Mills, pulling up his green Buick Regal. "Please come back," he called from the car as he shut the engine. "Please come back," he called as he got out. Under his horn-rimmed glasses his eyes looked worn.

I stepped aside as Candy went to him and they touched and talked. Then they made a sort of affectionate, heartfelt handshake, all four hands, like an athletic duo bonding just before facing opposition. Then that broke into a sort of hug. Candy turned to me, made an effort at a smile, and the two of us joined her father in the front seat—after laying our "bundles" in the rear.

On our return her mother seemed at least to be holding a stiff upper lip. None of us pretended differences had been resolved, but no one fought.

By then it was early evening. Soon friends would join hosts and house guests who'd returned in our absence. We had something to eat, then socializing and bridge-playing became the order of the evening: "When the Mills and the Sanders get together on a Saturday night, watch out!" Candy's mother shouted at one rollicking high point. Mouths sprang open in laughter, glasses clinked in abandon. Candy and I hung around nearby, trying to be friendly as we abstained from the drinking.

We went for a walk, then returned, sat around. Yet another couple had dropped by, revving things up to new heights; the partying now seemed as if it wouldn't end. Candy went up to her parents and told them we were going for a long walk on the beach, that we might even stay the night there, not to worry: we'd be back midmorning.

We slipped our sleeping bags over our shoulders once more as we set out on foot once again. It was now near midnight and dark, except the sky was clear with a few bright stars. We headed toward the beach, stepped into the water's edge, beheld waves roar and crash farther out, then soothe their way in up close. Up in the velvet sky a shy moon was fading in, bright enough to sparkle the tear and roll of the waves. The water was mild as it rushed our bare tired feet, begging its foamy way above our ankles.

We retreated ten yards from the water's edge back under supporting beams and trusses, behind boardwalk piers where all was dark: now we could still see and hear the ocean without getting wet. We slipped off our bags—and took the acid. Again we were taking liberty with Leary's stipulation regarding setting: we were in an unfamiliar spot. Also, weren't we still in at least a somewhat disturbed mind-set following the earlier wholesale upheaval? Nevertheless, we felt we "knew" the acid we had—and we weren't adding ritalin to it.

In twenty minutes I could feel it start, that same not unpleasant sensation in the back of the neck. After another twenty or thirty, as the waves coursed their inevitable path toward us and away from us, I began to enter a state of mind reminiscent of lines from Whitman. In "Out of the Cradle Endlessly Rocking" he'd written:

> . . . the sea,
> Delaying not, hurrying not,
> Whisper'd me through the night . . .
> Lisp'd to me the low and delicious word death,
> And again death, death, death, death,
> Hissing melodious . . .
> . . . edging near as privately for me rustling at my feet,
> Creeping thence steadily up to my ears and laving me softly all over,
> Death, death, death, death, death.

Farther out they rose and cracked in massive plunge and might and thud and yell; there they suggested to me, called to me, impressed upon me, the death of all that lived. It was the utter truth about the universe, and there was nothing I could do about it. I sat there saying subvocally "I'm dying, I'm not dying;" I was putting up ego resistance when all I needed do was recognize Yes I am, like all else. Or perhaps see and accept the cyclic, illusory nature of it—as I'd failed to at Millbrook.

Thus for me it was a matter of internal endurance for about three quarters of an hour: Candy at my side, my feelings unspoken, only a few brief and occasional exchanges between us. Then suddenly we noticed a moving light on the beach, out under old stars and a now stronger moon, between water and boardwalk; and it was coming closer. Then we heard a command: "Who's there?! Come out!"

Gordon Ball

I could see a silhouette—there was just enough light to make out the bluish tinge of a uniform—some ten or so feet beyond the darkness of our boardwalk structure. In good faith I got up, advanced toward it. Half a dozen steps later, I left the enclosing shadow of beam and board and pier—the entire invisible realm—and suddenly manifested before my interlocutor in the world of star and moonlight. I was but a few feet from him, as if materialized instantaneously from nothingness.

He seemed startled and quickly took one step back as he drew a dark yet reflecting metallic object from his right hip and pointed it at my face. "Raise your hands. Who are you? What are you doing here?"

My hands raised themselves. We stood less than six feet from each other. He seemed young, shorthaired, about my size. "We're just looking at the ocean," I explained.

"Do you have identification?"

I reached in my hip pocket for my wallet, handed him my North Carolina driver's license. "I'm sorry if I startled you," I said. I didn't want to use the word "scared"; I didn't want to risk making him feel worse, or excite him further. He returned his pistol to its holster and took my license with his right hand, holding his flashlight on it with his left. By now Candy had appeared near me from under the boardwalk; her manifestation, fortunately, didn't surprise him like mine.

He studied the ID. "No one's allowed on the beach after 11 P.M.—so you can't stay."

"Oh, we didn't know—" I started.

"We were just visiting my folks who have a house here, and thought to take a late-night walk out under the stars, maybe even sleep out here," Candy's whiskeyish voice came in.

"Okay, but not around here. . . . Have you been drinking?"

"No," we chimed, in silent amusement.

He held out my license. As I took it I asked on a hunch, "Are you in college?"

"Yeah, during the year. This is how I pay for school."

"Oh, good."

"You can go farther down that way," he added, pointing with his light before he shut it off, "once the boardwalk ends there are no restrictions." Now we both thanked him and turned and started up the rickety wooden stairs.

'66 Frames

Then he called after us. "So you're a Capricorn," he said.
"Yes," I answered, "and you?"
"Aquarius."
"Oh, neat—water!" I answered. "Well, good night."
"Good night."

(2)

We remembered our sleeping bags and came back for them. At a some-
what higher prospect, we found a spot in the sand beyond the boardwalk,
facing ocean and horizon. I had no worries about death now and slowly,
slowly, as we sat watching the waves glimmer vaguely—a little haze was
building up—a broad arc of the lower horizon began to mutate into light.
Then as more time passed, the tip of a flat persimmon-colored disk
expressed itself like a seed sprouting from earth, slowly fading into the
consciousness of the horizon. It began to rise. It looked flat and empty and
as I stared at its expanding, rising flatness, I began to conceive of all nature
as a prop like any man-made artifice, like those I'd seen before on LSD: city
streets at 4:00 A.M. when I'd noted the two-dimensional stage-set like out-
lines of buildings—whole blocks of streets like a theater set deserted by
actors, crew, audience. It was as I'd see four years later, riding with friends
under the stars on the back of a truck hairpinning down mountains in
Sonoma County hours after a September midnight: all trees left and right
near and far as flat as a pressed leaf against the sky, all nature a dark aban-
doned set.

Now I said to Candy, my face to the horizon, a tinge of salt on my lips,
"The sun is Pop," as it swelled to immense flattened breadth. It was like
an item in some Universe Supermarket, available every day, always in
stock. It was as thin and illusionistic as the label on a can of Campbell's
Soup, as the mirror of it held by Andy.

Gordon Ball

ROSH HASHANAH DINNER AT STANLEY'S MOTHER'S

Some weeks after Maylee's visit to his apartment—one or two after our return from the beach—Stanley extended Candy and me a special invitation. Following a discussion one evening in which he startled us by proposing we move in with him and Carri, he made us feel honored: would we join them, he asked, for a Rosh Hashanah festival at his mother's Brooklyn apartment?

The next Saturday afternoon, cool, early fall, Stanley wore a light jumper, Carri a sweater buttoned over her blouse. A light breeze tugged at our heels as we started down the dark steps into the hollow embrace of the passageway at Sheridan Square. In the subway car, amidst a dozen bored faces, we argued over LSD. Recently Lyndon Johnson's federal government had tried its "It makes you blind" and "It damages your chromosomes" tacks. Many of us could see through such claims, which were later disproven.

"Stanley, our government has bald-facedly lied so many times to us in so many ways about drugs—we know so many people who've taken acid for years—surely you don't believe them—you know what their interests and their ignorances are. . . .

"Well, if our government says there's a danger with something I need to consider it."

"Well, sure, consider it, but apply it to what you know from your own experience—and from observing others all around you. If you took everything our government said about drugs at face value you'd have to stop smoking reefer!"

For once it appeared, however transiently, that I might have the last word with Stanley Fisher. No matter. For the rest of the afternoon and early evening—in his mother's small three-room home—arguments with Stanley Fisher, everyone else's interlocutor—would come from a different source. At a formica-topped kitchen table spread with Manischewitz and round Hallah bread, apples in honey, chicken soup, and a handsome roast, Stanley was on the defensive. Batting an occasional gray wisp from her forehead, Mrs Fisher (whose welcome of Candy and me was more than generous) repeatedly questioned and pleaded with her son. Now forty-two, Stanley made $34 a day—when he was asked to teach. Most of the time in her presence he sat erect and silent—or offered brief, clipped, matter-of-fact answers ("I choose to live this way, Mother")—as she asked:

"When are you going to get a real job?"

"Why do you only rent an apartment?"

"Why do you sleep on a mattress on the floor? Why not a real bed, Stanley?"

"What are your goals in life?"

"When will you and her get married?"

"Why don't you come see me more?"

TO ACAPULCO

One early autumn night, I lay next to Candy on our sheeted mattress as we started to sleep, sounds from the family overhead only a vague murmur. I'd worked two days at the Coop that week. And I'd have three days more this week, five days the next, five the next after that. . . . I thought of Wednesday morning, sitting at the Coop at the same desk working the same typewriter, filling in the same accounts, answering the same telephone, looking out the same window at Thirty-First and Lexington. And there was Leslie, for whom work for the Coop was virtually a twenty-four affair. . . .

My feet were tired and I thought of all the time I spent walking concrete, starting with block upon block to the subway at Broadway and Lafayette, then Times Square to the shuttle, up and out at Park and Twenty-Eighth and over to Lexington and Thirty-First, then reversing it all after six o'clock. By the time I retraced the last few blocks home in the evening, the day a ghost, the large looming cast-iron warehouses emptied of their eight-hour mania, I ached.

I thought of what I felt to be my failure as a filmmaker after Jonas's earlier enthusiasm, which seemed quite generous—his writing about *Georgia*, his scheduling showings with personal appearances, his transcriptions of our talk for the *Voice,* in spite of my saying very little. He now gave few signs of support or interest—and how could I blame him? I hadn't known what to do next—I was twenty-two years old, his age when interned by the Nazis—though I did have an idea for a new film. . . . But I'd asked Jonas if he'd take *Georgia* to Europe!

I speculated about the handling of the interview with Richard Aldcroft. I wondered what was going on in Jonas's life at this moment, was he on schedule, doing his own film work, 9:30 P.M. till midnight? I thought of the enormous admiration and affection I felt for him and even his solemn, almost sanctified work. I thought of his profound inspiration. I thought of Johnny Carson, his gentleness and his warped, sunset of a face after his beating. I saw Louie lying there on the concrete in the airshaft looking up glassy-eyed and expressionless, breathing his last. I thought about my family in North Carolina, about Candy's and my failure with her parents, of their nearly wholesale rejection of us. I thought of Richard Aldcroft alone or accompanied somewhere, behind cold steel, and Richie's brother Art, too. I even wondered about Robert Du Peintre, whom I hadn't seen in months: where might he be, what doing? What magic, what strong metaphysics or despair or charm, or love? And what of Andy, whom I'd scarcely seen since early summer? I asked myself of my friend Billy's work and commitment and the new woman he'd just met; I thought again of Leslie Trumbull and his endless hours at the Coop; I thought of Candy, sweet auburn-haired whiskey-voiced companion at my side, of her strength in the world. I thought of Barbara and David, wondering, doubtfully, if they'd last; I sensed the distance Candy and I felt growing between Stan-ley and Carri and us. Moved by their recent kindness, we had drawn back from living our lives with them. I thought of Candy's disaffection with the city, her still-running argument on it with her closest friend.

And so finally, many moments later, my head yet full of such ruminations, I who was always afraid to speak, spoke. In the quiet, in the darkness, I uttered the syllables: "Candy."

"Yes."

"Are you still awake?"

"Yes—what's up?"

"I—I don't know. I don't like being here in the city—anymore. But I don't know what to do about it." I turned and eyed her as she lay on her back in a realm of shadows, head partly tilted toward me. At my feet, Miss Lyn rolled, still sleeping, onto her belly. I thought I could see a small smile take over Candy's face.

"I do."

"You do?"

"Yep. We can go to Acapulco. It's paradise there."

"Really?"

"Yes. It's paradise there."

Gordon Ball

song lyrics acknowledgments

lyrics by Bob Dylan:

All Rights reserved. International copyright secured. Reprinted by permission.
"Visions of Johanna" copyright © 1966 by Dwarf Music
"Just Like a Woman" copyright © 1966 by Dwarf Music
"Bob Dylan's 115th Dream" copyright © 1965 by Warner Bros. Inc.
Copyright renewed 1993 by Special Rider Music.

"Call of the Far-A-Way Hills" copyright © 1962 & 1963 by Paramount Music Corporation. Copyright renewed 1980 & 1981 and assigned to Paramount Music Corporation. Written by Mack David and Victor Young.

print acknowledgments

"Please Do Not Clutch at the Gossamer Web" from Timothy Leary's *Psychedelic Prayers* copyright © 1966, reprinted by permission of the Futique Trust.

Use of a May 13, 1965 letter written by Jack Kerouac to Bill Trotter in response to a review of *Desolation Angels* reprinted by permission of Sterling Lord Literistic, Inc. Copyright © 1998 The estate of Stella Kerouac, John Sampas, Literary Representative.

Sections exerpted from the *Village Voice* copyright © V.V. Publishing Corporation, reprinted by permission of the *Village Voice.*

Sections exerpted from *Newsweek,* 11/14/66 and 2/13/67 © 1966, 1967, Newsweek, Inc. All rights reserved.

Sections reprinted from *The New York Times* copyright © 1966 and 1967 by *The New York Times.* Reprinted by permission.

Sections reprinted from *Esquire* reprinted by permission of *Esquire* Magazine. © Hearst Communications, Inc. Also, Esquire is a trademark of Hearst Magazines Property, Inc. All Rights Reserved.

Exerpt from "Wichita Vortex Sutra" reprinted by permission of the Allen Ginsberg trust.

The chapter entitled "Millbrook" is adapted from the voice-over narration of the film *Millbrook* by Gordon Ball, distributed by Canyon Cinema.

All copyrights for other materials exerpted and cited in the text remain the possession of the author and/or the periodical/book in which it appears. Exerpts from letters remain copyrighted by the authors of those letters.